CLEVELAND'S FINEST

Sports Heroes from the Greatest Location in the Nation

Vince McKee

Clerisy Press

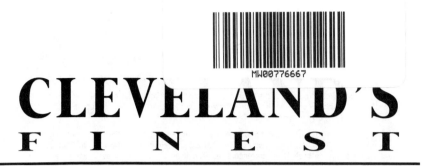

Cleveland's Finest: Sports Heroes from the Greatest Location in the Nation

Some names and identifying details have been changed to protect the privacy of individuals. All factual information was verified through **baseball-reference.com, pro-football-reference.com,** and **basketball-reference.com,** as well as with the athletes, coaches, and announcers themselves.

For further information, please contact the publisher:

CLERISY PRESS
An imprint of Keen Communications, LLC
306 Greenup St.
Covington, KY 41011
clerisypress.com

Library of Congress Cataloging-in-Publication Data

McKee, Vince.
Cleveland's finest : sports heroes from the greatest location in the nation / Vince McKee. — First edition.
pages cm
"Distributed by Publishers Group West"—T.p. verso.
ISBN 978-1-57860-573-6 — ISBN 1-57860-573-3 — ISBN 978-1-57860-574-3 (eISBN)
1. Sports—Ohio—Cleveland—History. 2. Athletes—Ohio—Cleveland. 3. Sports teams—Ohio—Cleveland. I. Title.
GV584.5.C58M35 2015
796.09771'32—dc23

2015020432

Distributed by Publishers Group West
Printed in the United States of America
First edition, first printing

Editor: Vanessa Lynn Rusch
Cover design: Scott McGrew
Text design: Annie Long
Cover and interior photos: © Vince McKee, except as noted
Copyeditor: Emily C. Beaumont
Indexer: Rich Carlson

This book is dedicated to my beautiful wife, Emily,

and my incredibly adorable daughter, Maggie. I love you both deeply,

and you remain the best reason to wake up every morning

and come back home from work every day.

My life is better because of you.

Contents

Acknowledgments

I want to thank my wife, Emily, for providing me the time to work on this book and always being 100 percent supportive. I want to thank my parents; my brother, Don; and my sister, Abbie: You all have always been my biggest fans. Most importantly, thank you to my Lord and Savior, Jesus Christ, through whose light all work is done.

Introduction

No one can measure the heart of a champion. It is the one distinct quality that can make any challenger a champion. Cleveland has been a part of some of the greatest moments in sports history. The city produced a football dynasty in the 1940s and 1950s and won two World Series (and came within a few outs of winning a third). The basketball franchise has risen from the ashes to produce a miracle—a Chosen One. Cleveland has had rookie sensations offering near perfection from the mound and has produced a soccer team that electrified the world of indoor soccer with multiple championships. The loyalty of Cleveland's fans is unfailing, as they have stuck by their teams in good times and bad. The fighting spirit of Cleveland can never be denied—offering the finest in all of sports cities.

This book highlights the best moments, players, and media members in Cleveland sports history. It has in-depth interviews with some of the top names in Cleveland sports. Each interview is a no-holds-barred tell-all of the most intimate and sometimes controversial details of the largest impact moments in Cleveland sports. This is the first book written from the players' points of view combined with media coverage and perspectives from fans. This book will change the way the entire sports nation perceives Cleveland, as finally its true sports stories are told!

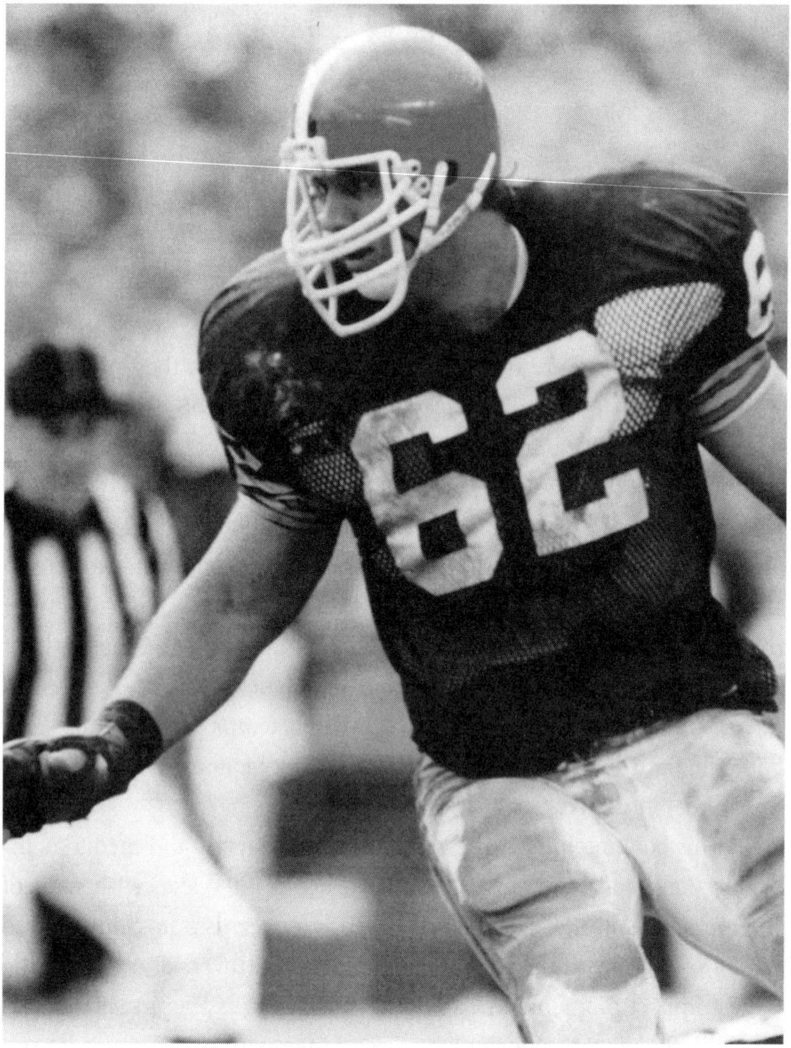

Photo: George Lilja

George Lilja came to Cleveland in 1984 and was the starting left guard on the 1985–86 Browns teams that won the AFC Central Division championship.

CHAPTER ONE

The Golden Years

There was a time in Cleveland sports when winning wasn't just hoped for—it was expected. There have been those in the sports media across the country who have made the mistake in recent years of mocking Cleveland's teams for not winning a world-championship title in over 49 years. What those pundits don't realize is that this city was built on winning and that its fans can and will survive anything.

Cleveland is a blue-collar city with hardworking people who support their hardworking teams. No matter the previous season's record, the loyal fan base in Cleveland is confident that the current season will be their season. Times have been tough for Cleveland sports teams, but it wasn't always that way. In fact, from the late 1940s through the early 1960s, Cleveland served as the marquee sports city on the planet.

Joe DeLuca, who grew up in Cleveland, has many stories about the winning years of the past. Things were much different then, when winning wasn't a gift but a birthright. Born in 1933, Joe had the incredible opportunity to watch the first-ever Cleveland Browns football game in person. Throughout the first 15 years of his life, he witnessed multiple championship seasons, not only in football but also in hockey and baseball.

The Cleveland Barons were a professional minor-league team in the American Hockey League who played their home games at the Cleveland Arena from 1937 to 1973. The Barons won nine Calder Cups, which was the minor-league equivalent of the NHL's Stanley Cup. As DeLuca once recalled, "The owner of the team, Al Sutphin, was beloved by fans for his aggressive nature in trying to build a winning team. The Barons were so dominant that most people around the country considered them good enough to be the NHL's seventh pro team. If it wasn't for a long-standing feud between Sutphin and NHL president Clarence Campbell, the Barons may have been the seventh NHL team at one point."

DeLuca remembered having to take streetcars from West 105th Street to Euclid Avenue downtown to see games at the old Cleveland Arena: "The cars had the old stove heat in them and weren't very warm. We would try to sit as close as possible to the front to keep warm and not freeze." Braving the cold of the streetcar rides paid off when he arrived at the famous arena in search of another Cleveland Barons win. He fondly recalled the packed lobby area where fans lined up to buy tickets, not to mention beer and soda. Soldiers who were home from the war would wear their uniforms to the arena, bringing their girlfriends with them. Going to games was a special occasion, and everyone would wear hats, men and women alike.

The Cleveland Arena hosted great events such as the Ice Capades, circus performances, area high school basketball championship games, and even Knights of Columbus track meets. It was a long, narrow hockey rink, regulation-size with stands that could comfortably seat 10,000 fans with another 1,000 fans standing. But with 90 percent of games selling out, it was always a packed house to watch the city's favorite maulers on ice. A general-admission ticket to a hockey game cost $1.25, while a Grand Stand ticket cost $2.25. For those in the crowd who had the money to spend, a box seat sold for the hefty price of $3.25. DeLuca explained that most people at the time only made about $40 a week, so these prices were steep for the league's best team. The atmosphere of the crowd was very different, however. "Back then just about everyone who went to a game would smoke cigarettes," DeLuca detailed. "It was much more commonplace, and the arena officials saw no harm in allowing the fans to smoke in their seats. A thick haze of smoke would fill the arena to the point that you could barely see the scoreboard. The fans who didn't smoke didn't mind because they just wanted to be there and root on their winning franchise. Fans back then were such die-hards that it didn't matter where they sat because they just wanted to be there."

DeLuca rooted for all players but held the Italian-American players closest to his heart. He explained that, being Italian himself, it was only natural to root for them, with his favorite player being Ab Demarco. Because he had to attend school during the day, most of the games DeLuca went to took place on Friday and Saturday nights with the occasional Sunday-afternoon matinee. "People in this town loved hockey, and if it wasn't for Jim Hendy buying the team and sticking a knife in the Cleveland hockey fan's heart, it would still be around today," DeLuca said. In 1948, the Cleveland Barons won the Calder Cup again in a four-game sweep over the Buffalo Bison team. As thrilling as the victory was, it paled in comparison to the wild ride the 1948 Cleveland Indians were about to take DeLuca and the rest of Cleveland on.

DeLuca's earliest memory of baseball came from sitting on his Italian immigrant grandfather's lap listening to Jack Graney call games on the radio. His grandpa would have a cloth hanky present at all times. When the Indians were winning, he would keep the hanky nice and smooth, folded neatly on his lap. When things weren't going well, he would twist and bite on it in a sign of frustration and worry. Joe had three uncles who listened to the games with him—Prosper, Jimmy, and Rocco—who were New York Yankees fans because of Joe DiMaggio. It was important to DeLuca that he grew up as an Indians fan and make his grandfather proud, despite his uncles' love for the dreaded Yankees. DeLuca was such a devoted fan of the Cleveland Indians that he would sneak into League Park on off days and ran around the bases. It wasn't until then-groundskeeper Emil Bossard caught him and kicked him out that his fun ended.

In 1920, the Cleveland Indians won the World Series in seven games over the Brooklyn Dodgers. The series was unique in that it was actually a best-of-nine series. The amazing game five of the series contained the first World Series triple play, a grand slam, and a home run hit by a pitcher. Years later, the team's owner, Bill Veeck, moved the team from League Park to Municipal Stadium. DeLuca's uncle Rocco had a weekend job delivering soda pop to the Municipal Stadium. It was on these trips that young DeLuca tagged along, just to run out of the truck at each stop and catch a glimpse of the inside of the ballpark. Memories like these only increased his passion for the team and strengthened his support. Then along came the famed 1948 season.

During DeLuca's junior-high years, kids who made all A's were rewarded with sports tickets. DeLuca never won any, so he would trade different items with star students in exchange for their prized tickets. It never mattered to DeLuca that these giveaway tickets were always for games against lowly teams such as the Philadelphia Athletics and Washington Senators—he was just happy to be there. As he recalled, "There was a city-wide essay contest amongst Cleveland teenagers to decide who would be the visiting team's bat boy that season. It was won by my classmate, Alan Broyles, from Audubon Junior High. It wasn't so much that Alan was a baseball fan, more so just a really good writer, which drove his classmates crazy that he would win. At school, Alan refused to discuss the players he got to meet, which only increased the jealousy of his classmates for landing such a sweet gig."

The Indians succeeded thanks to a new owner and a roster of great upcoming players, including the boy manager and star player Lou Boudreau. They boasted an amazing pitching staff led by Bob Feller, Bob Lemon, and Gene Bearden. They even had the first African American player in the American league, Larry Doby. The 1948 season provided incredible memories for the fans and players alike. "You could walk down the street at anytime and hear what was going on in the game because every store window and home had it on the radio blaring loudly. The excitement of Cleveland Indians baseball filled the air wherever you went," DeLuca recalled.

Owner Bill Veeck was called a showman by the media and the rest of the owners in the league. He ran such promotions as free-nylon night to boost female attendance. Another highlight was free-TV night and even free-washer-and-dryer night. Veeck went as far to allow midget auto races on the field track due to high pressure from Cleveland's mayor at the time, Thomas A. Burke. Veeck did whatever it took to get fans into his stadium and behind his ball club. His love for baseball started early in life when his father was the general manager of the Chicago Cubs. The young Veeck got his start by planting ivy on the walls of Wrigley Field at the age of just 15. Veeck would always make it a point to sit in the stands with the fans. He did his best to build excitement by relating to the fans as much as possible. He never wore a traditional tie and dressed in the same fashion as the average blue-collar worker in the mills. No matter where he went or what he did, he always carried a flair about him that sparked enthusiasm wherever he went.

The chance to play in the 1948 World Series came down to a one-game playoff between the Cleveland Indians and the Boston Red Sox. The beloved Indians traveled to Fenway Stadium and chose knuckleballer Gene Bearden to take the mound for this crucial game. Red Sox manager Joe McCarthy made an odd choice in Denny Galehouse, who had won only eight games that season, to start. On the strength of Ken Keltner's incredible game, in which he clubbed three hits, including a three-run home run off the famed Green Monster, the Indians cruised to victory and a trip to the World Series.

It was also on this day that DeLuca and his classmates discovered that their principal and teachers actually were normal people: He was shocked when he arrived at school and heard the announcement from the principal that the game would be played over the loudspeaker. DeLuca and his classmates felt as if Christmas had come early upon hearing this unthinkable announcement. When the Indians won that game, all of the children ran out of the school building screaming in celebration. "Church bells were ringing and factory whistles blaring," remembered DeLuca, with the last celebration of that magnitude having come in 1945 when World War II had ended. Later that evening, DeLuca's parents tried to take him and his sister downtown to celebrate the victory, but they were unable to make it all the way there because the streets were packed with people celebrating. It was almost impossible for DeLuca to wait for the morning paper to arrive the next day and read the article written by his favorite sports columnist, Gordon Cobbledick.

The 1948 World Series was played against another team from Boston, the Boston Braves of the National League. Game one was decided when a beautiful pick-off play at second base between pitcher Bob Feller and second-baseman Joe Gordon was called safe, even though the runner was clearly out. The runner was able to stay on base and came home to score shortly thereafter, giving the Braves an eighth-inning 1–0 lead that they would not surrender.

"The Indians were down but not out," stated DeLuca. The next two games were Indians victories due to excellent pitching performances by Bob Lemon and Gene Bearden. Game two was a victory against the phenomenal Boston Brave pitcher Warren Spahn. Cleveland went on to win game four, thanks to a great pitching effort by Steve Gromek and a game-winning home run by Larry Doby. After a rare shaky performance by Bob Feller, the Indians lost game five 11–5, taking the series back to Boston.

October 11, 1948, was the last time Cleveland celebrated a World Championship win in baseball. It came on the heels of another great performance by pitcher Bob Lemon, where the Indians beat the Braves 4–3. Cleveland had held off a Boston two-run rally in the eighth inning to hold on for the win and the World Championship title.

The next day, Cleveland's public schools were closed so that the children could join in the downtown celebration. A 20-car escort led the parade route, with Bill Veeck and Lou Boudreau sitting in the lead car while the crowds of people alongside the parade screamed in pure joy. In the mass of people, DeLuca found himself standing alongside none other than the visiting team's bat boy, Alan Broyles. For the first time all season, Broyles was actually showing emotion as DeLuca saw a single tear trickle down his cheek. It turned out that he was a fan after all.

In 1946, professional football returned to Cleveland when Mickey McBride, real estate agent and owner of the Yellow Cab Taxi Company, founded the Cleveland Browns. Cleveland had a prior professional football team in town called the Cleveland Rams; however, after winning a championship in 1945, the team's owner, Dan Reeves, relocated the Rams to another town.

Mickey McBride's first order of business was to move the Cleveland Browns from League Park to the new Cleveland Municipal Stadium downtown. If not for this improvement, there might not have been a football team in Cleveland for many years. Many fans have the false impression that the team was named after the "Brown Bomber," Joe Louis, when in fact the Cleveland Browns were actually named after legendary coach Paul Brown, whom McBride hired to coach his new team. This naming came after a failed attempt in the local Cleveland newspaper to let the fans decide on a name for the team. Though the fans had voted for the Panthers as the name, Paul Brown shot that down, stating that the Panthers were associated with past failed team in another town.

Brown was brought in to coach the Cleveland Browns after years of serving in the US Navy and following very successful coaching stints at Massilon High School and Ohio State University. He signed a contract worth a reported $17,500 yearly, which at the time was the highest paid coaching contract in football. McBride even reportedly offered Brown a stipend for the rest of his time in the military.

Brown wasted no time signing as many players as he felt were needed to help the team win immediately. With some of the biggest and best players brought aboard, including Northwestern quarterback Otto Graham, eventual Hall of Famer running back Marion Motley, star wide receiver Dante Lavelli, and placekicker Lou "The Toe" Groza, the new team in town proved to be a force to reckon with. The Browns began practicing at the campus of Bowling Green State University, located a few hours west of Cleveland. The team colors, brown and orange, came from the Bowling Green Falcons.

"The Browns were being led by a great disciplinarian," detailed now-80-year-old Browns fan Joe DeLuca. "Brown was such a strict coach that he even enforced a dress code, but that was why his players respected him. He even fired the team's captain, Jim Daniel, after he had gotten drunk a week before the 1946 championship game. Daniel had gotten so drunk that he took a swing at a cop. In order to set an example for the rest of his team, Paul Brown didn't hesitate to cut his captain."

The Browns joined the All-American Football Conference in 1946. Brown was so well prepared that he convinced McBride to keep a list of reserves who didn't make the team employed on his taxicab payroll just in case of an injury. The part-time taxi drivers were fondly known as the Taxi Squad. Brown searched the entire country to bring in the best talent he could find.

The Browns took the field at Municipal Stadium for their first game against the Miami Seahawks in front of 63,000 fans on September 6, 1946. DeLuca can still close his eyes and recall the moment: "The lights were shut off in the whole stadium, the only light coming from the exits signs, when a spotlight from the right-field stands turned on. The light shone into the dugout, where the Miami Seahawks players were about to run out and take the field. As the announcer spoke and the first player from the Seahawks ran across the field, he kicked up a little dust as he ran across the dirt infield. I remember getting chills seeing this, thinking something great was happening. I still get goose bumps as I think about it all these years later."

DeLuca can still name every single player from the 1946 roster, the position they played, and their number without even having to look at a team picture. Years later, he would meet Lou Groza at a laundromat and tell him that it was the greatest team in Browns history. When Groza asked him why he felt that team was the best ever, DeLuca replied, "If that team was lousy, no one would have come and they would have left town." It was vital that the 1946 Cleveland Browns be great.

Coach Brown's winning team brought packed houses for each game. Cleveland fans quickly forgot about the Rams when the Browns crushed the Seahawks and kept the ball rolling all season. McBride was a smart businessman who took full advantage of the team's success, selling tickets at the premium price of 25 cents apiece. Included in each paid program was a raffle ticket that entered fans in a drawing to win a brand-new car. McBride even promised a big celebrity would appear at every home game as well.

In 1946, the Cleveland Browns won their first league championship against the New York Yankees, 14–9. This completed a magical first season that spilled over into a 1947 season. In their second year, the Browns defeated the Baltimore Colts 42–0 for a second consecutive championship. Heading into 1948, nothing would change: The Browns won their third championship with a 49–7 trouncing over the Buffalo Bills. The Cleveland Browns did not lose a single game the entire 1948 season, making them a dominant force in the league.

The year 1948 in sports had been so amazing for Cleveland that the city was now known simply as "The City of Champions." As DeLuca shared, "We were so spoiled with all the winning, it was as if it would never end." In 1949, the Browns won the championship title yet again under the direction of Brown with a 21–7 win over the San Francisco 49ers. In 1950, the Cleveland Browns moved into the NFL and remained dominant, winning the championship on Christmas Eve over the Los Angeles Rams 30–28. Paul Brown was proving he could win in any league at any level. DeLuca attended that game with hundreds of other rabid fans, freezing but winning! The irony was sweet, because they had just beaten the former Cleveland Rams.

The Browns would go on to reach the championship finals for the next three years, but they did not win those championships. Changes for Coach Brown started before the 1953 season when McBride sold the team to a group of local businessmen led by David Jones for $600,000. Brown was upset that McBride did not consult him about the deal, even though the new owners assured him they would stay out of the picture and let Brown run the team. This was a vital issue for Brown, who needed full control over personnel decisions in order for his system to work successfully.

Brown remained unfazed with the ownership change and led the Browns to back-to-back NFL championship wins over the Detroit Lions and the Los Angeles Rams in 1954 and 1955. The 1955 championship would be the last one for which Brown retained Otto Graham, who announced his retirement following that final game.

In 1956, the Browns suffered their first losing season under Coach Brown as they struggled to go 5–7. It was their first season without Graham as quarterback, and the team had problems adjusting. In the following year's draft, the team selected Jim Brown out of Syracuse University. Loaded with talent, Jim Brown was one of the greatest runners to ever play the game. The problem, however, was his lack of discipline, which he later used to misalign his teammates against Coach Brown. It didn't help matters that Coach Brown was critical of some aspects of Jim Brown's game, including his extreme lack of blocking. Where Jim Brown excelled was running, not blocking or being an all-around good teammate. In Brown's first season, the team would reach the championship game but go on to lose 59–14.

As Jim Brown rose as a star, players began to question Paul Brown's leadership and play-calling. By the late 1950s, Jim had turned his teammates and the media against the proven coach. It was Jim Brown's play on the field that allowed more people to side with him over the seasoned coach. Fans were in awe of Brown's running ability, and they willingly looked past his off-the-field antics. Jim Brown later started a weekly radio show, which Coach Brown did not like as it undercut his control over the team. The team finished second in its division in 1959 and 1960, but these finishes didn't bother Jim Brown because he continued to lead the league in rushing every season.

A dark cloud soon rose over Cleveland in 1961 when Art Modell, a New York advertising executive, bought the Browns in 1961 for almost $4 million. At first it looked as if Modell would not be all that bad as an owner—he gave Paul Brown a new eight-year contract and stated that he and Brown would have a "working partnership."

It didn't take long, however, for Modell to get in Brown's way and start playing a heavy hand in the team's field affairs. This upset Coach Brown, who was used to having total control in football matters.

Only 35, Modell was close in age to many of the players, and he took it upon himself to try to buddy up to many of them. Modell became very close with Jim Brown, which was the kiss of death for the disciplinarian coach. Modell could be heard during games second-guessing Paul Brown's play calling.

Things finally came to a head between owner and coach when Paul Brown traded Bobby Mitchell for the rights to Ernie Davis, a Heisman Trophy–winning running back out of Syracuse. Davis was no stranger to the end zone, having broken all of Jim Brown's rushing records at Syracuse. This was a trade that did not sit well with Jim Brown, and he was not happy to have Davis as a teammate. Sharing the spotlight was not something Jim Brown preferred. Sadly, Ernie Davis never played a single game as a Cleveland Brown—he was diagnosed with leukemia before the start of the 1962 season.

Paul Brown was a methodical and disciplined coach who tolerated no deviation from his system. He ran a well-oiled machine, which was simply not the way Jim Brown wanted to be coached. In the end, Modell sided with Jim Brown and fired the legendary coach on January 7, 1963. This was right in the middle of a newspaper strike that allowed Modell to keep this move under the radar. It was the first of many shocking moves and disappointing decisions that Cleveland sports fans would have to endure by Modell that would occur over the next forty-plus years. Blanton Collier, Paul Brown's longtime assistant, was later named as the team's new head coach.

Paul Brown would only stay away from the game for less than five years; he was quick to throw in his hat for team ownership of the AFL franchise that was starting in Cincinnati. Brown was the third-largest investor in the team and was given the title of coach and general manager, two roles he would succeed in. The Bengals joined the NFL in 1970 as a result of the AFL–NFL merger and were placed in the newly formed American Football Conference. In his years as the Bengals head coach, Brown took the team to the playoffs three times but was never able to win a championship for the Queen City.

Coach Paul Brown was a great leader. Many of the men who worked directly underneath him continued on to amazing careers, including Don Shula, Blanton Collier, Weeb Ewbank, Bill Walsh, and Chuck Knoll, to name a few. Coach Brown finished with seven league championships during his tenure with Cleveland. He led the Browns to 11 straight title games in that stretch. It was the most dominant run of any head coach in the history of football. As one of the greatest head coach in the history of professional football, Paul Brown will forever be remembered as the man whose coaching ways, attention to detail, and discipline reshaped the landscape and model of pro football.

CHAPTER TWO

Richfield

Richfield Coliseum was built in the early 1970s and first opened to the public in 1974 as home to the NBA's Cleveland Cavaliers, the WHA's Cleveland Crusaders, the NHL's Cleveland Barons, and, in later years, the AFL's Cleveland Thunderbolts, as well as indoor soccer teams the Cleveland Force and the Cleveland Crunch. The Coliseum hosted major sporting events, such as the 1981 NBA All-Star Game and showcased several professional-wrestling events seen worldwide on pay-per-view. It also served as a venue for music concerts by big names from Frank Sinatra and Stevie Wonder to U2 and Bruce Springsteen. Hall of Fame basketball star Larry Bird mentioned that Richfield Coliseum was his favorite place to play on the road.

The building, in the middle of a large area of farmland, was 30 minutes south of downtown Cleveland and stuck out like a sore thumb. This massive structure held more than 20,000 seats and was one of the first arenas to include luxury boxes. Joe Tait, legendary announcer for the Cavaliers, remembered his first impression of the coliseum as "a beautiful building in comparison to the old Cleveland Arena—it was like going from the ghetto to the palace. The one question was if people would still show up because of the long distance many had to travel to get there. At the time, that part of Summit County was surrounded by farms. It was in the middle of nowhere, and there was a sheep ranch right next to it. I thought it was an absolutely beautiful building."

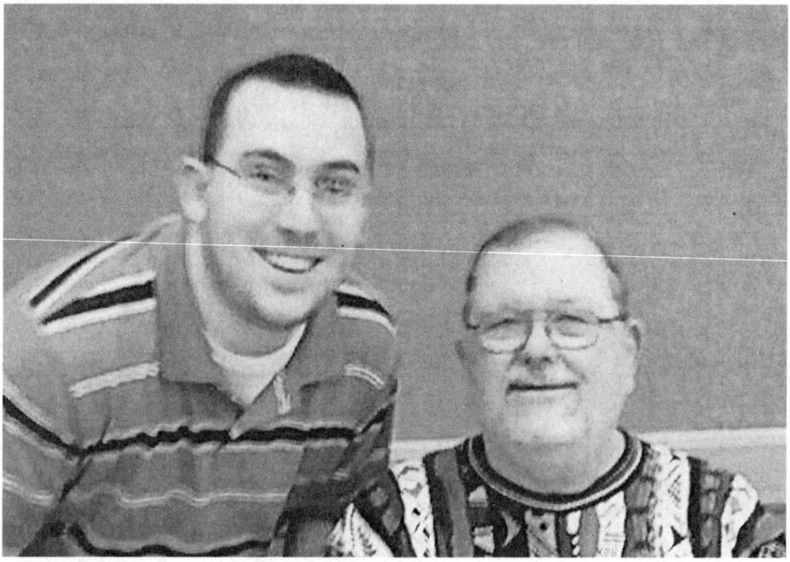

Vince McKee with the legendary voice of the Cavs, Joe Tait

The Cavaliers had a new home; now they just needed to start winning. Owner Nick Mileti built Richfield Coliseum for his recently formed basketball team. Until then, they had been playing at the Cleveland Arena but hadn't enjoyed much success. Since the team's 1970 opening season, the Cavs hadn't had a single winning season. Shortly after the move to Richfield in 1974, however, they record started to improve. The team won 40 games that year but fell just short of the playoffs. Tait recalled the 1974–75 season positively in that "things were changing because we were starting to get better ballplayers. We had not yet won a lot of ballgames in the history of the team, so the upgrade in the talent of the roster was crucial. The fact that we came within one game was frustrating but also encouraging because it showed you how close they were to bigger and better things."

During the 1975–76 season, NBA Coach of the Year Bill Fitch led the Cavaliers to a record of 49–33 and a National Basketball League Central Division title. The team boasted a roster filled with talent such as Austin Carr, Bobby "Bingo" Smith, Jim Chones, Dick Snyder, and the newly acquired perennial All-Star Nate Thurmond. Years had passed since Cleveland had won anything, 1964 being the last time a Cleveland team had won a championship. The team's newfound success had fans across Northeastern Ohio excited about sports again. "After the horrible start to the season, head coach Bill Fitch made the trade for Nate Thurmond, which was the catalyst that turned that ball club around. Nate was a great player and also a tremendous leader. He came in and really galvanized the team to get them aimed in the right direction and then went on to win the division," Tait said.

Tait became the man lucky enough to call the action of this new miracle team. In his childhood, he had tried to play basketball but never fared too well, as he wasn't athletically inclined. And because he didn't have a television growing up, any form of basketball he experienced came through the radio. To make money while attending the University of Missouri in Monmouth, Tait took a job as a janitor at a local radio station. The station offered him a chance to do two five-minute sports radio spots a day. In 1970, the newly formed Cleveland Cavaliers basketball team of the NBA hired Tait as the lead radio play-by-play man, a job he performed until his retirement in 2011. It was an amazing career that resulted in his being inducted into the Broadcast Hall of Fame in 1992.

The first unit of the Cavaliers consisted of Jim Cleamons and Dick Snyder at guard, Jim Chones at center, with Jim Brewer and Bobby "Bingo" Smith holding up the frontcourt. Coming off the bench were Austin Carr, Campy Russell, Foots Walker, and Nate Thurmond. The bench players were just as good as some of the starting lineups that season. The Cavaliers boasted a solid rotation of players who would take them well into the postseason. Joe Lustek, from North Ridgeville, had no bones about sharing his love for that team and those players:

> *I remember the flashy uniforms standing out among other teams. They were stylish at the time but funny looking back at them now with the short shorts. I used to love Bobby "Bingo" Smith, not only because of his talent but also because of the Afro haircut. Few could ever forget the*

great energy of Joe Tait on the microphone. An incredible adrenaline and excitement arose from the fans in the crowd. I remember the endless smack talking with other students at school, especially the dreaded Boston fans.

Cleveland Cavaliers fans' enthusiasm helped lift and shape some of Tait's broadcasting as well, and he vividly recalled the fans' excitement:

Sure, you get swept up in the enthusiasm and excitement of the whole thing. If anything, you have to make sure that you don't overdo it yourself because it is very easy to do so. I know a couple of times listening back to old tapes that I probably did go too far. It was hard not to get totally involved in that series because of the extreme nail-biting results of those games. The crowd really did pick up the team and pick me up as well. It was a rare experience because it was the first time the team had ever been

Vince with the "Miracle of Richfield" Cavaliers

to the playoffs and had, at best, a mediocre performance prior to that season. They beat Washington and, because most people considered the fact they were even there a miracle, the name stuck.

The first playoff-round matchup for the Cavaliers took place against the Washington Bullets, who later became the Washington Wizards. The Bullets were impressive opponents whose lineup included all-stars Elvin Hayes and Wes Unseld, both of whom went on to become Hall of Famers. So formidable was the Bullets lineup that they went on to win the NBA championship title the following season. The Cavaliers were known for their quick offense and their well-rounded attack on both sides of the ball; nevertheless, they would need all of their skills at hand to take down the Bullets. With Joe Tait on the microphone calling the action to hungry sports fans everywhere, the series was ready to kick off with a bang.

Game one ended in heartbreak for the Cavaliers, who lost 100–95 in front of the hometown crowd. The team bounced back during game two in Washington, though, defeating the Bullets 80–79 on a 25-foot jump shot by Bobby "Bingo" Smith in the final seconds. The thrilling one-point win was a sign of things to come later in the series. The men in wine and gold kept the momentum going in game three with a hard-fought win in Richfield, outscoring the Bullets 88–76. Desperate for a win back home in game four, the Bullets came out with a 109–98 victory. The Cavaliers won game five at home 92–91 when Jim Cleamons rebound a shot by Smith and put it back in to beat the buzzer. Matt Morino, COO of Morino Ventures LLC and a current Strongsville resident, shared his memories of this playoff series:

I was lucky to be able to go to a playoff game with my mom, who along with me was a big Cavaliers fan. It was game five of the series with the series tied at 2–2, so that game was critical as the series would be moving back to Washington for game six—a tough place to play, so we did not want that one to be a possible closeout game for the Bullets. I'll never forget arriving at Richfield Coliseum more than an hour before game

> *time and seeing the place packed. You could feel the electricity in the air with 20,000 fans chanting "Lets Go Cavs!" an hour before game time—no fire from the rafters, no blaring audio system with recorded chants, this was real! And when that old 1970s Cavs theme song, "C'mon Cavs," began to play, the place went bananas—standing ovations with deafening cheers as the Cavs came out for warm-ups. The game was nip-and-tuck the whole way and, in what had become par for the course, it was going down to the wire. The Cavaliers had the ball and had called time-out to set up the final play for a basket they had to get in a game that was, up to this point, their biggest one ever. The ball was inbounded and went to Bingo Smith for a shot at another buzzer-beating jumper. But this time Bingo was forced much further away from the basket by that stingy Washington defense. Obviously, Bingo's buzzer-beater in game three was still very fresh on the Bullets minds, and he really had to force this one up. Things looked bleak in those final few seconds, but then, out of nowhere, our point guard, Jimmy Cleamons, had somehow managed to sneak under the basket and, leaping high into the air, caught Bingo's air ball and laid it in the basket all in one motion as the buzzer went off and the place exploded!*

The series only grew more exciting and intense by the day. Following game five, game six went into overtime, but the Bullets managed to bounce back and bring in a win at 102–98.

There are few moments in sports that can match the buildup and thrill of a game seven. The feeling of do-or-die is one of pure anxiety that can only be cured with a win. Yells and excitement from the fans had the ground of Richfield Coliseum shaking an hour before the start of game seven. During warm-ups, the crowd containing more than 20,000 cheering fans chanted, "Let's go Cavs!" If the fans had anything to do with it, the Cavaliers would not be having a first-round exit. Ruben Rodriguez, who was from Cleveland but had been stationed by the Navy in Norfolk, Virginia, was given tickets and flew back home for the final game in the series. He had these vivid memories of the game to share:

> *I will never forget that game; it was the loudest crowd anywhere for any sport. You could actually feel the place shake! When Phil Chenier missed the last shot, there weren't enough cops to stop the fans from cutting loose. There were dudes climbing on the baskets as if they were tearing down goalposts instead.*

Sulaiman Ahmad, from Euclid, also shared his thoughts from the time spent at the series:

> *The main thing I remember about the Miracle of Richfield was the noise. I have never heard a crowd that was that loud. At times, Richfield Coliseum felt like it was literally moving.*

Joe Tait had a special viewpoint of the fan's reaction from the broadcast table on the court:

> *It was a "natural" crowd reaction, and that's what made it so special. Nate Thurmond had his brother, George, come to one of the games and place a tape recorder on his lap so he could record the amazing sound of the crowd at the packed Coliseum. There had never been anything like what we were all experiencing. That entire season, the crowd response was just unbelievable. Those things don't happen anymore because of the artificial commercial atmosphere produced at arenas now.*

As fate would have it, game seven would be an even more intense game than the previous six thrillers that the fans had witnessed. Local Cleveland fans were unable to watch the game due to an NBA blackout, but as Matt Morino shared, fans were still able to listen to and watch snippets of it:

> *My whole family gathered around our radio at home to listen to Joe Tait call the biggest basketball game in Cleveland history. The TV news*

stations also had something called "Action Cams" that were stationed at the game and would interrupt TV programming for short snippets of film from this huge game. It was hard to hear Joe's voice at times—the crowd was deafening. The game was tied at 86 with just seconds to go, and the Cavs had the ball and had called time-out to set up for the last shot again. We watched—yes, watched; even the NBA couldn't keep their blackout for these last few seconds—as the Action Cams had interrupted all Cleveland TV stations to show this final, fateful play.

Just like in previous games, it came down once again to the final shot. Dick Snyder was called upon to take the final shot with just under 5 seconds remaining. As his running 5-foot bank shot hit off the glass and went in, the Richfield crowd came unglued. The city had just witnessed the completion of a miracle.

Although they would fall short in the next round of the playoffs, losing to the highly touted Boston Celtics in six games, no one could take away the pure joy Cleveland fans felt during game six of the Bullets series. Many believe that if starting center Jim Chones hadn't broken his foot in a practice between the two series, taking the steam out of the red-hot locomotive engine that had become Cleveland basketball, the Cavaliers might have even upset the Celtics. The Cavaliers did manage to win two games in the series with outstanding plays at home in front of rabid fans. Backup center Nate Thurmond did his best to fill in for Chones, but the Celtics' John Havlicek was too much for him. Joe Tait gave his firsthand account of what happened during those games against Boston:

Nobody expected the Cavaliers to beat Boston at that particular time, and the fact that they came back in that series got people pumped up to an even higher level. People began to think that even without Chones this team could still be a team of destiny. It was in the fans' minds that they could pull off one of the all-time greatest upsets. It was easy for the fans to get swept away in it. The problem was that Thurmond had to pick up extra minutes for the hurt Chones, and it was simply too much to ask. Despite their best efforts, we fell short in six games.

North Olmsted native John Rehak, a noted child psychologist and youth basketball coach for many years, also shared his memories of the series:

It is my honest opinion that if Jim Chones didn't break his foot, that the team would have won the NBA Championship. It was a magical time for our city, and one that I will never forget.

Bruce Rice of North Olmsted, a retired mailman and an avid Cleveland sports fan, recalled:

We brought a banner to each game with a giant rear end on it that said, "Hey Cowens, Stuff This!"

The truth, however, was that Cleveland sports teams were in the middle of a miserable run. The Browns hadn't been good in years. The Indians never made it back to the playoffs after getting swept in the World Series in 1954 against the San Francisco Giants. The Cavaliers had been terrible until this magical run. They gave the city some desperately needed hope. It didn't matter if it was the clever nicknames or the colorful uniforms—Cleveland fans were just happy to have a winner.

CHAPTER THREE

Super Joe

The Cleveland Indians had suffered through some very lean seasons for three straight decades. They were in need of a change, in need of a player with so much talent and charisma he could singlehandedly change the face of Cleveland Indians baseball for the better.

In the spring of 1980, a player came out of nowhere to do just that for one unforgettable season. He was more than just an average Joe—he was super!

Joe Charboneau grew up in California with his single mother in search of a dream. He was taught the game of baseball by his older brother, Rick. Six years older than Joe, Rick had an extreme passion for

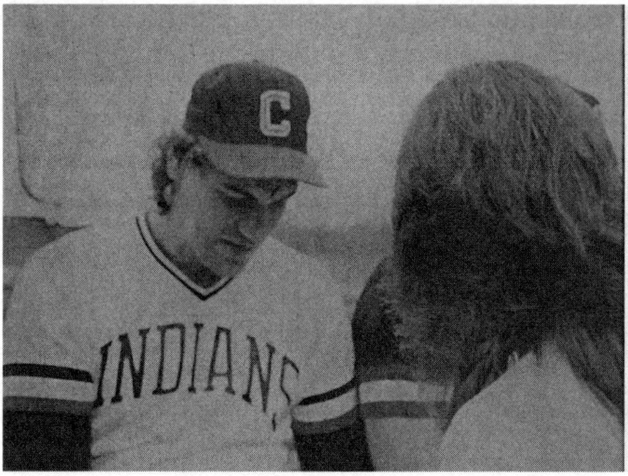

Photo: Garry Gosky

Joe Charboneau meets with a fan.

baseball. A great athlete in baseball and hockey, Rick spent a lot of time with Joe, molding him as a young man both on and off the field. The older Charboneau trained his younger sibling in the weight room as well. The brothers were so close that Rick helped Joe in weight training from the age of fourteen all the way through his playing days in the major leagues. The guidance Joe received from Rick helped prepare him mentally and physically to reach the professional level.

Joe Charboneau would be the first person to say that the main trait of a good hitter is to be tenacious. It isn't just an hour-a-day thing, but rather a skill that needs daily practice for hours at a time. During an interview at his Cleveland-area home, Charboneau described what he thinks it takes to be a good hitter:

> *I didn't have a lot of natural talent, so I had to work every day to groove my swing and keep everything in order. It's a constant, ongoing project to be a good hitter. You have to imagine yourself doing a lot of it as well, hitting doubles, triples, and home runs. You have to picture yourself succeeding so when you're not physically doing the work you still have to do it mentally.*

Charboneau's insight provides further evidence that any good ballplayer is blessed not only with physical tools but mental ones as well.

Growing up with his older brother constantly watching baseball, Charboneau had many heroes. He fondly recalled having a Carl Yastrzemski poster in his room, next to a Raquel Welch poster. Not only did he look up to Yastrzemski, but he also idolized both Al Kaline and Stan Musial. His fondness for Musial was so great that he used his bat model to hit with in the majors.

In 1976, after playing ball at Brooksville High School in California, the Minnesota Twins drafted Charboneau. Minnesota had a good program that also had produced major league pitcher Mark Langston. When scout Lee Irwin showed up at Charboneau's house to sign the contract, it was predetermined that the signing bonus would only be $500. Joe was still trying to take care of his single mother and could not take such a small amount of money, so instead he asked for $5,000—an

Photo: Garry Gosky

1980 American League Rookie of the Year Joe Charboneau

amount that was promptly denied by the Twins. The Philadelphia Phillies took a chance by drafting Charboneau later that same year. During his time with the Phillies organization, Charboneau met Cal Emery, the last player to hit .400 in Triple A. Charboneau developed his skills further by working with Emery in the Phillies Instructional League. He also had the chance to work with Tony Oliva and Willie Stargell, both great major-leaguers in their own right.

Charboneau was traded to the Cleveland Indians before the 1979 season began after having a very good 1978 season at the minor league level. He had the fourth-best average in the minor leagues in 1978, a record that caught the attention of the Indians. The team was able to acquire him by trading pitcher Cardell Camper. Charboneau continued his minor league dominance in 1979 by hitting .352 for the Indians' Double A team—and seemed destined to arrive at the Indians' Triple A Charleston, South Carolina, affiliate—when he was called up to the majors sooner than anyone might have thought possible. Regular left fielder André Thornton was sidelined with an injured knee, giving Charboneau his shot at the big league club. Playing in front of a huge Cleveland crowd is always special for a ball player, and Charboneau described his first game in the big leagues at Cleveland Municipal Stadium:

Our first opening day after coming home from the road, we played on a sunny afternoon of 74 degrees and in front of 72,000 people. I thought it was going to be like that every day. The next day it was very cold and we only had 3,000 fans in the stands. But Indians fans are great fans, and I really enjoyed them. I had a good relationship with them and they treated me really well. It was a great place to play. I wouldn't have won Rookie of the Year any place but Cleveland, and 1980 would have not worked out like it did if I didn't play in Cleveland.

Charboneau's rookie season became a thing of beauty. He fit in well with his teammates and hit for an impressive .289 average. He also showed signs of serious power, belting 27 home runs and knocking in 87 RBIs. During Joe's rookie season, Indians fans fell in love with him instantly. A song written about him, "Go Joe Charboneau," climbed to number three on the local radio record charts.

Charboneau recalled that having all that attention on him "was weird, and it was really strange having a song out. It was overwhelming because I didn't expect any of that; I just came to play baseball. I never expected any of that—it was just so different. The cool thing was that a lot of the profits went to charity, so I was okay with it." A number of larger-than-life stories about him made the rounds, including a couple of anecdotes asserting that he could open beer bottles with his eye and fix a broken nose with pliers and a bottle of Jack Daniel's. Joe explained how these stories

Photo: Garry Gosky

Joe gets ready to step into the batter's box.

came about, offering, "it was stuff that happened mostly in college. I attended a junior college in California called West Valley Junior College. One of my old college friends came down to Cleveland one night and told local reporter Dan Coughlin about things that had occurred back in college, and that's how some of those crazy stories got out."

Photo: Garry Gosky

Joe Charboneau was quite popular with the fans.

Charboneau was quick to give credit to Cleveland's fans for his success. He has been quoted as saying that "Cleveland was a great place to play," and he believed that it was his relationship with the fans that helped him to achieve his rookie success. His incredible season caught the attention of nationwide sports analysts as he was voted American League Rookie of the Year—the first Cleveland Indian to achieve that honor in nine seasons. (The last Indian to win the award prior to Charboneau was Chris Chambliss in 1971, and it wouldn't happen again until 1990 with famed catcher Sandy Alomar Jr.)

The guidance Joe received from his third-base coach, Joe Nossek, brought out the best in his abilities. Charboneau would credit Nossek for keeping him grounded during some tough times during games. He kept him level-headed if he was having a bad night at the plate. It was also Nossek who worked with Charboneau in the outfield to further hone his skills.

Nossek wasn't the only person guiding young Joe that season. Assistant coach Dave Duncan took time to work with Joe and help him refine certain skills that were necessary to be a big-leaguer. Hitting coach Tommy McCraw played a crucial role in developing Charboneau's swing at the plate and in making sure the young rookie was able to adjust to certain pitchers.

It was the preparation of the 1978 and 1979 minor league seasons that helped Charboneau succeed in his rookie year in Cleveland. Those seasons gave him the confidence that he would need to excel at the professional level. He credits those seasons, along with the weight-training guidance of his brother, with helping his body develop as well. In the late 1970s and early 1980s, major league clubs didn't have the techniques and equipment they do now, so it was those extra workouts that made a huge difference.

Joe Charboneau's rookie campaign will never be forgotten. In many ways it changed the landscape of baseball, proving that a player who was not highly touted could come out of nowhere and have a great season. It also gave the Cleveland Indians a new outlook, showing that the team could have a winner again after so many years of losing. Super Joe gave new life to the franchise, and to the city.

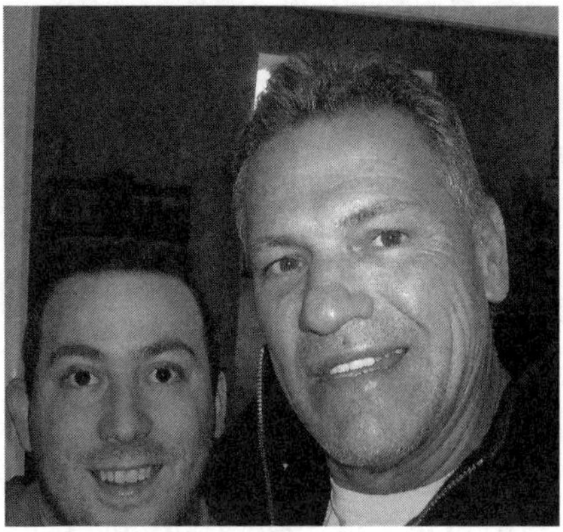

Photo: Garry Gosky

Joe Charboneau today with Vince McKee

CHAPTER FOUR

Perfection!

In the spring of 1981, the Cleveland Indians were led by manager Dave Garcia and played under the ownership of Francis J. "Steve" O'Neill. It was a roster carefully put together by general manager Phil Seghi. Bruce Drennan and Joe Tait were calling the Indians game on WUAB-TV, while Nev Chandler and Herb Score were the play-by-play duo for Indians radio games.

The Cleveland Indians roster included the 1980 rookie sensation Joe Charboneau fresh off his amazing first year in the big leagues. Rick Manning joined Charboneau in the outfield, along with Larry Littleton. The team was anchored by "The Human Rain Delay" Mike Hargrove at first base, Duane Kuiper at second, Toby Harrah at third, and shortstop Tommy Veryzer. The team also had Pat Kelly and André Thornton ready to come off the bench at any time, Chris Bando sharing time behind the plate with veteran Ron Hassey, and future Hall of Fame pitcher Bert Blyleven to lead the starting rotation.

On Friday, May 15, 1981, the Indians were ahead 15–8, surprising everyone by spending 16 days in first place in their division. The team never was more than a game ahead of the other teams in the division, but it didn't matter because they gave hope to their fans. A five-game winning streak at one point in April had fans already talking postseason.

Lenny Barker grew up in Rose Tree, Pennsylvania, with two brothers and two sisters, although he was the only one to play baseball. He enjoyed playing not only in organized leagues but also in the

Photo: Garry Gosky

Bert Blyleven was the ace of the 1981 Cleveland Indians.

streets with his friends. Barker recounted that he wanted to be a pitcher at an early age, stating, "At the age of seven or eight, I felt that I would excel at it. I always liked pitching, and I would have kids in the neighborhood come over and catch for me. I knew at an early age that I wanted to be a pitcher."

Barker and his friends would play in any field they could find and pretend to be their idols—Whitey Ford, Sandy Koufax, Willie Mays, Hank Aaron, and Barker's own personal hero, Mickey Mantle. Barker revealed that it was his dream to play in the major leagues: "My aspirations of playing big league baseball started when I was 10 years old. By the time I got to high school, I knew I had a chance to play. It didn't matter to me who I got drafted by because I just wanted to play professional baseball."

Barker played baseball at Neshaminy High School near Philadelphia, where he excelled and was eventually drafted by the Texas Rangers. Barker said he found out that he was drafted by Texas when he "got a call from a scout in their farm system letting me know I had been drafted. A short while later, they started coming over and we got working on a signing bonus." Barker made his major league debut in 1976; looking back over his three years as a Texas Ranger, he noted:

> *It felt great because it was a dream come true when I was picked first in the third round. All my life as a little kid I wanted to be a pro athlete, and this was my opportunity to get the ball rolling and show them what I could do. I have nothing bad to say about the Rangers because they treated me good and it was a great learning process. I learned a lot in the*

minor league system. I had a great time in the minor leagues; I didn't make much money, but I still had a great time.

However, going from Philadelphia was a culture shock for the young player:

It was the first time I ever had to step on an airplane when I flew to Sarasota, Florida, where the rookie league was located for the Texas Rangers. It was a kind of shock just getting into an airplane for the first time. I was the type of guy who was large in size and, because my parents were divorced when I was a young age, I had to become a man pretty quick. I knew I had a lot of confidence in my ability when I got there, so it worked out good.

Barker showed signs of brilliance at times, but he also struggled with command before being traded to Cleveland in 1979. Revealing how friendly and welcoming the Indians were to him, Barker received the nickname "Big Donkey" from Cy Buynak, the Indians' clubhouse manager:

We had great times, and we would have parties all of the time with our families. We had a lot of team unity back then. On the road, we would have a group of eight to ten guys go out to dinner together. I got traded to Cleveland after the 1978 season, when I was traded with Bobby Bonds. The first time you get traded, you're kind of shocked in the beginning and feel like the other team didn't want you. Then I started thinking about it and realized that the team trading for you really wanted you. I also realized that I had more of an opportunity to become a starting pitcher in Cleveland because in Texas they had four All-Stars in their starting rotation. They had Fergie Jenkins, Gaylord Perry, Bert Blyleven, and John Matlock. It would have been very hard to break the rotation. I was happy to be here because it was someone who wanted me. I was happy to play in the major leagues and I didn't care where. Cleveland gave me the opportunity to start, and that's why I still live here today. I love this city.

The Indians were happy to have Barker, who went on to win 19 games in 1980—a breakout season after they won only six games in 1979. Barker explained what made the 1980 season special:

I played winter ball in Puerto Rico after the 1979 season and concentrated on my pitching and getting command of all my pitches. We had a pretty decent team in 1980, and everything started working for me. I was able to throw a lot more strikes, as I threw over 240 innings. I had over 180 strikeouts with only 80 walks. It was a great ratio for a power pitcher. I believe that it was the concentration level and everything finally clicking. I was becoming a major league pitcher instead of a major league thrower. I started getting better and better at my control, and that, with my work ethic, turned everything around.

Barker was off to a good start in 1981 and was proving the Indians' faith in him to be correct. Later that year, on May 15, 1981, Barker took to the mound, just as he had done on previous game days, in front of a crowd of 7,290 fans at Cleveland Municipal Stadium:

It was a normal spring day with some sprinkles and coolness in the air. I didn't do anything different from my normal routine. I ate a little food, but not much because I didn't like to eat a lot on the days that I pitched. I laid around the house and relaxed a bit before leaving to pick up my brother from the airport. I left my house around 4 p.m. to pick him up, but his plane was late and I had to wait. When he finally arrived, we had to speed to the ballpark. When I finally got there, I had trainer Jimmy Warfield put some heat on my arm real quick so I could rush out and warm up. Once I got out there and starting stretching, I was fine. We didn't realize right away that when I was warming up I was throwing almost all fastballs.

Cleveland's opponents for the game were the struggling Toronto Blue Jays, led by manager Bobby Mattick. Taking the mound for the Jays was Luis Leal, who at that point in the season was a modest 2–3. Barker had come into the contest with a record of 2–1. The balmy 49-degree Cleveland spring weather was perfect for a pitcher's duel. Behind the plate calling the balls and strikes was Rich Garcia, with Greg Kosc, Don Denkinger, and Jim McKean handling the calls on the base paths. Pitchers and umpires don't really mix, but Barker knew Rich Garcia and was familiar with his strike zone:

> *I knew Richie before that game; he was a good umpire who called a good game. Over time, you get to know the umpires and you can tell their strike zones. Most of them keep the same strike zones and some don't. Being a pitcher, you don't become friendly with umpires, but you know who they are and remain cordial with them. There are a lot of good umpires, but there are also a lot of bad ones.*

The fans in the stands—who just wanted to kick back and watch some baseball—had no idea what a special moment they were in store for. Little did anyone know that Lenny Barker was about to catch the attention of not only the fans in the stadium but also of baseball fans nationwide. The battery mate for Barker that evening was Ron Hassey, who went on to catch another perfect game later in his career with pitcher Dennis Martínez in 1991. Barker looked back at working with Ron Hassey, stating,

> *I felt really comfortable with Ron Hassey. He was a guy who was an All-American third-baseman out of Arizona. He was able to make a successful transition from third base to catcher. It was amazing to see how he progressed. He actually was a pretty darn good catcher who did a good job and called a great game. He worked hard back there and was the only catcher to catch two perfect games, so he must have done something right. We also had Bo Díaz, who was an All-Star in 1981. He was a pretty good catcher who caught for me down in Venezuela numerous*

times. I was used to both, and they were both excellent catchers. Sometimes you get a relationship with a certain guy who you feel comfortable with. The manager can tell when you get in a groove with a certain guy, and they will keep that tandem working together.

All eyes were on Barker from the first pitch. As he wound up to throw, the seal of history was about to be broken in epic fashion. Barker managed to get each of the first two batters to ground out to shortstop Tom Veryzer. The third out came when George Bell grounded out to first-baseman Mike Hargrove. A rather routine trip through the top of the order became a common occurrence as the night went on. Len walked (no pun intended) through what he felt during the early part of the game: "It started off feeling like a normal game, and I was throwing nothing but fastballs early. The guys behind me made a couple of incredible plays in the first inning. As we got later in the game, I started striking out batters at a good pace."

In the bottom of the first inning, a leadoff single by Rick Manning got the Tribe off to a good start. After second-baseman Jorge Orta popped out to the shortstop, Mike Hargrove reached first base on an error by first-baseman John Mayberry. André Thornton wasted no time hitting a sacrifice fly deep enough to score Manning from third, giving the Indians an early 1–0 lead. Moments later, Ron Hassey singled and the lead grew to 2–0. Harrah ended the inning with a called third strike from Leal. The score, and the Indians' lead, was more than Barker was going to need. Barker said that the early lead helped him to relax and focus going into the second inning: "It helps out for sure. In tight games,

Photo: Garry Gosky

Mike Hargrove played first base the night of the perfect game.

you can make one bad pitch and lose a game. We didn't average a lot of runs back then, so every time we got up on a team it was nice. It made it easier to pitch, but still a two-run lead is not a huge lead. When you're pitching well and have a lead like that, you can get your team a win."

Facing Barker to lead off the top of the second was cleanup hitter—and the person responsible for the first inning error—John Mayberry. His fly ball to center field started the inning off for the Indians right-hander. After Upshaw grounded out to second base, Garcia flew out to center field, which ended the second inning in the same way as the first: perfect for Barker.

After a bottom of the second that saw the Indians fail to add to their lead, Barker took the mound to face the bottom of the Blue Jays order. Back-to-back ground outs by Bosetti and Ainge set the table for a fly out by Martínez that ended the inning. Barker had made it through the Blue Jays lineup once without allowing a single hit or base runner. At the top of the fourth, after the Indians failed to score again, Barker began his warm-up tosses to prepare to face the top of the Blue Jays order for a second time. Griffin managed to hit the ball out of the infield this time, but right into the glove of left fielder Joe Charboneau. Barker recorded his first strikeout of the game by getting Lloyd Moseby to swing and miss. It was quickly followed by another strikeout by Bell. Twelve Toronto batters had come to the plate, and each one had failed to reach base.

A quick bottom of the fourth didn't give Barker too much time to rest between innings, but it also kept him from getting cold. Leading off the top of the fifth was cleanup hitter Mayberry, who became yet another strikeout victim, the third in a row and all swinging. After an Upshaw foul ball fly out to third base, and another strikeout, this time by Garcia, to close out the top half of the inning, Barker was more than halfway through the perfecto. During the bottom of the fifth, Orta hit a two-out single only to get thrown out at second while trying to steal with Hargrove at bat. Bosetti led off the top of the sixth by grounding out to second-baseman Duane Kuiper. Danny Ainge and Buck Martinez followed with back-to-back strikeouts; they both went down swinging. Barker had earned every one of his strikeouts that same way, as his pitching arsenal appeared to be more and more unhittable inning after inning.

The Indians continued to make things interesting by trying to add to their lead in the bottom of the sixth. They had hits by both Hargrove and Harrah. Leal managed to strand both runners on base by forcing fly outs from Thornton and Hassey. He followed that with a ground out from Charboneau that closed out the inning and kept Cleveland still ahead 2–0.

With 18 outs down and only 9 more to go, the chance of a perfect game entered everyone's minds—even Barker's. He disclosed when he felt that he could be pitching a perfect game: "After the seventh inning, and then truly in the ninth inning, that's when I went out there and knew my pitches were working. I still had great command of them, and the Blue Jays couldn't hit them." The once unlikely feat was now suddenly possible, even close enough to hope for. Barker wasted no time in getting Griffin to ground out to start off the seventh inning. Barker then took matters into his own hands by getting both Moseby and Bell to strike out swinging. Barker was red-hot as he now set down 21 batters in order. All of his strikeouts resulted from Toronto batters swinging. Barker was in full command of all of his pitches and headed toward a perfect game. Barker didn't have time to think about a perfect game too much, though, because again the Indians went down in order to close out the seventh. With the top of the eighth inning on tap, the Cleveland Indians were beating the Toronto Blue Jays 2–0. But the real story was that starting pitcher Lenny Barker was now a mere six outs away from tossing a perfect game.

For the third time that evening, Mayberry went down swinging. With just five outs to go, the 7,290 fans in attendance at the Cleveland Municipal Stadium roared at every pitch as if there were ten times that number of fans present. The atmosphere became intense and exciting as Barker closed in on what only a few hours earlier seemed impossible to imagine. After an Upshaw ground out to second-baseman Kuiper, the crowd began to sense magic in the air. When Garcia struck out swinging to close out the top of the eighth inning, the Indians crowd roared again with excitement, because the team was just three outs away from seeing baseball history.

Orta, perhaps filled with adrenaline from a possible perfect game, started off the bottom of the eighth with a solo home run off of relief pitcher Leal. It was an insurance run that brought the score to 3–0. Barker had a chance to breathe a sigh of relief before taking the mound at the top of the ninth. When Barker walked to the mound in the top of the ninth inning, he was no longer just another major league player—he was a man just moments away from achieving baseball immortality. He was on the verge of pitching only the tenth perfect game in major league baseball history. He was no longer the hard-throwing righty that the Texas Rangers had sent away after early control problems: Barker was a man on a mission and no one was going to stop him from achieving it. He was so focused that he didn't think of the possibility of Toronto laying down a bunt in the ninth inning, "It didn't cross my mind. I had a no-hitter going against the White Sox once when their leadoff hitter bunted to reach base to start the seventh inning. The next time he came to bat, I drilled him. That is part of baseball."

Vince with perfect-game hurler Lenny Barker

Bosetti completed his 0–3 night with a foul ball pop out to the left side of the infield to start the ninth. Desperate to try anything to break up the no hitter, Blue Jays manager Bobby Mattick chose pinch hitter Al Woods to bat for Danny Ainge. The move proved futile—Woods also struck out swinging, giving Barker his 11th strikeout of the game. When Mattick then substituted Buck Martinez for Ernie Whitt, it was his last move. The tension in the crowd and the fans watching at home was thick. Barker had come so far and everyone knew they were just seconds away from witnessing history. Barker forced Whitt to fly out to center fielder (and current Indians television broadcaster) Rick Manning. The perfect game was complete, and the city of Cleveland erupted in joy and pride for their beloved starter.

The crowd went wild with excitement after the last out of the perfect game. Barker had just pitched only the tenth perfect game in Major League Baseball history. His teammates stormed the field to greet him in celebration. How did the perfect-gamer celebrate? Barker described it as a pretty low-key affair: "We went back to my condo back in Parma and we celebrated for a while. We were on the game of the week the next day, which was an early day game, so some of us celebrated longer than others." It took a few days for the great accomplishment of the game to sink in for Barker: "It pretty much set in a couple of days later when I started thinking about it. Everyone was waiting to see if I could do it again. It was never in the back of my mind, as I believe the next game I threw a three hitter only to lose 3–0 because all three hits were solo home runs. So it was back to reality real quick because that is what the major leagues does to you." Out of the 104 pitches that Barker threw that perfect night, 84 of them were strikes:

> *I always had a good curveball and threw it hard, but that night I was able to throw it over the plate with ease. I just had such good control over it, and Hassey and I were able to realize it quickly. That night we threw more curveballs, as I would normally throw mostly fastballs. It was just knowing that when you get something working well that you don't change it. They were trying to hit the ball because every strikeout was swinging. My concentration was unbelievable that night, and my confidence was high from having a good season thus far. The whole staff was having a great year until the work stoppage. That night belonged to my curveball because I could throw it anywhere and they weren't hitting it.*

Barker only made one adjustment to his pitching during the game, stating, "I threw one changeup that Mayberry hit for a line drive out, so we got rid of that pitch and stuck to the fastball and curve." After Rick Manning caught the last out and Barker had achieved the perfect game, he described the feeling in detail:

> *All the air was sucked out of my body as I took a big sigh of relief that it was over. I felt like a 1,000-pound weight was lifted off my shoulders. It was one of the best feelings I have ever had in my life, besides having my children. It was a tremendous feeling having all my teammates celebrate with me. In the clubhouse, they rolled out a whole lane of towels leading up to my locker filled with Champagne. It was a great feeling not just for me but for my teammates as we all celebrated. Everyone was so much a part of it back then because of the loyalty from the city and players. Cleveland had so many negative things said about them that it was nice to have our team in first place and then have the perfect game to go along with it. It was something that hadn't been done in a long time, and for it to happen in Cleveland was great for the city and for everyone as we all shared in it. It wasn't just my game, it was everyone's!*

CHAPTER FIVE

The Orange and Blue Era

"Show people how to have success and then you can push their expectations up."

—Lenny Wilkens

The Gund brothers now owned Richfield Coliseum, so it seemed like a natural move for them to also purchase the venue's main revenue producer, the Cleveland Cavaliers. It didn't take long for the Gund brothers to shake things up by changing the team's colors from wine and gold to orange and blue. They also replaced the swordsman mascot to the word *Cavs,* with the *V* as a net. Theses changes, although small, made a huge impact on the direction of the franchise for years to come. It was a new era in Cleveland basketball, one that would provide fans with hope once again.

The Gunds were new to the world of professional basketball, but it didn't take them long to place an NBA veteran in their front office to build the team: Wayne Embry. He was chosen to assemble a team that could make a quick turnaround and once again make the Cavaliers a playoff contender. Born in Springfield, Ohio, in 1937, Embry attended and played basketball for Tecumseh High School and from there went on to play basketball at Miami University of Ohio. The St. Louis Hawks drafted him in 1958 before he was traded to the Cincinnati Royals. His pro career covered eleven years playing for the Boston Celtics and Milwaukee Bucks. After a lot of behind-the-scenes front-office work while playing in Milwaukee, Embry eventually became the first African American general manager of an NBA team after retirement as a player.

The Milwaukee Bucks made history by having Embry as their GM for seven seasons. After his seven-year run in Milwaukee, Embry decided that it was time to take a break, and he stepped away from the game for a few years. In 1986, the Gund brothers brought Embry back to the Cleveland Cavaliers headquarters to begin building a dynasty.

Embry's first move was to bring in a coach to help guide the team. His choice was Lenny Wilkens, a man who would eventually go down as one of the greatest basketball coaches of all time. Wilkens was born on October 28, 1937, in Brooklyn, New York. Wilkens graduated from Providence College, where he was a two-time All-American who led his team to its first appearance in the NIT tournament. His time playing at the school was so impressive that years later, in 1996, they decided to retire his number 14 jersey. At the time of his graduation, he was the second all-time leading scorer in school history.

Lenny followed up an impressive college career with an even better professional stint in the NBA. He was drafted by the St. Louis Hawks in 1960 and went on to play eight seasons for them. In his rookie year with the Hawks, the team made the championship round, losing to the Boston Celtics. For the next seven years in Boston, they made the playoffs routinely but never again returned to the championship. Perhaps his most impressive season was in 1967–68, when he finished second to the great Wilt Chamberlain in the season's MVP voting.

In a surprising move, the Hawks dealt Wilkens to the Seattle SuperSonics in 1968 for Walt Hazzard. Wilkens was named head coach while still playing for the SuperSonics prior to the 1969–1970 season. He was able to perform well, even with the added pressure of coaching, making the All-Star team three more times during his days with Seattle. Not only did the team's record improve under the direction of Wilkens, but he also managed to average more than 20 points, over 6 rebounds, and 8 assists per game during his playing days there. Those statistics would be great for any player, let alone one who was also focusing his time on coaching. Wilkens was traded from Seattle to Cleveland in 1972 and spent two seasons with the Cavaliers before finishing his career with the Portland Trail

Blazers. He retired as a Trail Blazer after the 1974–75 season and then went on to coach with them for the 1976 season.

When Wilkens's playing career was finished, it would be considered one of the best of all time. He was voted into the Naismith Memorial Basketball Hall of Fame in 1989 for his playing career. He was a nine-time All-Star and the league's MVP in the 1971 All-Star game. He was masterful at both scoring and assists. He showed how he was an unselfish teammate by leading the league in assists for the 1969–1970 season. The Seattle SuperSonics retired his jersey number, 19, and he was also voted into the All-Time Fiftieth Anniversary NBA team.

Wilkens enjoyed his time as a player and coach in both Seattle and Portland. It was only a matter of time after he retired from playing that he would once again roam the sidelines as a coach. He returned to Seattle, replacing Bob Hopkins, a quarter of the way through the 1977–78 season. The team had only five victories at that point in the season, and the pressure was placed on Wilkens to turn things around. It didn't take long for him to do so, because the SuperSonics began to dramatically improve: They won 11 of their first 12 games under his direction and never looked back. They used the momentum of the winning streak, along with the masterful coaching skills of Wilkens, to take them all the way to the NBA championship series. The SuperSonics eventually lost to the talented Washington Bullets in the finals. Despite the loss in the championship, it was a sign that Wilkens would have a long and successful career as a coach.

The SuperSonics returned to the championship series the very next season. They faced the Washington Bullets again, this time winning the series in a mere five games. The championship was the first and only in Seattle NBA history. Wilkens showed that he could manage a team of All-Stars, including such talents as Gus Williams, Jack Sikma, and finals MVP Dennis Johnson. He also proved he could handle bench talent with his use of reserves Paul Silas and Fred Brown.

When Wilkens left his coaching position in Seattle, it didn't take long for Wayne Embry to offer him a contract coaching the Cavaliers for the 1986–87 season. This move proved the team was headed in the right direction with the ownership, general manager, and head coach all in place. It would be only a matter of time before winning ways would return to Cleveland.

Cavaliers who played under Wilkens described him as one of the smartest and best coaches they ever played for. They respected him because he played the game of basketball and had a true understanding of what it took to win. As Larry Nance said,

> *Coach Wilkens understood how to communicate with his players without yelling at them, and that is why he was so successful. We were a great group, and it was because we had the best coach ever. As a person, he was even better because he cared about you and never yelled at you. He was stern and would let you know what you were doing wrong, but then after practice sit down with you and talk about family. He was that kind of coach, and it made us feel like we were part of a family. If I ever coach, or if my children decide to coach, I want them to be identical to that man because he was awesome.*

The Cavalier roster was decent but also in need of improvements in certain areas. The pressure was on Embry to make the proper selections in the upcoming draft. It would also be crucial for him to lure free agents to play in Cleveland.

June 17, 1986, would be the day that changed the course of history for Cleveland basketball for many years to come. It was on that day that the Cavaliers drafted Brad Daugherty, a center out of the University of North Carolina. Cleveland acquired the first pick, which Embry used on Daugherty, in a trade the day before that sent Roy Hinson to the Philadelphia 76ers. It was one of the smartest moves in Embry's career as general manager. Seven picks later, the Cavaliers selected Ron Harper out of Miami University in Oxford, Ohio. Both players were highly touted college players. The Cavaliers then went on to select Johnny Newman, Kevin Henderson, Warren Martin, Ben Davis, Gilbert Wilburn, and Ralph Dalton in the draft as well. Embry

Photo: Sheryl Scanlon

Mark Price

was not done dealing yet on that fateful day, though: He would send a future 1989 second-round draft pick to the Dallas Mavericks in exchange for the draft rights of Mark Price, who was also a first-round pick coming out of the Georgia Institute of Technology. With the acquisition of Price, the Cavaliers now had three first-round talents on their roster.

Born in Black Mountain, North Carolina, in 1965, Brad Daugherty grew into a seven-foot frame that was destined for the hardwood. Daugherty excelled at basketball while playing at Charles D. Owen High School. With Daugherty's leadership on the court, his high school team reached the 1982 State Finals before losing in the championship game.

Daugherty was a top recruit later that year for Dean Smith and the University of North Carolina at Chapel Hill Tar Heels, and he would be remembered as one of the few players to play for a Hall of Fame coach in both college and then the pros. Many considered Daugherty to be one of the best centers to ever play for UNC. He was a two-time All-ACC first-team selection and a first-team All-American in his senior season, during which he averaged more than 20 points a game. Based on his impressive college basketball career, Daugherty was later inducted into the North Carolina Sports Hall of Fame in 2002.

Joining Daugherty on the Cavaliers that year was fellow first-round draft pick Ron Harper, who had been a collegiate All-Star and drew many comparisons to Julius Erving for his high-flying style. Harper was a two-time MAC player of the year and made the NCAA All-American second team in his senior season. He immediately showed that Embry's faith in him was warranted, averaging more than 22 points a game in his rookie season. Harper was voted second for the Rookie of the Year to Indiana Pacer Chuck Person.

Mark Price was the player in charge of keeping things running smoothly. A fellow first-round pick of the Dallas Mavericks, he was the perfect man to lead the charge. Price had grown up in Bartlesville, Oklahoma, where he attended Enid High School. After graduation, he went to play college basketball at Georgia Tech and, with hard work and court savvy, he managed to establish himself as the leader of the team. He was a two-time All-American and the recipient of All-ACC honors for all four years of his college career. In the 1984–85 ACC championship game, he led his team to a win over UNC and his future teammate, Brad Daugherty. He was also named ACC player of the year. Price's jersey number at Georgia Tech was retired in acknowledgment of his great college career.

Joining forces with the top three draft picks was Cavaliers 1985 draft pick John "Hot Rod" Williams. Legal problems forced him to sit out his rookie season after being selected by Cleveland in the draft. He'd had a solid career at Tulane University and under Embry, and the Cavaliers were willing to look past his somewhat checkered past and place him full into the fold. Former teammate Larry Nance disclosed how it was to play with "Hot Rod": "He was very underrated as one of the best low-post defensive players that have ever been around. He was a great defensive guy and also a great friend. Once you're his friend, he will do anything in the world for you. We became great friends and we still talk today."

Midway through the 1986–87 season, Embry decided to sign free agent guard Craig Ehlo. Ehlo reflected on growing up learning the game:

> *There was only one game a week on television when I was growing up, so I didn't really have any one athlete I molded myself after. The most influential person in my life who helped me with basketball was*

my high school coach Joe Mahaga at Monterey. He was influential in teaching me the fundamentals of the game. He taught us a continuity-type offense, where we would pass the ball about six times before we got anything to look at shot wise. I was blessed in that area because he was determined to teach us the strict fundamentals and the teamwork part of the game, which helped me develop as a player. I wasn't a very big kid in high school at 6-foot 4-inches tall, so I had to find ways to perform well with using my size against larger opponents. My junior college coach, Ron Mayberry, was also very influential in helping me develop every aspect of my game. I was built to be a swing-type player because I could handle the ball and shoot the ball well at my size.

Ehlo attended Odessa College and Washington State after that. He reflected on that time in his life and his basketball career:

My high school team made it to the regional championships in Texas, and I was lucky enough to lead my team in scoring. However, I think my size may have deterred any school from recruiting me. I didn't have a lot of offers out of high school, even though my team was successful. I did have a few accolades such as being All-State and things like that. I just chose junior college because it was a better avenue for me and close to my home in Lubbock, Texas. I went down there for two years and that was a big part of my life because I was able to put on some more weight. It allowed me to play more and get better as I played 36 games my freshman year and 31 my sophomore year. I was able to average about 24 points a game my sophomore year with 6 rebounds a game and 7 assists. I think that is what caught the attention of several schools. I received letters from the University of Texas, Houston, Oklahoma, Iowa, and some other smaller schools such as Baylor and SMU. It was Washington State that caught my attention the most, because at the time the PAC 10 was a dominant conference. I felt that it was a chance to play in one of the nation's premiere conferences. I had a great coach in George Raveling. He taught me a tremendous amount of respect for the game. He taught me how to use my skills, and we were able to finish my senior season in second place in the PAC 10. We only lost by one game to UCLA and were ranked fourth in the country at that time. We made it to the NCAA tournament and beat Weber State in the first round before losing to the University of Virginia in the second round.

Ehlo was picked by the Houston Rockets in the 1983 draft and played for three years in a limited role. Ehlo explained that the draft back then was much different than the draft today:

The draft was not celebrated and exposed as it is today with ESPN covering the whole thing. I was at Washington State working at our summer camps when the draft was happening. I was on an outdoor court helping out with some young children, chasing them around when the camp director came and told me I was drafted by Houston in the third round. I didn't do much celebrating. Instead, I just went back to work at the camp. That was when they had rookie camps in the middle of the summer and then we would get invited to the veteran's camp after that. I made that team for the first three years under one-year contracts each time. It was like $40,000 coming out of a college, and I thought I was a very rich man.

After his third season, Ehlo moved into free agency, which allowed Embry to sign him. The Rockets reached the NBA finals in 1986 before losing to the perennial powerhouse—the Boston Celtics. Ehlo's championship-round experience made him even more inviting to the Cleveland Cavaliers organization. He shared how it felt to play for the Rockets, and later in that championship series against the Celtics:

In the next year's draft, we selected Hakeem Olajuwon and he completed the twin towers that the team had, so I didn't play a lot. I only got into a handful of games, but I can say I was part of the one-man roster that beat the Lakers in five games in the conference finals before losing to Larry Bird, Kevin McHale, and those guys in the finals. That was the Celtics year, as they went 40–1 at home and couldn't be beat. We hung in there, but lost in six games. The last game was a blowout, and I got to play the last few minutes and be out there to score the last basketball before the fans rushed the court. That was my one brief moment in the NBA finals.

Ehlo also explained his decision to sign with Cleveland for the 1986–87 season:

My coach in Houston was Bill Fitch, who was one of the first Cleveland coaches. Cleveland did not have a good team at that point, so coach Fitch would always tease us and say "I'm going to send you to Cleveland" when we weren't playing well. I was in the Western Conference and only had to go to Cleveland once, and that was when the Coliseum was out there so I wasn't familiar with Cleveland at all. I grew up a Dallas Cowboys fan, so I was somewhat familiar with the Browns. I knew that Cleveland fans were a very sports-minded group of people. I got signed to a ten-day contract with the Cavaliers when Mark Price came down with tendinitis. Coach Wilkens was familiar with me from coaching in Seattle when I was at Washington State. I had talked with him several times when I was doing the rookie camps. When Bagley went down with a sprained ankle, it left me with a few others to play as the guards. It was a baptism by fire. We played five games in the ten days I was there, which gave me a chance to perform for them. I was able to sign with them for the rest of the year after that stint. It was a weird way of getting to Cleveland, but I'm very glad that I did. I was brought up loyal to keep your word, and when Houston had called me asking me to come back, I knew that even though it would have been easy to go back to Houston, I had given my word to Cleveland and owed it to them to stay there and start fresh.

The 1986–87 season was a learning and growing experience for the Cavaliers that upper management had expected. The team finished with only 31 wins but showed growth in many ways. John Williams, Brad Daugherty, and Ron Harper all made the NBA All-Rookie team. Despite the sixth place finish, the rookies' playing skills gave Cleveland fans hope.

The 1987–88 season brought low expectations from many outside of the Cavaliers organization, however. The team had gotten off to a mediocre start before Embry pulled the trigger on a blockbuster deal that brought seasoned veteran Larry Nance to town. On February 25, 1988, the Cavaliers traded away Tyrone Corbin, Kevin Johnson, Mark West, and two future draft picks to the Phoenix Suns. In exchange, Phoenix sent Larry Nance, Mike Sanders, and a future first-round pick to Cleveland.

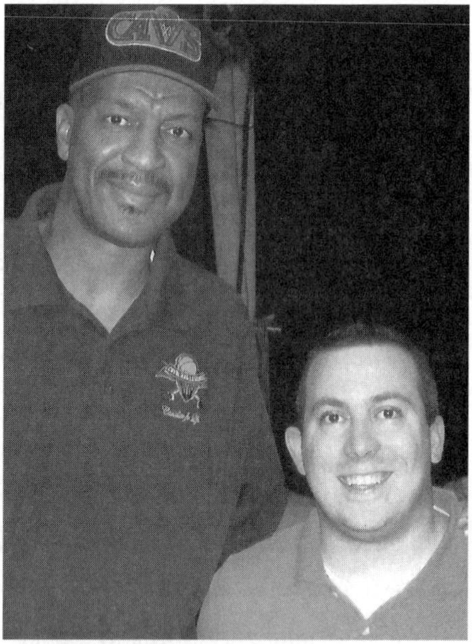

Vince with Larry Nance

Many in the media saw Nance's acquisition as placing the final piece in the Cavaliers rebuilding puzzle. Larry Nance grew up in Anderson, South Carolina, the youngest in a large family of great athletes. He learned the game of basketball from his brothers, cousins, and uncles. At first his older relatives would not allow him to play with them because he was too small, but then as he grew older and taller, he became very talented, and the family allowed him to play all the time. He spent most of his childhood on the court with his family learning to play and perfecting his skills.

Nance grew up idolizing the great Julius Erving. He was glued to his television every time he had the chance to watch him play. He spent every Sunday afternoon in his own backyard, which he named The Spectrum, pretending to be Dr. J. Nance would later say that Erving was his favorite player until he reached the NBA and played against his idol.

Nance went to a trade school in McDuffie, South Carolina, following in the footsteps of his father, who was a truck driver. While studying basic academics at the school, he also played basketball. Anderson Junior College recruited him to play for a year, but then Clemson recruited Nance. Clemson head coach Bill Foster had already seen Nance play and offered him the last "available" scholarship. Foster's faith in Nance was strong, and he knew that Nance would be more than worth taking a chance on. It was a loss of a top recruit for Anderson Junior College, but choosing Clemson over Anderson was a no-brainer for Nance. It's not often that a major ACC college would happen to have an extra scholarship—call it fate, or whatever, but for Nance and Clemson it was the start of a beautiful partnership.

Nance was picked by the Phoenix Suns in the first round of the 1981 NBA draft following a good career at Clemson. Nance reflected on the excitement and emotion of being drafted by Phoenix:

> *To come from a small town like Anderson, it felt really good because making the pros was never a realistic expectation growing up. I just loved to play basketball and playing hard, and because of playing hard, things worked out. When I realized I was going to get the opportunity to go to Phoenix and play, it was just awesome. Upon arriving in the pros, I continued to play the only way that I knew how to play, and that's just work hard and try to develop to make myself better. That approach turned out a successful basketball career.*

It didn't take Nance long to blossom into a superstar. He participated in and won the 1984 Slam Dunk Championship contest, following in the high-flying footsteps of his hero, Dr. J. The trade that brought Nance to Cleveland would go down as one of the signature moves of the Wayne Embry era, but it was a rough trade at first for Nance, as he explained:

> *At the time it was the worst thing that could happen to me because I loved playing in Phoenix, plus I loved racecars and was able to get to the track several times a week. I was under the impression that if you played hard and kept your nose clean you would always be with the same team. The night I got traded I was upset because it was cold in Cleveland. There were two places I never wanted to play: Cleveland and New York. It was the worst time in my life, filled with pressure because I was supposed to bring the change. Then I met my new teammates and things began to change. I started to be around them and play with them, and I realized what great people they were with the great coaches that we had and things started changing—we started winning. All of a sudden this trade turned out to be the best thing in my life. I became best friends with "Hot Rod." We became a very successful team with a great point guard. Things just began to work out better, and I became very happy to be here.*

The Cavaliers played well for the final 27 games of the season because of Nance's addition. They had a modest 42–40 season record, finishing fifth in the Eastern Conference Central Division. They made the playoffs for the first time in several years. The Cavaliers lost to Chicago in the first round, taking the Bulls to the limit by forcing a deciding game five in the best of five. It was the first trip to the playoffs for this young group, and also the first showdown with a player who would become a familiar enemy: Michael Jordan.

It didn't matter to the team who the leading scorer was each night. Their philosophy was to feed the hot hand on any given night. They were unselfish, which was the key component to why they were so good. There weren't any egos on the team, a true sign of teamwork and great coaching. Longtime radio play-by-play man Joe Tait had these words to share about the team dynamics:

> *That was a ball club from top to bottom that was a more talented team then the "Miracle Team," but in the same token the league was much better as well. Michael Jordan was playing in a league of his own. You had Isiah Thomas with the Pistons, Malone and Stockton with the Jazz, and the best pound-for-pound player, Magic Johnson, who could play all five positions. It was the same in the standpoint that the fans really got pumped, but in the same token the league was loaded with talented teams at that particular time.*

It was common for the Cavaliers to have a two-hour practice followed by a one-hour meeting in the locker room. They loved to talk and spend time with each other so much that after most practices they would all go over to a teammate's house to bond some more! Larry Nance shared his view of this magical time:

> *I think it is because we loved each other and it didn't matter night to night who was the leading scorer. We didn't care who was going to be the leading scorer—we just wanted to win. Our goal was to find the guys with the hot hands and keep feeding them the ball. There were no egos ever, anywhere or anytime! We never got into an argument about someone taking too many shots; it never happened. We truly loved being around each other, and so did our wives and families. I was never part of a group that was like that before or after. That kind of teamwork and chemistry is what made us successful. I don't see that type of thing anymore with today's athletes and teams. That's why so many people when I go places say they loved our group. They enjoyed watching unselfish team basketball.*

This kind of team bond was and still is very rare in professional sports. Craig Ehlo explains the camaraderie of the team during this time:

The main thing was team chemistry and that we made ourselves available for fans by living in the local area. Our chemistry was built with several factors in place, one of which was the fact that Larry Nance had a pond we would go fishing in before practice behind his house. We played together, and it didn't matter that we had All-Stars because we still played together. I think people really enjoyed our team because of our method of playing. It didn't matter who led the team in scoring as long as we won. I think it was a fun time for people to come out and watch a team play together like that. Then in the off-season we all stayed in town and none of us moved out of state. I lived in Fairlawn, Mark and Brad lived in Hudson, Larry lived in Bath, and "Hot Rod" lived in Akron, so we were visible. We would go to Summit Mall and constantly interact with fans. I think because we were visible and stayed in the community through the year it helped the fans' relationship with us. I think it helped having Joe Tait around, too, because if he was doing something with his horses at the racetracks or events with women's groups, it was amazing. I never thought I would spend my summers in Cleveland, but then I found that there was lots to do by sticking around. There were plenty of golf courses and many other things to do. I think our visibility in the community is what won over the hearts of the fans.

Ehlo went on to explain how everyone on the team got along so well together:

Our wives would get mad at us after the games because we would sit in the shower for over an hour after the game like a bunch of old women just talking. We would walk out in that cold garage in the Richfield Coliseum and our wives would be like, "What is taking you so long?" It was just an amazing time listening to "Hot Rod" talking about Louisiana or Larry talking about cars, or even listening to Tree Rollins talk about how many kids he had. Gary Briggs, our trainer, was the glue that held us together.

The fans flocked to the Coliseum to see this unique and unselfish team-orientated basketball. The Coliseum was rocking nightly as the fans gravitated to the players on the court because of their workmanlike approach. The total season attendance was 730,925, a number good enough to finish 5th out of 25 teams in the league. It proved once again that when Cleveland produces a winner, the fans show up to the games.

The 1988–89 season was the first full season with the core team in place, and it quickly showed as the Cavaliers continued to improve. They managed to win a club-record 57 games, good enough to finish second in the Eastern Conference Central Division. The key factor to the improvement was how well the team bonded. They were friends on and off the court and truly cared for one another. This was a factor in building their chemistry and made them dangerous to any opponent.

The first-round playoffs matchup was against the Chicago Bulls, a team they had beaten all six times that they faced them in the regular season. With homecourt advantage and the dominant regular season record in place, it seemed that the Cavaliers would easily get revenge for the previous season's playoff outcome. Sadly, with expectations high, they promptly lost game one of the series at home 88–95. They bounced back with a game two victory of 96–88 and traveled to Chicago with the series tied. The Bulls wasted no time in reclaiming the lead in the series with a 101–94 game-three win. A thrilling game-four overtime win for the Cavaliers sent the series back home to Cleveland for the deciding game five.

In game five, Craig Ehlo played the game of his life, scoring 24 points, 4 assists, and 4 three pointers off the bench, and gave the Chicago defenders fits all afternoon. His last-few-seconds go-ahead layup gave the Cavaliers a 100–99 lead. Then Chicago called their last timeout to set up a final play. Seconds later, Jordan hit "the shot," and

Cleveland was knocked out of the playoffs for the second straight year by the greatest basketball player of all time. Jordan finished with a game-high 44 points, and his game-winning shot would go down as one of the most famous of all time. Larry Nance related why, after such a great season, things went wrong in the playoffs:

> *Not to make excuses because the team from Chicago was very good, but injuries hurt us late in the season. I know I had some ankle problems that may have held me out of the next round. I truly feel that when our team was healthy we could beat any team in the league, including Chicago. I'm not making excuses, but I'm just saying we weren't healthy and they went on to win. It's just part of life in basketball.*

This was an incredible 1989 season in which the Cavaliers beat the Chicago Bulls six times but just couldn't get past them in the playoffs. Craig Ehlo shared what he thought happened during that playoff run:

> *We just owned the Bulls that season, as we won a lot more games than they did. We secured the three seed and they had the six seed, which led to the matchup in the first round. It was the first year the Bulls decided to wear black socks and black shoes and it gave them this special mojo. It's not that Michael needed the extra help, but it seemed to make his teammates play better. We had played poorly in game four and should have lost that game, but Jordan missed two free throws. It allowed us to take that game in overtime and win. It gave Jordan some added fuel as we headed back home for the fifth and final game. Every time you hear Michael Jordan talk about playing against Cleveland, he mentions he hated the fans because it was such a great rivalry, despite the amazing games he had against us. We were such competitive teams, and it led to some great games between us.*

Ehlo elaborated on what happened with "the shot":

We had a simple give-and-go play moments before with me and Larry Nance that led to me hitting the go-ahead shot to put us up by one point with seconds to go. The play worked to perfection—all five of us on the court did our job to execute it. The problem was that it left three seconds for the greatest player of our lifetime. To tell you the truth, we did something that we never did before. Coach Wilkens was one of the coaches that kept someone on the vision of the ball, but for some reason he chose to pull Nance off that assignment and called for a double team on Jordan. I think if I had been playing one-on-one with him, I would have played him harder, but because I had the help I may have slacked off a little bit. When Jordan juked Larry on the first move, I ran over to catch him and by the time I got there Jordan was already coming back the other way, so I went flying across him like E.T. across the moon and went right by him. I kept my hand in his face as long as I could, but he had the ability to stop on a dime, pull up, and hit the shot. When I watched it go in, it was the agony of defeat. Those three seconds seemed like slow motion to watch him get that shot off and make that play. When you talk to Michael or anyone with the Bulls at that time, they will all say that shot was exactly what propelled them into their championships.

The following 1989–1990 season was known for some critical injuries to Daugherty and Nance, as well as a controversial trade. Wayne Embry took a major chance that never panned out when he traded away young phenomenon Ron Harper. On November 16, 1989, the Cavaliers traded Ron Harper and three future draft picks to the Los Angeles Clippers for Danny Ferry and Reggie Williams. It was a calculated risk based on the large amount of hype surrounding Danny Ferry's amateur career.

Danny Ferry went to Duke University after being considered one of the best high school athletes in America. He was voted *Parade* magazine's "Prep Player of the Year" from DeMatha Catholic High School in Maryland. Because Ferry played so well during his college basketball career, many considered him to be the next Larry Bird. He was a two-time ACC player of the year as well as a 1989 NCAA All-American first-team member. Also that year, United Press International voted him College Player of the Year. He was drafted by the Los Angeles Clippers as the second overall pick in the 1989 draft. However, Ferry had no interest in ever playing for the Clippers. Instead, he chose to play in Europe for the Italian League. He continued to excel while playing in Europe, averaging 23 points a game. The Clippers eventually grew tired of waiting for Ferry to come home to play for them, so they traded his rights to the Cavaliers. Once Ferry agreed to play for Cleveland, Embry signed him to a 10-year contract. Sadly for Cleveland fans everywhere, Ferry would go down as one of the biggest NBA busts of all time, because he never lived up to his expectations. He averaged just double digits in scoring twice for his entire NBA career.

The Cavaliers did manage to make the playoffs that year despite the injuries. They finished with a 42–40 record, good enough for fourth place in the Eastern Conference Central Division. They ran into Charles Barkley and the Philadelphia 76ers in the first round of the playoffs. Sir Charles and his teammates eliminated the Cavaliers in five games.

The 1990–91 season got off to a horrible start because the Cavaliers lacked their full complement of draft picks due to the Danny Ferry trade. Things went from bad to worse as All-Star point guard Mark Price suffered multiple injuries and appeared in only sixteen games all season. Power forward John "Hot Rod" Williams suffered season-long injuries as well, and the Cavaliers finished with their worst record in years at 33–49.

The 1991–92 season, on the other hand, would be remembered as one of the best in Cleveland Cavaliers history. It was a perfect mix of players in their prime, young players improving daily, and veterans playing with the energy of rookies, blended together with a Hall of Fame head coach. With a full roster all season and confidence growing daily, the Cavaliers cruised to an impressive 57–25 record. They finished in second place in the Eastern Conference Central Division with high hopes to go far into the playoffs.

The Cavaliers promptly disposed of Dražen Petrović, Derrick Coleman, and the New Jersey Nets in the first round of the playoffs, earning a matchup with the elite caliber arsenal of the Boston Celtics. The matchup with Boston proved to be a classic as it was a back-and-forth battle that went on for all seven games. Early on, the Cavaliers fell behind in the series 2–1. Then pivotal game four went into overtime at the Boston Garden. Behind a 32-point performance from Larry Nance, the Cavaliers left Boston with the win. Game five at the Richfield Coliseum was a tight one throughout the first half, with neither team able to pull away. The Cavaliers, behind the halftime adjustments from Wilkens, came out in the second half with full guns blazing. They outscored the Celtics by 11 in the third quarter and never looked back, winning the game and taking a 3–2 lead in the series. Craig Ehlo described how it felt to advance so far so quickly in the playoffs after early exits in previous years:

> *The final game of Larry Bird's career was in the old Richfield Coliseum, and it was very loud. It was a rough go for me because I had torn my MCL about six weeks prior. So when we got into the playoffs, I was still reeling and had to guard Petrović in the first round. Then in the second round I had to guard Reggie, who had been averaging 35 points a game against us. In the finals, we had to face Chicago again, and even with Gerald Wilkins it was a nightmare. I thought we had finally reached the pinnacle of all those years that we had put together before losing in six games to the Bulls.*

Unfortunately, after a great fifth game, many Cleveland fans would like to forget game six as the Cavaliers got crushed 122–91. Nance reflected on reaching the Eastern Conference championship by beating Boston and on the overall atmosphere in the Coliseum that day:

> *Derrick Coleman wore me out in the first round; he was very tough. Then it was incredible to beat Boston, with it being Larry Bird's last ride. I thought that if another team played together as well as we did, it was Boston because they really did play as a team. That series was two great teams out there playing great team ball, which made it very enjoyable. Then we ran into "the man" again.*

A loud crowd packed the Richfield Coliseum on May 17, 1992, to see the final game of the exciting series. The Cavaliers ended Larry Bird's Hall of Fame career on a losing note when they defeated the Celtics 122–104. Just like many times that season, the win was a total team effort with all five starters scoring in double digits. John "Hot Rod" Williams, who was coming off the bench in that series, also managed to have 20 points. The Cavaliers were off to the Eastern Conference Championship round for the first time since the "miracle season."

Waiting for the Cavaliers in the 1992 Eastern Conference Championship round was their old friend Michael Jordan and his Chicago Bulls. The Cavaliers managed to make the series interesting by winning a couple of games, but in the end the developing dynasty of the Bulls was too much for the Cavaliers to overcome.

The following season, Cleveland would reach the playoffs yet again, this time making it to the second round before getting swept by Chicago. The addition of superstar Gerald Wilkins from the New York Knicks proved to be helpful but still not enough to get past the Bulls. Sadly, that series marked the last Lenny Wilkens would spend in Cleveland as head coach. The Cavaliers made the decision after the playoffs to go with Mike Fratello, a former head coach from the Atlanta Hawks turned analyst. It was a move that brought to a close one of the brightest eras in Cleveland basketball history.

Lenny Wilkens went on to become one of the greatest coaches of all time. He coached in Atlanta, Toronto, and New York before retiring from the bench in 2005. By the time his career was over, he was inducted into the Hall of Fame again, this time as a coach who had won 1,332 games during his tenure. By the time he retired from active coaching, he had the most wins in NBA coaching history (before Don Nelson broke that record in 2010). In 1996, the NBA voted Wilkens as one of its all-time 10 greatest coaches. Craig Ehlo also shares his admiration of Coach Wilkens, saying,

> *It was unbelievable, as I had watched him with his Sonics teams. He had a mild-mannered disposition, but he also had a rip-your-heart-out competitiveness in him as well. You may not see it in his body language, but that was the way he plays and coaches. I loved that and that's exactly what I wanted to be like. I remember I rode with him on the plane the first day I got there, and he was trying to explain to me some of the offensive things we were going to try and do. I remember after that the game when I didn't play, he called me in and told me I would play the next night, which was a great thing because he really took me under his wing. He made me feel wanted and needed, and it was all because of him having that kind of demeanor. He loved us no matter what because it was a hard-working town and hard-working team. The people of Cleveland still loved us no matter what happened.*

Larry Nance wrapped up his playing career after the 1994 season, retiring as a Cavalier. The Cavaliers decided to retire his jersey number, 22, which now proudly hangs in the rafters at Quicken Loans Arena. Nance finished his career as a three-time All-Star and was known for being one of the best shot blockers of all time. While playing in Cleveland, Nance was voted to the All-Defensive first team once and the All-Defensive second team twice. Nance described his ability to play defense and shot-block:

> *Those are the stats I love, because to me I consider those to be effort stats. I learned how to block shots from my uncle because he told me that most people are right handed, so if I learned how to block shots with my left hand it would keep me out of foul trouble. So I had a God-given ability*

> *to be able to jump, and I loved blocking shots because it was a definitive positive and a sign of hard work. It was something I loved to do, and a lot of time once you start blocking shots the other team will start looking to avoid shooting on you, then you know you have them. As long as what I do on the court can help my team win, I'm all about that stat—it is the only one that matters.*

Nance also disclosed how it felt to have his jersey number retired and what encouraged him to stay in Ohio after retirement:

> *It feels great because this organization is filled with classy people and great owners. I think the owner now makes it a great place to be. I still live in Akron, Ohio, the same place I lived when I played here because I love the fans, not the weather. Right now, I have a son in Wyoming, a daughter who just graduated from Dayton, and a thirteen-year-old son who lives with us. I spend a lot of time with them. I'm close to opening up my own basketball facility down in Akron to teach basketball to kids. I want to teach these kids old-school basketball of playing the game the right way. I would love to have my hands in the racing, but it is so expensive and I can't do it without sponsors. I still love racing just as much as I always have.*

Brad Daugherty would go on to be celebrated as one of the greatest players in Cavalier history. By the time his career ended in 1994, he had five All-Star game appearances. He averaged nearly 20 points a game and, to that point, was the Cavaliers' all-time leading scorer and rebounder. He went on to hold both of those records for several years. His jersey number, 43, also proudly hangs in the rafters of Quicken Loans Arena. His career could have reached even greater heights if he hadn't been forced to retire at age 28 because of chronic back injuries. Nance, who was in awe of his teammate, said, "Brad was very skilled and didn't beat his chest, but he killed the best in the league on a nightly basis. He was also the best passing center and had a true understanding for the game. He could score and rebound with the best of them."

Mark Price is widely considered the most popular player to ever wear a Cleveland Cavaliers uniform. He seemed to be good at everything he did on the court, and the fans loved him for it. He knew how to score, how to pass, and how to shoot foul shots with a precision seldom seen before. He left the Cavaliers after the 1995 season and spent a few more years in the league before retiring. He would be remembered as one of the league's most consistent shooters, finishing with an incredible 90 percent foul-shooting percentage and a 40 percent rate from beyond the three-point arc. His retired jersey also hangs proudly in the rafters of Quicken Loans Arena. Nance praised Price as "a great, smart, energetic point guard who made everything easy for his teammates around him. He just knew how to play ball!"

Craig Ehlo followed Lenny Wilkens to the Atlanta Hawks for a couple of years before ending his career in Seattle as a SuperSonic. Nearly 30 years after his time in Cleveland, Ehlo is still seen as one of the most beloved figures in Cleveland sports history. He had a solid career and was respected by his teammates and fans because of his work ethic and approach. Larry shared his thoughts about playing with Ehlo, "A hard worker who came to play hard every game and always gave 100 percent of his effort. He always had to guard the toughest guys and that was okay with him because he wanted to." Ehlo has also had a few chances to meet Michael Jordan since he retired. He described that experience:

> *I took my son down to Santa Barbara to Jordan's camp he runs for kids. On the last day he signs autographs for everyone as they put him in the middle of a room. When my son came through there, he asked Jordan to sign his shoe. When Michael asked who he was, and my son said, "I'm Austin Ehlo," and Jordan called him in closer. He told my son that I had hit the shot to put the Cavaliers up before "the shot" took place right after that. I thought that was pretty cool of him to do that.*

Ehlo has led a happy and busy life since retiring from the game, detailing:

I was lucky that after basketball—after I retired—I was able to get into broadcasting with the Seattle Sonics television. I got to announce with Kevin Calabro, who was one of the best play-by-play guys in the business. I did that for two years before arriving in Spokane, where I started broadcasting Gonzaga basketball for the next seven years. I was able to work with Fox also doing PAC 10 games. I coached high school for a couple years after that because I love being around the game, and as a broadcaster you don't have ownership in wins and losses. Sometimes after broadcasting a game, I would go home feeling vacant because of that fact. Now I'm 51 years old with a 24-year-old daughter that just graduated from college, and I never thought I would hear myself say those words. I have a 21-year-old son who is playing football for Eastern Washington. I am currently coaching as an assistant football coach here with Eastern Washington. I spend my days in the gym as well as having a son who is a sophomore in high school. He is a football player, too; I grew up in Texas, so we have a love for football in our family as well. I come to work happy because I'm in shorts and a tank top, which is something that I did my whole life.

Ron Harper went on to enjoy a stellar career as well. After suffering some injuries with the Clippers, he found his way to the Chicago Bulls and never looked back. He won three championships while playing with the Bulls and won two more playing with the Lakers before retiring in 2001. The trade Danny Ferry made never quite panned out for Wayne Embry and the Cavaliers. However, Danny Ferry went on to become the general manager of the Cavaliers a few years after his playing days came to an end in 2003.

With players such as Nance and Ehlo, it was easy to see why the team had such great chemistry. They won and lost as a team without having one player get too much credit or blame. It was an organization that excelled on a teamwork philosophy that few teams follow in today's NBA. Nance portrayed his time playing for the Cleveland Cavs and the love and support of the Cleveland fans, saying,

I appreciated the fans when they cheered for us and still do now. They tell me how they loved our team because of how hard we played. I want the fans to know that when they see me they are always welcome to come up and say hello. I will always stop for an autograph and shake a hand. I really appreciate our fans because we have the best fans in the world! I just want to say, "Thank you!"

Craig Ehlo also shared this love of Cleveland fans when he said,

I have a picture of myself, Ozzie Newsome, and Joe Carter that hangs in my sports room and we are all wearing each other's uniforms. I see that picture every day, and it just reminds me of those seven years I was in Cleveland. The fans accepted you for who you were and patted you on the back when you did good and picked you up when you were down. They wore their hearts on their sleeves and supported us no matter what. That is the biggest thing I can say to them, the camaraderie that we had with our team had a lot to do with those 20,000 people at the Richfield Coliseum every night. They supported you no matter what and I have never come back to Cleveland where anyone said anything negative to me. Every time I go back, fans tell me that they had a wonderful time watching our group play. I just want to thank them for supporting us for all those years. Even though we never won a championship, they loved us through and through.

CHAPTER SIX

Cleveland Crunches the Drought

Our family wasn't blessed with much money, despite having two working parents. But with what little extra money my parents had, they would take us to the Richfield Coliseum to see the Cleveland Force soccer team. They wore solid-yellow jerseys with a white stripe across the chest with the team name; they also wore powder-blue jerseys of the same design. They had great talent on the field, combined with unique names such as P. J. Johns and Ali Kazemaini. And who could forget star players Kai Haaskivi and Benny Dargle, or even our arch-nemesis opponent, Tatu?

The Cleveland Force, named after the mystical Force from the *Star Wars* movies, was a charter member of the Major Indoor Soccer League, known as the MISL, with five other teams. The inaugural season for the league was from 1978 to 1979, with the original owner, Eric Henderson, selling the team to Bart Wolstein shortly thereafter.

Our family would go to the games as often as we could, and many times my dad was lucky enough to score us free tickets. At halftime of each game, me and my brother, Don, would take a little orange soccer ball and kick it around the top of the arena above our seats until the game was ready to resume. The Force also had a deal where they would toss Oh Henry! candy bars out to the fans in the crowd. It was a fun atmosphere that packed in entertainment for the entire family.

Over the next few years, the team kept improving. Bernie James won Defender of the Year in 1983. Then two years later, in 1985, Kazemaini won Rookie of the Year. Two years later, John Stollmeyer was given the same award. In the late 1980s, the team was led by Haaskivi, who could seemingly find the goal in his sleep.

The key addition for the Force was the hiring of new head coach Timo Liekoski for the 1982 season. The team started to win more often, even winning the Eastern Conference Championship for both the 1985–86 and 1986–87 seasons. In the 1987–88 season, the team made it to the championship series against the San Diego Sockers. Unfortunately for Cleveland fans, they saw their team swept by the high-powered San Diego team, who had won their seventh championship in the league's 14-year existence.

Wolstein then decided to fold the team shortly after getting swept in the 1988 championship series, despite the high level of success that they had been experiencing at Richfield Coliseum. It came as a shock to many fans, as indoor soccer was staring to catch on in northeast Ohio. At one playoff game against the Chicago Sting, more than 19,000 fans were in attendance. The Force were averaging at least 11,000 people per regular season game. Wolstein claimed that the reason that he shut down the team was because he was upset that other team's owners were not investing the same amount of time and money into their teams as he was with the Force.

My brother and I didn't have to mourn the loss of soccer in Cleveland for too long, however, because in 1989 Akron businessman George Hoffman created the expansion soccer team known as the Cleveland Crunch. Luckily, soccer was back in Cleveland not long after it had left. The first move by Hoffman was to acquire visionary general manager Al Miller. The games would still be played at the Coliseum, and they even brought back Force legend Haaskivi to be a player/coach. A trade by Miller to bring in Zoran Karić from San Diego to team with star player Hector Marinaro cemented the team's destiny of greatness. Karić and

Marinaro quickly became known as the Dynamic Duo because they dominated the league with their amazing scoring abilities.

The Crunch would go on to have a solid season in 1990–91, advancing to the MISL Finals before losing to the San Diego Sockers. The next year, they returned to the playoffs before being eliminated by the Dallas Sidekicks in the semifinals. To the surprise of many, the MISL ceased all operations in the summer of 1992. This left the Crunch without a major league soccer affiliation, not to mention no place to play. They wouldn't have to wait long before joining the National Professional Soccer League (NPSL) as one of three teams, including Baltimore and Wichita.

The Crunch was switching not only leagues but also venues and head coaches. The new home of the Crunch was the Convocation Center at Cleveland State University. The new head coach, Gary Hindley, was allowed to keep six players as part of the expansion. The decision to keep team leaders Marinaro and Karić came as a surprise to no one. Tommy Tanner, Andy Schmetzer, and George Fernandez were also chosen to be on the team. Hindley was insistent on keeping backup goalie Otto Orf, too, which came as a surprise to many fans. He felt that Orf's strong arm, combined with the smaller venue of the Convocation Center, would allow more breakouts to occur with Marinaro and Karić.

It didn't take long for the new coach's strategy to pay off: Orf quickly became a 25-game winner. The story of Orf is a marvelous one in itself, given the fact that he didn't start playing soccer until high school. As a child, Orf was interested in playing baseball and hockey even though he had always wanted to play football. He was a fan of both the Buffalo Bills of the National Football League and the Buffalo Sabers of the National Hockey League. Growing up, soccer was never an option, and it was a failed attempt at playing high school football that led him to give soccer a try. He had a strong arm, but he was still short for his age and had trouble seeing downfield over the lineman. He also had some personal adjustments from going to a Catholic school through eighth grade to attending a public high school. Starting in his sophomore year of high school, he decided to try playing soccer. The team did not have a goalkeeper, and Orf figured that if he went out for that position, then he wouldn't have to sit the bench:

> *In the beginning, the coaches kept it simple by telling me to focus on just stopping the ball and booting it down the field. As time went on and competition improved, I began to learn how to hold onto and position the ball better. As I got older and played more, the focus was on learning how to use your feet properly. Learning how to use your feet as you play goalie is very important. It is kind of a funny story, but I actually got Most Improved Player two years in a row, which shows just how much I had to learn and grow. By the time I was a senior in high school, the coaching and faith in me paid off, as I was able to obtain several shutouts.*

His early coaches made it simple for Orf, telling him to "just stop the ball" and "boot it down the field." As he got older and played more, Orf learned how to use his feet and continued to improve his game. He showed his incredible desire to win, improve, and compete at the highest level. Those are qualities found in every champion in and out of the sports world.

After a great senior year with several shutouts, Orf went to college at the University of Buffalo. It didn't take him long to prove he was worthy of a spot on any team—he walked onto both the soccer and baseball teams. After 18 months of playing college soccer, he decided to leave school for a spot on the Buffalo Storm of the United Soccer League. The Storm had to send their regular goalkeeper back to Poland because they were going broke and couldn't afford to pay him. They were looking for a local, low-salaried player to back up the new starter, and that is where Orf, now five inches taller, fit in. Orf, who was planning on making money painting houses for the summer, decided to take the Storm up on their offer.

The son of a blue-collar worker, Orf had a tremendous work ethic that impressed his teammates. Because of this, he was allowed to follow his teammates after the Storm folded. After the Storm, Orf went on to play for the Portuguese League in Boston and the Croatian League in Toronto, giving him the opportunity to play all over the world. In 1984, Orf was cut by the Canton Invaders and went back home to work in a machine shop. But his love for the sport led Orf back to playing for the Columbus Capitals, the Fort Wayne Flames, and the Toronto Italia in the Canadian League. Keith Weller, the assistant coach of the MISL's San Diego Sockers, saw Orf playing in a game in Fort Wayne, Indiana, and decided to bring him in to back up legendary goalkeeper Victor Nogueira. The Sockers were looking for a solid keeper who also had good foot skills. With Nogueira out for double bunion surgery, the Sockers needed Orf in uniform as soon as possible. The day after Weller saw him play in Fort Wayne, Orf was in San Diego with a Sockers jersey on.

The following year, Orf went to Cleveland to back up starting goalkeeper, P. J. Johns. Orf described his first impressions of playing in Cleveland and at Richfield Coliseum:

> *I was originally planning on going to Yugoslavia to see if I could make it in Europe. A week before I was to leave, I received a call from Kai Haasikvi asking me to try out to be a member of the Cleveland Crunch. He was the coach at the time and wanted me to compete for the backup job after they brought P. J. Johns back from Tacoma. In the last two games of the preseason, while competing for the backup job, something incredible happened against San Diego. They had pulled their goalie to have a sixth attacker during a free-kick attempt with the game tied and only a few seconds left on the clock. I was able to make the save, then ran to the top of the box and launched the ball all the way down the field into the opposing net. The referee blew the whistle before the ball went in and called a foul; we ended up losing in overtime. This bit of action must have been enough because the coaching staff decided to keep me over Chris Peak for the backup spot on the roster. It was a very nerve-racking tryout in front of almost 19,000 fans. It is like I tell my*

kids that I coach, you need to be able to make the saves you should, because even a simple mistake may cost you a spot. I was able to deal with the pressure well because making it in the professional ranks takes a little bit of luck as well.

Because of his rough experiences when he first came to the Crunch, Orf was ready to be a starter when Hindley finally needed him. Hindley's plan was to combine Orf's strong arm with the offensive outlets of Karić and Marinaro. Orf shared how Hindley's plan helped him to start on his road to be a great player:

The first couple years I played in Cleveland, I had a poor record. I didn't get to play at home, and most times would only get to play in the second half of a back-to-back on the road. My stats were not helped by this situation. At that time, salaries were based on statistics because of the players unions; it was very open and transparent. These factors did not help, and even winning half of your away games was seen as good. I had a prior relationship with Gary from 1990 when he took me down to Orlando, Florida, to play outdoors. Even with extremely limited playing time, Gary saw how hard I worked and made sure I got paid accordingly. He told me upfront that I would be the backup and I was to hold up my end of the bargain as he would hold up his. He wanted me to work my butt off to drive the team, and that's exactly what I did. Years later, when Gary got the job in Cleveland, I already happened to be here, which was a good thing given our previous history. He knew the arm that I had, and he was very smart because he knew he had the two best scorers in the league with Hector and Zoran. With my strong arm, it gave him the opportunity he saw to counterattack. This new element made it a lot of fun for me because it gave me the chance to be more involved in the game. It is difficult to stay mentally in the game as a goalkeeper when you're playing outdoors; however, the indoor game gave us a chance to become instrumental in the game on offense and defense. It was a great opportunity for me to fire the ball down the field at the feet of the two best players in the league. As time went on, we would develop plays to make us even stronger. The budget of our team was spent on offense. Our strength was not always on defense, so when we had the chance to make a good counterattack we scored at a much higher rate than other teams because of this new system in place. It was a risk-versus-reward, as we would have a forward hang back and not play defense; the percentages were in our favor with those two set to take the passes downfield and score.

As Orf was doing his best to stop everything that came at him in the goal, it was fellow star player Hector Marinaro who became a scoring dynamo every time he touched the ball. Marinaro possessed a soccer pedigree that few could beat. Growing up in Canada, Marinaro's dad, who was originally from Argentina, excelled at playing and then coaching soccer. Marinaro grew up in locker rooms and looking up to the players that his dad coached. He would dream of one day becoming a player himself. His dad was his hero, and Marinaro saw him as a great coach and a great dad—the whole package.

Marinaro played in a variety of international soccer leagues. He would play against different cultures such as the Croatians, British, Serbians, Latinos, Portuguese, and Greeks. He was around people who displayed great passion for the game, which helped to enhance his love of the game. Marinaro played on the championship Toronto Italia Soccer team in 1983, which was coached by his dad. His teammates included Donny Biggs and Peter Zezel, who both went on to play in the National Hockey League after they were finished playing soccer. A little later that year, Hector was offered a contract with the Cleveland Force of the MISL. Hector shared his first experiences and impressions of Cleveland and the Richfield Coliseum:

My first impressions of Cleveland were amazing. Quite honestly, when I came down here in 1983, I wasn't sure what I wanted to do with my life.

I decided to take a chance and play for the Force. The first year in Cleveland showed me what I wanted to do for the rest of my life. Being cut a year later was devastating and tough, but it made me much stronger and work harder to get back in the league. That first year in Cleveland went a long way in showing me what I wanted to do with my career. We were averaging 14,000 people a night for our games, then go to the Cavs game and see half that many. [Playing at Richfield Coliseum] was awesome. I hate driving by there now and seeing a big old empty field. I have great memories and respect for the Richfield Coliseum because of that first year.

After his short stint in Cleveland, Marinaro, who was only 19 years old, worked even harder to continue playing in the league. In 1986, he played for the Minnesota Strikers, coached by Allan Merrick. Merrick's decision to switch Marinaro from defenseman to forward altered the course of history for both indoor soccer and Marinaro. "I always had a knack for scoring goals. Even as a sweeper, I would try to push forward out of the back and try to score. I remember in the semifinals of the national championships in Canada when I scored three goals in one game as a defender. The transition was a little bit hard at first, but it came together pretty fast. As long as you get back and play defense and have the right teammates, you can make the switch."

The following season, Marinaro lived up to the faith that the coaches had in him by leading the league with 58 goals. He shared his memories of his time with the Strikers, saying,

I was lucky enough to be teamed up with South African David Byrne in my tryout in Minnesota. We actually lived together for two years in Minnesota, as he was my roommate and we formed a great bond. It is a funny story because I was in Minnesota on a trial and the teams back then were only allowed eight foreign players. And I would have made a ninth. Coach Allan Merrick wanted me to sign, but because they were full I could only go to practice but not play in the games. It was there that I met Bruce Miller, who was the assistant coach at the time. There was a point before I was officially on the team that I had to live in a hotel and when Bruce Miller found out, he invited me to stay in his home. I was lucky enough that the Strikers were a very veteran-laden team. It was there that I met Ray Hudson, who went on to call the play-by-play for soccer on the BN channel. He was a great player and better person. So it was a great team to really catch stride with.

The Minnesota Strikers folded at the end of the season, which led Marinaro to play for the L.A. Lazers. After the Lazers folded, he came to a crossroads in his career. Remembering his love for Cleveland in the short time he played there, Marinaro decided to return to Cleveland and play for the newly formed Crunch. The atmosphere he had experienced playing for the Force was unmatched to any other team he played for, so when the opportunity presented itself to play in front of the same excited fans as a member of the Crunch, he jumped on it. It also gave him the chance to be closer to his family in Canada. Hector revealed what brought him back to play in Cleveland:

Neither one of the cities I played with after Cleveland had the same atmosphere that I had in Cleveland. I once again wanted that atmosphere that only the Cleveland fans could create. I also wanted to be closer to my family living in Canada. When I was in Los Angeles, it was all away across the country and it was too far away from my family. I am very close to my family, and Cleveland was the closest city back to Toronto. It was a great reason to come back with the combination of playing close to family and in front of incredible fans.

This move showed not only Marinaro's loyalty to his family, but also his loyalty to the fans that were good to him years earlier. This demonstrates a great deal about his strong moral character and humbleness.

With Marinaro's great goal scoring, combined with the excellent defense in goal by Orf, the team only needed one more piece to complete the package: Zoran Karić. He had grown up playing soccer in his native country of Yugoslavia when his agent brought him to America to play for the San Diego Sockers of the MISL. He gave some background on the role of soccer in his life as a child in Yugoslavia, saying, "Back in my country, soccer was everything, and it was a privilege for me to play. I started at a very early age of five years old. Every kid would try to play soccer because of its immense popularity. It is the number one sport back home." He also shared what brought him to America to play for the Sockers. "My agent brought me here back in 1987. It was a hard adjustment to make because I had never played indoor soccer with the boards until then, and it took me a couple of weeks to adjust." Karić would go on to be named Rookie of the Year in 1988. The Crunch got away with a huge coup when they traded Paul Wright for him, pairing him up with Marinaro. Karić revealed his first impressions of Cleveland were after he was traded to the Crunch:

> *My first reaction was to be disappointed because I was traded. I was the leading goal scorer of that team at that point, so I didn't understand why they wanted to trade me. Where I come from, when someone trades you it meant you didn't mean much to them. I believe it was a business move because my contract was coming up and they couldn't afford to pay me. They had several high-dollar contracts already and knew they could trade me for Paul Wright and some cash. He was one of the top-notch players in the league. It was tough for me but ended up being one of the best moves I ever made coming to Cleveland.*

Karić is described by his teammates and coaches as the most competitive person they have ever played with and coached. It was his fiery spirit and will to win that separated him from most players in the league and built him into one of the greatest to ever play indoor soccer. Karić agreed with his teammates about his competitive nature and detailed how that helped him achieve so much in his career:

> *I have my own school now, and I have the chance to coach kids who are looking to improve. I cannot stand people who don't have the desire to win. You can challenge me at any game, and I want to beat you. I don't care if my opponent is 4 years old or 80 years old, I still want to win the game! That is how I approach anything, and it is a huge plus. Sometimes my teammates would get upset with me because I'm so competitive and sometimes may go over the line. But the bottom line is that I'm all about winning. I love to win!*

With Marinaro, Karić, and Orf in place, the 1992–93 NPSL Cleveland Crunch debut season was a strong one. The team advanced to the championship series, taking on the Kansas City Attack. With the help of Karić's and Marinaro's abilities to find the net combined with the shot blocking of Orf in net, the Crunch went on to take a commanding 2–1 lead in the best of five series. Unable to put the series away at home with a game-four loss, the Crunch was forced to travel back to Kansas City for game five. Like many times in life, it was a missed opportunity that would come back to haunt the Crunch, who played flat in game five and lost the series. The loss was heartbreaking for both the players and fans.

Marinaro described the loss as devastating and the toughest moment of his young career:

> *It was a championship series of the two best teams in the league, but they had the better record, so they secured home-field advantage in the playoffs. It was very depressing knowing that the season was over and having to wait an entire year to get back and try for redemption. It was the most devastating loss of my career. We played game five at Kansas City and played terrible. It was rough because I had just been named MVP of the league and I had a terrible game five. I sat on the floor in the tunnels of old Kemper Arena for at least 90 minutes following the game, crying. I was so disappointed in myself and that we had lost the*

> *series. It was very tough, and I was down and depressed for several weeks after that. My performance in game five really bothered me, but it also really fueled me for the next year. I knew we were good enough to win it all. I feel as though we should have won it all that year, but we didn't and I think that made us hungrier for the next year, knowing that we were so close. We all knew that we had the team to do it, but we just didn't get it done.*

The team was so close to winning it in game four that the letdown couldn't be overcome in game five. The loss, however, motivated the entire team to come back better and stronger the next year. Karić pointed out the feelings of the loss against Kansas City and how it motivated the team for the following season:

> *We had a chance to win the series in game four at home and lost—that was really tough, not being able to take advantage of that chance. Kansas City was a very good team back then. It made us realize how hard it was to win the championship. For 10 years, we won the most games in that timespan, but that means nothing when the playoffs come. You need to win in the playoffs for that to matter.*

The next year, the Crunch went on a mission to make up for the letdown of the previous season. The 1993–94 team was proof that sometimes you have to lose before you can win, as the Crunch dominated the season and returned back to the championship round. It had been 30 years since Cleveland fans had celebrated a championship in any sport. The series against the St. Louis Ambush gave the city one more chance at ending the painful drought.

Game one in St. Louis is one that Orf wouldn't soon forget. "In many ways it changed my career," said Orf when asked about it years later. The Crunch was blown out 26–6, and Orf had one of his worst showings as goalie. He gave up numerous goals in the first period, forcing Coach Hindley to pull him from the contest. After game one, the Crunch faced another uphill battle.

Orf and the rest of the Crunch proved just how mentally tough they all were, as they came back to win game two on the road 21–14, evening up the series heading back home to Cleveland. Orf learned from his mistakes in game one by playing great for the remainder of the series. His solid goalkeeping combined with the scoring attack of the Dynamic Duo, led to a game-three win of 29–8. In the identical scenario from a year earlier, the win placed the hometown heroes just one game away from winning the championship.

On April 27, 1994, a group of men who received far too little fanfare ended a 30-year curse that had haunted Cleveland sports teams. These men didn't play for large amounts of money or fame—they played for the love of the game and the hunger to win. They took the pressures and hopes of an entire city on their backs and in their hearts, and they didn't stop until they fulfilled the dreams of every fan watching and supporting them. One of the most epic games in soccer history took place on this fateful night.

The Crunch fought hard all night but still trailed by several goals late into the fourth period. With time against them, they needed to score quickly if they were to have any chance at coming back. With time winding down and the odds against them, Marinaro managed to score and tie the game at 15, sending the contest into overtime. Between the end of the fourth quarter and overtime, fans could see Orf being stretched out by the trainer on the sidelines. Many, including Orf himself, thought he was cramping up because of the length of the game and the intensity. It would be revealed later that Orf was playing on pulled hamstrings. Coach Hindley asked Orf if he wanted to leave the game because of the intense pain he was in. However, with Orf being a fierce competitor and loyal teammate, there was no way he would allow himself to leave the game. Not only did Orf play through the pain, but he also managed to excel and shut down St. Louis again for a scoreless first-overtime period. Orf's performance during game four would go down as one of the gutsiest in sports history.

> *We knew that we had to win that game to close the deal, because if we didn't win we would have to go back to St. Louis. It was the same scenario from a year before, and one we didn't want to face again. It was a nerve-racking night, and it was difficult to focus on the positive things because you're focused on avoiding the bad things that can happen. It was a tight game—we trailed for the majority of the night. It was Zoran and Hector connecting on a couple of free kicks to tie the game at 15 and send it into overtime. Both teams were very defensive and hesitant during the first overtime period, because no one wanted to make the mistake that would lead to a goal. To play a whole quarter with neither team scoring a goal was very rare for both of us. I had torn my hamstring and was in intense pain even with the adrenaline going. I thought I had cramps because of the length of the game and continued to have the trainers stretch me out during extended breaks in the action. I didn't realize it at the time, but that was actually making things worse. Coach Hindley offered to take me out, but there was no way I was coming out of that game. The final play started with me coming out of the box to head the ball to George Fernandez. I saw the St. Louis guy coming after it and wanted to make sure I got it before he did. Fernandez passed it along to Andy Schmetzer, who played it into the corner. He then bounced it off the board where Hector was sitting up front for the tap-in goal to win it.*
>
> *Honestly, as much as I would love to say how much I remember that game, I actually remember much more from watching the tape than actual memory because I was so focused on not letting up any goals. It was almost difficult to enjoy while playing it because I wanted to win so badly. I did enjoy playing the game and playing for the fans most of the time, but in this specific game, I was more focused on not making any mistakes and doing whatever I could to keep the ball out*

of the goal. I recall lying on the ground as Hector was running around the field with endless energy in celebration. It was one of the greatest memories for me in my entire career. That game gave me the confidence that I could perform at the highest level as a starting goalkeeper. It gave us as a team the confidence that we could win despite whatever the deficit was that we were facing. It led to numerous championships after that, but the first one set the tone for the rest of my time in Cleveland.

As the second overtime began, the crowd became louder as the intensity on the field began to grow. It was as loud as any arena in the world for any sporting event or rock concert. The players fed off of that support and excitement from the fans. With the clock running down once again in double overtime, it was now the time for the Crunch to satisfy everyone's hopes and put the fears to rest. With the ball flying toward Orf in goal, he managed to leap out and head the ball away, stopping a fast break chance for the Ambush. Seconds later, Schmetzer recovered the header from Orf and advanced it up the field to set up the winning goal. Schmetzer played it off the board to a wide-open Marinaro, who tapped it in high off the goal into the net. In that one brief moment, Marinaro and his teammates managed to erase 30 years of pain for all Cleveland sports fans. Marinaro described the feeling of exhilaration and pressure that he felt playing that game:

The atmosphere in the stadium that day was incredible. From a personal standpoint, it was a sense of urgency, thinking back to the year before. We had a chance to win it at home the year before and couldn't, so we knew that we didn't want to return to St. Louis. We knew deep down that if we were going to win the series we had to win tonight, because a trip back to St. Louis for game five would have been almost impossible to win. We wanted to win it in front of our hometown fans;

> *the place was packed and going crazy. It was a tremendous atmosphere because of the extremely loud fans. We were down two goals in the fourth quarter 15–11 and couldn't seem to score. When Zoran Karić came out of the penalty box, he was able to set me up on two restart goals to tie the game. I remember those goals every bit as much as the game winner in double overtime. The first overtime was crazy, as everyone was on edge not wanting to make a mistake. There were chances at both ends, as Otto played unbelievable to hold them scoreless by making some amazing saves. Both goalkeepers played great and everyone was putting everything on the line. George Fernandez, Tim Tyma, and Andy Schmetzer played amazing defense.*
>
> *I still get chills just thinking about it because it was unbelievable. It all started with Otto as a long ball came though and he came out of his goal to head it to George Fernandez. From there, they played it along the side with Andy Schmetzer by his side. I was waiting inside the box with the St. Louis defender playing me really tight. I saw Andy go deep in the corner, so I knew he was going to play it deep off the boards. I spun to lose my defender and found myself literally wide open two feet from the goal with the ball coming off the boards with a spin on it. It's funny because, even from two feet out, I roofed it and almost missed it. My adrenaline after the ball went in the goal was pumping as I ran around the field twice before anybody caught me. It was a tremendous night! When the on-field celebration was over, I went into the stands and hugged my dad. I just broke down crying before going back down on the field. It was just awesome!*

Orf described what it was like to return to the championship by defeating the St. Louis Ambush and bringing a championship to Cleveland:

> *In game one of that series, we were down by 10 points in the first quarter and I was pulled from the game. It was a turning point for me in*

> *my career because at that point I was the starter the year before and we couldn't close the deal. I let up some goals in that first quarter that I shouldn't have. The next night, Gary Hindley had to make the decision to go back to me or keep me on the bench. He decided to give me another chance and I was able to capitalize with a very good game. It was a turning point for me because I had very little sleep the night before with questions from the media about if I had what it took to win in pressure situations like those. Winning the game in St. Louis gave us the home-field advantage and me the confidence I needed to have a strong series. As a goalkeeper, you have to try and keep the negative thoughts out of your mind. It is a story that could have gone either way, but I was lucky enough that I was able to use it as a positive motivator, and we went on to win the series in four games.*

Karić also weighed in about what it felt like winning the NPSL championship:

> *I remember every moment of that double-overtime game because it was the greatest highlight of my time playing in Cleveland. We wanted to make the most of our chance to win and end the series because we didn't want to run the risk of having to go back to St. Louis for a game five. I seemed to be having trouble with the referees all game and spent a large amount of time in the penalty box. I think I spent an entire quarter in there at one point. I couldn't wait to get out of the box because I felt as though I was letting my team down not being able to play. I'm glad that once I got back on the field we were able to score and take advantage of some of those restarts.*

The packed house at the Convocation Center erupted with excitement. It was a moment of the purest of joys for everyone in attendance and those watching on television. Marinaro shared that the team didn't feel the pressure of winning a championship as much as a pressure to play well:

We knew the history of Cleveland and knew that it was a Browns town with all the suffering the Cleveland fans had to go through. I don't think the team felt the pressure so much as we felt our own. After the year before, and being so close losing in the fifth and the deciding game, we knew that we had to get it done that night. We felt that we were ready and we came out pumped up, even with St. Louis playing great. We had the opportunity to win it and clinch it at home and didn't want to lose because of that. I had been playing 11 years and it was my first championship. I was frustrated that we had been to the championship a couple of times and couldn't get it done. I felt the pressure on myself to get it done, because I was already 28 years old and had won a couple of MVPs but had not yet won the big one. The championship ring was the big thing. It was great because my family and my fiancée were there.

Orf also shared that the pressure of winning a championship for a city that was in dire need of one was pretty far from his mind:

It didn't come into play for me. We had heard about all the terrible things to happen to Cleveland sports teams in the past, but it didn't really dawn on me at the time. It wasn't until after we won that I was made much more aware of it. To me, it was my own personal kind of drought because I had gone my entire pro career as a starting goalkeeper without a championship. I had been on a championship-winning team before but never as the starter, so I knew what it would take. I had only been in Cleveland for four years, so I was just getting to know all the Cleveland sports personalities and stories.

All of the players knew that it had been years since Cleveland had a championship. Karić expressed his feelings about being part of a championship-winning team:

I had been in Cleveland from 1989 to 1993 without a championship, so it was more of a redemption for those years we went without winning it all. In those previous years, we always made the playoffs but could never seem to close the deal. It took me five years to win it, so it was getting frustrating not winning it. Believe me, any sport you play when you win the championship, it is a special thing because it is not easy to do.

The Crunch may have been a distant fourth when it came to notoriety behind the Browns, the Cavaliers, and the Indians, but on that night they were first in everyone's hearts. The Crunch roster was a group of blue-collar workers who used past defeats to motivate them to bring home the gold. They weren't driven by money or ego, just an incredible thirst to compete and win at the highest level. In a day and age where million-dollar athletes are sometimes more concerned with their image than wining, this group of warriors put it all on the line every night.

The fans who witnessed it live have memories that will last a lifetime. Patrick Goggin, a North Olmsted resident, fondly recalled being at the championship game:

I was with my dad and brother, as we had already been to several games that year. We had nosebleed seats, but in the Convocation Center there wasn't a bad seat in the house. The stands were packed and I believe it was even a sellout for the big game. My best memory is when the crowd went crazy as Hector Marinaro's goal hit the back of the net to win the game. The crowd had erupted and the feeling was awesome as everyone was giving high fives and hugs. As a 12-year-old soccer player at the time, it was an unforgettable experience for me to be there. My brother and I looked up to Hector Marinaro and Zoran Karić. Clevelanders tend to forget about the Crunch winning the championship, which is a shame because it is a major championship. The team never gets the credit it deserves. People make fun of soccer, but I think the ones who make fun of soccer are the ones who can't play it. It is such a great memory for me because not only did the Crunch win the championship, but I got to see it with my brother and my dad.

Hindley went on to coach for one more year before he was replaced by Bruce Miller. Miller had been friends with Hector Marinaro in the past and had a great desire for the game of soccer. Marinaro explained the difference between Hindley and Miller thus:

> *They were very different people, as Gary was very detail-oriented in every aspect of the game. Gary was technical in every aspect of the game, from substitutions to penalty kills. The practices under him were very specific, as he had an exact plan to be followed. Bruce Miller was a former player in the old North American Soccer League and even played against some of the greats. His philosophy was not to ruin a great team. With all that being said, it was his philosophy to keep everyone happy. We had a lot of personalities and great players, so his job was to keep everyone getting along.*

At the time Bruce Miller took over, he was told by general manager Al Miller and owner George Hoffman, "Here are the keys to a very expensive fast car, don't crash it." Miller revealed what brought him to Cleveland to become the coach of the Crunch:

> *I had known the general manager, Al Miller, from some previous interactions in the league. At the time, I was working as the director of sports programming at a facility called the National Sports Center. It was a 20-million-dollar sports complex built for the Olympic Sports Festival in 1990. It was also the home of the USA Cup Youth Tournament, which is the largest youth soccer tournament in North America and the world. When Gary Hindley left the Crunch, they had several tier-one coaches lined up to interview. These were men with highly regarded resumes with head coaching experience. When they all passed on the job, I was part of the tier-two listing. It didn't hurt that I had a friendship and past history with Hector. It was on September 3 when I got the call for them to fly me out for the interview. They made me an offer, which was*

> *a pay cut from what I was doing, but they wanted me to try it out for six months. My girlfriend at the time encouraged me to give it try as long as we got married first. So we got married on September 14, 1995, and left for Cleveland three days later with our 7-month-old son. I wasn't sure if it was going to be a long-term deal. We got off to a hot start at 22–3 and, after the early season success, they made me a three-year offer so I decided to stay.*

It didn't take Miller long to justify the ownership's faith in him. He coached the Crunch to another league championship in the spring of 1996. The Crunch avenged the previous championship-round loss to Kansas City in 1993, beating them in six games to claim their second championship in three years.

The Crunch was unable to win the championship in both of the following two seasons. They did return to the championship series at the end of the 1998–99 season against the St. Louis Ambush. The series proved to be just as dramatic as years earlier when these two teams battled for the championship. After a hard-fought series, the Crunch once again won the NPSL championship trophy. Marinaro described what contributed to the Crunch's long run of success in the 1990s:

> *The owner of the Crunch, George Hoffman, along with the general manager, Al Miller, did a great job putting the teams together. Al Miller did a great job bringing in the pieces that we needed while keeping the core players together. George Hoffman was never shy from giving Miller the needed finances to build the winner and sustain it. It is never easy to repeat as a champion, I played 21 seasons and only won three championships, so there was 18 seasons when the last game was a loss. Once you taste that first championship, it is easy to stay motivated because you want it again. The feeling of hoisting the trophy with the crowd going crazy is incredible. The great thing was*

that all three championships we won at home. It was always great to celebrate with all the fans. The soccer fans in Cleveland are a lot of great people that have been around for a long time; it was great to share it with them.

Orf also explained the differences between the two coaches, saying,

Gary was very much a perfectionist with the philosophy that indoor soccer is an unpredictable game, so we needed to master all the predictable parts of the game. We worked hard on special teams all the time, such as power-play and penalty-kill situations. We scored a lot of our goals on free kicks, so this was also drilled relentlessly under Gary at practice. Gary had bonus systems set up for how we did in certain situations. His whole system of coaching was disciplined and organized. Gary wanted to become the general manager after the first few years of great success, but because we already had Al Miller in place, it was time for Gary and the Crunch to part ways. Bruce Miller stepped in next; he was good friends with Hector. He was a different kind of coach, as he let the leaders of the team lead the team. He spent his time trying to work more with the younger players in perfecting their roles. As far as I went, it was difficult at times because Gary coached with a lot of discipline and made each player responsible. As Bruce coached, the discipline started to erode away, as he was more of a player's coach. As we got older, the discipline that we were lacking started to show. It was just the way I saw the game. I yelled at a lot of players because it was difficult on me as the last line of defense if someone blew their assignment. I was willing to do just about anything to win, so when I needed to yell at younger players or whomever, I didn't hesitate. We had Andy Schmetzer and Tommy Tanner playing their tails off on defense helping me out, and Hector and Zoran downfield scoring goals, so the system did work.

Karić, too, expressed what it was like to play for Gary Hindley and then switching to Bruce Miller: "They were both good coaches and good people. Bruce was more of a player's coach and was totally behind myself and Hector, even asking for advice at certain times. Bruce Miller made us feel very important. I give Bruce a lot of credit, because it wasn't easy coaching me as I'm very competitive and want to do a lot of stuff my way."

Bruce Miller was able to show his incredible coaching skills by keeping the team together and focused after the first championship in 1994. He then went on to lead them to a few more during his time as coach. Miller pointed out the main attributes every team should have to be successful:

I was a player's coach with a simple philosophy: At the end of the day, if everything is equal, talent will win out. My attitude was keeping them healthy and happy. If you can keep good players happy and healthy and give them a simple framework to play in, you will be fairly successful. I found that keeping the guys on the bench happy was harder than keeping the starts. We field eleven guys at once, with the twelfth and thirteenth guy being the hardest to keep happy. We were so stacked with talent that we had guys on the bench that would start for any other team in the league. It was a forty-eight-game season, and we had our moments of things going wrong, but it was my job as the coach to solve it.

The Crunch played for two more seasons after the NPSL switched to the MISL. At the start of the 2002–03 season in the MISL, the team once again was called the Cleveland Force. But poor ownership took over and things would never be the same. The team had four different coaches after Miller left, and unfortunately things just didn't work out. Hindley and Miller had been amazing with their coaching skills and leadership ability during their time with the Crunch and Force. The Force would eventually fold after the 2004–05 season.

Despite the sad end to an amazing franchise, no one could ever take away the incredible memories that the team created. The combination of Marinaro, Karić, and Orf under the leadership of Hindley and Miller was a dynasty that Cleveland may never see again in any sport. It is one of the greatest stories, not only in soccer, but in any major professional sport. The Brazilians can tell their children about the glory years of Pelé, and Cleveland fans lucky enough to see it can tell their children about the dynasty that was Marinaro, Karić, and Orf.

Karić described the relationship that he had with Marinaro and Orf:

> *It was the highlight of my career, playing with both of them. Hector was my roommate for 11 years on the road. We became very close friends because we developed a bond both on and off the field. We began to understand each other so well on the field as well. He was such a smart player and was able to take full advantage of my skill. He was one of the smartest players I ever played with, as well as one of the greatest finishers. Otto Orf is also a great guy; I have known him since my days playing in San Diego. He is a big-time winner and loves to win, which is a great quality to have. We have been very close friends for all these years. I get to talk to Otto a lot, as he is a good friend of mine.*

Coach Miller shared his feelings about his star players, starting with Marinaro: "He was a fantastic player, an unbelievable competitor and leader. He was one of the best, pure scorers I have ever seen with an unbelievable shot. He had a nose for the goal and was just a pure goal scorer."

Bruce then went into detail about Karić:

> *Zoran is the most competitive guy I have ever coached. You don't coach Zoran, as he is a talent unto himself. He didn't like to lose at anything: There could be two bucks on the line, but it didn't matter because he just wanted to win. He was very creative, and when you combine that with*

> *his flaming desire to win, he was incredible! His own teammates loved and hated him because he expected so much from himself he would go off on teammates. He wanted everybody to play at top level. He was a winner and someone you wanted on your team. It didn't matter if it was golf or just playing cards, he just wanted to win.*

Lastly, Miller related his feelings about Orf: "His large frame covered so much of the goal. He was an orthopedic mess because of how much he busted his butt to help the team win. He was the ultimate team guy—he went through any pain to help the team win. He was big and strong with a fiery temper to win. He had a strong personality with a character that I had to manage at times when needed."

In Marinaro's 19-year career, he won the league MVP seven times, more than any other person in any professional league. Later, in May 2005, the MISL named their MVP award after him. Marinaro reflected on what made him such a great player for so many years, and he provided some advice for future players:

> *I don't consider myself the greatest of all time. I feel as though I played against and with players better than me. I just happened to play longer, because some of them played outdoor soccer and some played in Europe. I think what my stats say is that I scored the most goals ever, but I still wouldn't consider myself the greatest. It was a tremendous honor when the MISL named their award after me; I never expected anything like that. It was special and really hit home with me and my family. When I started playing, I really had no idea what I wanted to do with my life, but the first year in Cleveland really showed me that indoor soccer was the life that I wanted to lead. The message I would tell anyone is to never give up on your dreams. I was cut from the Force nine months after they signed me, and it took me two years to get back into the league, but I just never gave up. I would recommend that athletes never stop working on their game. Zoran Karić and I are considered great because we used to stay every day after practice and keep working harder. We would stay after and take countless shots,*

giving the goalkeepers extra practice too. That is how we became good at our craft—with constant practice and hard work. I took pride at what I was doing at practice. I wanted to pick corners and do everything right.

Marinaro then went on to explain his decision to retire:

Things were happening behind the scenes that no one knew about. I was on a guaranteed contract for a long time, making well into the six figures. In 1999, the new ownership came and starting changing things around. In 2003, they offered me a new contract for only $25,000 after making six figures. They were trying to force me out like they did with Zoran Karić and Tommy Tanner. They were trying to get rid of the whole core of the Crunch, including changing the uniforms and team name. Most of the decisions they made killed soccer in this city. I signed for a cheap extension because I wanted to go out on my own terms and didn't want them pushing me out. So I signed for $25,000 with a bunch of incentives. I simply did not want to be pushed out. When the season was over, the contract stated they would pay me to do summer camps. I had a wife and two kids and I needed to support them. That is when they blew me off, didn't let me do the summer camps, and also did not pay me. It was later that summer when Chicago picked me in the expansion draft. The management team started to say they would do anything to get me back after stabbing me in the back. I was angry with them and said I wouldn't play for Cleveland again. I wasn't about to move my family and everything, so I decided to retire. It was a forced retirement because the new ownership wanted to go in a different direction for every aspect. It was a disappointing ending to a great career after a lot of great times. The new management team of Paul Garofolo and Richard Dietrich ran the team into the ground. They pushed out Al Miller, and the team was never the same. It was a sad situation because I felt we had done a lot to grow soccer in Cleveland. To watch it get run to the ground in just a couple short years was frustrating to take. In the end, Garofolo was *the one paying the bills and he was the one who had to suffer from his poor decision-making.*

Marinaro now coaches soccer at John Carroll University. He distinguished the differences between being a player and a coach and how he made the decision to coach:

Ali Kazemaini, who currently coaches at Cleveland State University and who was a teammate of mine with the Crunch, was the previous coach here at John Carroll. He had heard through the rumor mill that I wanted to get into coaching and reached out to me when he left. He told the athletic director about me and we talked. They offered me the position, which was perfect for me because it was something I wanted to do without having to move my family. My children and my wife were all born in Cleveland, so it was perfect because I didn't want to move them around the country for a coaching job. I wanted my children to have the stability of growing up in the same neighborhood and going to the same schools and getting to keep all of their friends. I love coaching at this school because of the great friends and community in general. The most rewarding thing about coaching is the quality of the kids. They are tremendous kids who want a good education first and foremost and then to play soccer secondly. The difficult thing at the NCAA level is that we can only have hands on for about three months. It is hard because we spend so much time getting close with them, and then it's all over so quickly. It's tough to sit around and not have the daily competitive challenges.

Marinaro described Orf as a great teammate and family man who many times put his body on the line for the sake of the team. He described Orf as having an unbelievable arm and an even more unbelievable character. Orf portrayed what made him such a great goalie and soccer player:

The drive and the will to win. I would also have to give my parents a ton of credit. My mother gave me creativity and my father instilled the work ethic. Indoor soccer was beautiful that way because you could use the boards and try different things to deceive the defenders. It was my mother's creativity that helped with this. My father's work ethic helped when I played under Gary Hindley, who was a perfectionist. Once you look at those things as a positive, then you become a better player because of it. I worked hard playing backup for years, so once I got the chance to start, I was not going to let any game pass me by without giving it my best. It was enjoying and playing as hard as I could every minute, which is probably why I limp around so much now. The broken toes, fingers, and concussions were well worth it.

Orf is now the director of a program called the Hands On Sports Foundation. He described how he got involved in the project:

Hands On Soccer started as a goalkeeper's camp in the summer of 1994. It did well for a couple of years, so I expanded it to all aspects of the game because I thought it was important for kids to learn the fundamentals. We are still doing that today, and it's been a great twenty-two years of teaching children. With the shift of indoor soccer to futsal internationally, as well as now in the United States, it has made the winter season mandated for futsal for academy teams across the country. This is our sixth year in northeast Ohio working with kids in futsal. It is a great way to pass on the experiences and the knowledge that we have to the next generation of soccer players, so they can become much better than we ever were as kids.

Along with teaching, Orf is very active in the community, developing and helping host charity and other community events:

I was able to develop a golf outing at the Aurora Country Club to help with a charity to help those with spina bifida, a disease my sister suffered from. We were able to donate the money to the hospital for those

> *who suffered. After a few years of doing that, we were able to apply for our own 501(c)(3), and now we are doing the inner-city soccer initiative. I have also been lucky enough to work with Coach Sam Rutigliano's foundation called "Coach Sam's Inner Circle" for the last several years. It has given me the chance to teach kids in the inner city of Cleveland. We are planning on opening up our futsal court in the inner city of Akron this coming spring. It is just one more way to spread the word of the international game of soccer. It is such a great game because it breaks downs so many barriers between cultures. Everything has now come full circle, as I have been given the chance to spend some time with the kids. The best thing for me was being able to coach kids that I watched go on to become professionals. It feels amazing to know that we had a small part in their success.*

The one common trend I noticed as I interviewed each player was his desire to win combined with a great work ethic. It didn't matter the position or the size of the player, they all had that same inner passion to succeed burning deep inside of them. The fact that they could go through a major head-coaching change and still remain dominant in the NPSL speaks volumes not only about their talent and dedication, but also their character.

Marinaro shared a final message to the fans of Cleveland, who have supported for years:

> *The Cleveland fans were tremendous, and I'm still friends with a lot of people who were fans of the team. I consider them more friends than fans at this point. It is a great sports town and the fans are tremendous. I loved playing here and representing Cleveland; it was an honor. I want to thank everyone for all the years of support, and I hope I did Cleveland proud. It was a great ride, but it is unfortunate that athletes have to get old because it was a lot of fun.*

Karić also thanked the Cleveland fans, saying, "Thank you, it was a great experience playing for such passionate fans. My years playing in front of them were just incredible. I want to say thank you because playing in Cleveland was the best 10 years of my life."

Coach Miller also shared what he felt for Cleveland's fans:

> *It was a great time in this city for soccer, and it hasn't been the same since. The relationships between the players and the fans were truly special. The players weren't making a ton of money, so the fans' relationship with us meant a lot. I remember after winning my first championship walking around the Convocation Center and meeting so many of them. I came from a six-kid, one-income family and never forgot where I came from. The fans were great, and we cared as much for them as they did for us.*

CHAPTER SEVEN

Tribe Fever!

The most exciting time in the history of Cleveland sports occurred between the 1995 and the 1999 seasons, when the Cleveland Indians won five straight division titles. They won the American League Pennant twice and even came within a few outs of winning the World Series. It all started years earlier when Richard Jacobs bought the team and envisioned what would happen if they played in a stadium that drew a good crowd. Jacobs proved his gamble correct by building a new

The Indians moved into Jacobs Field in 1994.

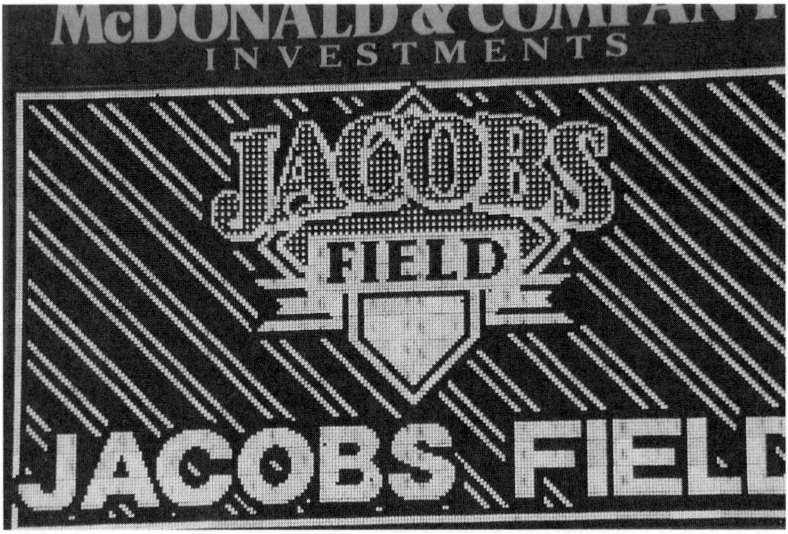

stadium where a 455-game sellout streak happened that only ended when he sold the team.

Jacobs bought the team in 1986 with his brother, David. At the time, the Indians were one of the worst teams in baseball. Among the plans for new players and coaches, the new owners believed that a new stadium devoted exclusively to baseball would be needed, as the Indians had been sharing Municipal Stadium with the Cleveland Browns.

In May 1990, the Cuyahoga County voters approved a 15-year "sin tax" on alcohol and cigarette sales to finance the new Gateway Sports and Entertainment Complex. Construction started eighteen months later, and a new era in Cleveland baseball was born on the corner of Carnegie and Ontario in downtown Cleveland. The construction was completed in October 1993, just in time for the next spring's baseball season. The stadium cost nearly $175 million, with Jacobs funding over half of that. Sports talk host and avid Cleveland Sports fan Jerry Mires remembered the opening season at Jacobs Field fondly:

> *Everyone says that Cleveland is a Browns town, but Art Model can thank the Indians for being so lousy for so long during that stretch. The Indians had such terrible ownership throughout the late 1960s, 1970s, and early 1980s before the Jacobs brothers bought the team. That is the whole reason why they took over the city—because if the Indians had been successful, many things would have gone differently. I remember hearing all the different things, like the team might get a dome or even move. You heard about things like sin tax and didn't even know what they were about. My whole childhood was memories of the original stadium. I was lucky enough to be at the last series against Chicago and things of that nature. I remember Alex Cole stole six bases in one night, and I was there in a crowd of no one. I used to love walking down and seeing the old big nose Wahoo with the big Marlboro sign. The thing that got me was going downtown to the Westside Market with my grandma all the time, and it amazed me to see how*

> *quick they were building Jacobs Field. Maybe it took two years, but it seemed like it flew by as I watched it grow week by week. That first season was crazy because they had such drastic improvement. With all the garbage going on with the Browns, it was nice to see the Indians and this beautiful ballpark grow.*

As baseball was set to begin in the spring of 1994, Indians fans were wildly excited about the prospects of finally having a winning team in Cleveland. They had the perfect mixture of free agent veterans with young players in their prime. It was a plan set in motion by high-profile general manager John Hart several years earlier. Hart talked about his good relationship with Indians owner Dick Jacobs and manager Mike Hargrove:

> *When you look at any sporting venue, and especially baseball, it comes down to the owner, general manager, and manager being connected. Mike Hargrove, as the manager, was very much included in everything we did, all the way up to the ownership level. The thing I wanted to do as a general manager was to make sure that it was a locked-in group. I had Mike sit in on financial meetings so he could see what the club was facing economically. We would also bring in Dick and Mike to talk about the state of the team, so there was a blending of the people who knew. The worst thing that can happen in an organization is a lack of communication. We had a good connection because Mike was a field guy who was pretty secure in his own skin. He was the perfect manager for this young club and good players guy. There were never any real issues, as we all knew our roles. I could walk into Mike's office and talk about what was going on on the field, and he could sit in an owners' meeting.*

Hart had been around the game of baseball for years, beginning when he played in the minor league system of the Montreal Expos. He eventually left pro ball and returned to college at the University of Central Florida, graduating with a degree in history and physical education. Hart couldn't get baseball out of his blood, however, and decided to return to the game he loved. In 1982, he entered the Baltimore Orioles organization, becoming a manager in their minor league system. He reached the pro level as a third-base coach for the Orioles before he left for Cleveland in 1989.

Hart had several special roles in the Cleveland Indians organization, including team manager after Doc Edwards was fired. At one point, he ascended to director of baseball operations. In 1991, Hart replaced Hank Peters as general manager and was named executive vice president of the team. He related the transition from the field to the front office for the Cleveland Indians:

> *I saw generations of fans that were so hungry for a winner because they hadn't had one. They had been through so many bad years, and they were fans that were loyal and connected with their players. I felt the excitement to be a part of a turnaround. I also understood the baggage that the Indians had been carrying with them. I thought it was a tremendous opportunity and also realized that this was an original American League franchise. There was a rich history of baseball in Cleveland, and it gave me the "why not us" approach. We had been struggling through some low-win seasons, and when I came in we had the chance to strip it bare and make as many good trades as we could. We wanted to have a development and scouting system in place to strip it and rebuild it. The last piece of this was getting Jacobs Field. I think it gave us the ability to add the pieces to the puzzle.*

One major factor in Hart's success as general manager was that the team manager was already in place when he took over. He wasn't saddled with making this key decision, however; it was the faith that Hart had in Hargrove rather than making his own selection that paid dividends.

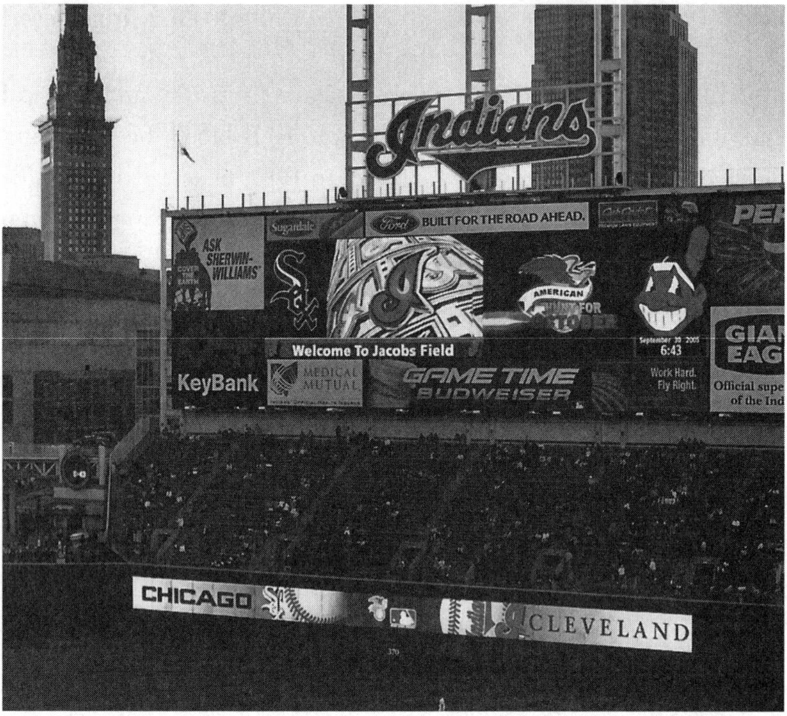

Jacobs Field

Hargrove was a former professional ball player who had spent time as a Cleveland Indian. He had a good career that spanned several seasons with Texas, San Diego, and Cleveland. He was named American League Rookie of the Year in 1974 after he hit an incredible .323. He was the first Texas Ranger to ever receive that honor. Hargrove was also noted for taking extra time at the plate to check his batting gloves and hat, among other items, that earned him the nickname, "The Human Rain Delay."

In 1985, Hargrove ended his playing career as a Cleveland Indian. Years later, his career path would bring him back to Cleveland, but this time he would be in the dugout. Midway through the 1991 season, he replaced John McNamara as the head coach of the Indians. Hargrove disclosed why he chose Cleveland as the best place to begin his career as a big-league manager: "I knew Dan O'Brien and Joe Kline well from my days playing back in Texas. I felt as though my best chance to get back to the big leagues, either as a coach or manager, was with the Indians because they had all suggested that I should continue in a managerial position when I got done playing baseball. It was a comfort thing as much as anything." However, the Indians faded away that season and they finished up only winning 32 of their final 85 games. The next year was only a little better, as they managed to win 76 games in his first full season of coaching the team. The 1993 season was a year of transition, as they wrapped up play at the old stadium and overcame a boating accident tragedy in spring training that cost the lives of two of their players.

Heading into the 1994 season, everyone around baseball realized that Cleveland was on the upswing; it would be up to Hargrove to guide the team that Hart had masterfully put together over the last several years. The amazing off-season trades and dealings between 1993 and 1994 cemented Hart's reputation as a genius. Hart disclosed some of the selling points that he used to bring free agents into Cleveland:

> *For the first time we had a core [group] of players that were really good and that people around baseball were aware of how good they were. There was an opportunity in Cleveland that we should be considered among the elite because we had a very talented team. Those guys we brought in still had gas in the tank and understood how to win. I think the new stadium and the energy and excitement around Cleveland helped. People around the league were starting to talk about the energy that we were starting to build. That was the first year we ever made any of those phone calls to try and bring in veteran talent to go with our core group of young talent. We didn't even attempt to do it in prior years. We were met with a very positive reception from a lot of those guys who, just a year or two before, wouldn't have bothered with that sort of a deal.*

Following the 1993 season, Hart pulled the trigger on a deal that would singlehandedly change the course of Indians baseball for years to come when he traded Reggie Jefferson and Félix Fermín to Seattle for Omar Vizquel. Known as "Little O" to many of his teammates, Vizquel became one of the greatest shortstops to ever play the game.

Vizquel had won his first Rawlings Gold Glove Award playing shortstop with Seattle; he would go on to win 11 more before his playing career ended in 2012. He was also the perfect one-two punch with Kenny Lofton in the lineup. A great bunter, Vizquel had no problem getting Lofton over to third base after he had reached base and stole second. His excellent play in the field also brought out the best in second-baseman Carlos Baerga. The Indians had unknowingly struck gold.

Baerga shared what he liked most about playing with Vizquel in the middle infield:

> *It was awesome! He was the best shortstop I have ever played with in my life. He was a guy who taught me how to play defense and prepare myself for a game. He made me work to become a good player. His first day on the team, I agreed to teach him how to hit and he agreed to help me become a better fielder. He was a very complete player who could bunt and hit and play great defense. He concentrated so hard on defense that every day we went to the field he made me take at least 30 ground balls at live speed and turn the double play like with a real hitter. He taught me so many good habits on how to prepare for a game.*

When Hart wasn't trading for infielders, he was signing future Hall of Famers such as Eddie Murray. The signing of a living legend like Murray meant that the Indians were on the verge of bigger and better things.

Murray began his career when he was selected by the Baltimore Orioles in the 1973 amateur draft. Four years later, he won the American League Rookie of the Year by hitting .283 with 27 home runs and 88 RBI. Over the course of the next 11 years, he averaged 28 home runs and 99 RBI a season. Not a year went by that sports writers didn't consider him for a possible MVP award, and twice he finished as second place in the voting. Murray also teamed up with future Hall of Famer Cal Ripken Jr. and caused havoc around the rest of the league. In 1983, the tandem became so dangerous that Murray hit for a .306 batting average, along with 110 RBI and a career-high 33 home runs. This incredible season led to a World Series title for the

Baltimore Orioles. Eddie was eventually traded to the Los Angeles Dodgers prior to the 1989 season for three players. He had two solid seasons in Dodger blue as he continued hitting his way to a future spot in Cooperstown. Leaving the Dodgers a few years later, he signed with the New York Mets, hoping to combine his talent with other high-priced players to make a pennant run. But it never worked out for him in New York, so when he became available after the 1993 season, Hart wasted no time bringing him to Cleveland.

Adding Murray gave Cleveland the credibility it needed as well as a team leader both on and off the field. It was Murray who found a comfortable spot behind Albert Belle in the lineup that provided the protection Belle needed. He would be the team's designated hitter but also serve as first-baseman when regular first basemen Paul Sorrento needed a day's rest.

The Murray pickup was big, but Hart was not done dealing yet—he managed to bring in veteran ace pitcher Dennis Martínez. Nicknamed "El Presidente," he was considered one of the top Latin pitchers of all time. As the first Nicaraguan to ever reach the major leagues, Martínez was also on the 1983 World Series Championship Baltimore Orioles team with Murray. He played for the Orioles from 1976 to 1986 and was a perennial ace in their rotation, leading the league in wins in 1981.

In 1991, while pitching for the Montreal Expos, Martínez managed to throw only the 13th perfect game in major league history. He went on to lead the league in both ERA and shutouts that same season. Martínez was well respected by his peers ,and his nickname stuck with him wherever he played. He won 100 games in Montreal before leaving the Expos after the 1993 season. He is one of only nine major league pitchers to win 100 games in both the National and American Leagues.

The addition of Martínez on December 2, 1993, was just the spark the Indians needed to collaborate with proven starter Charles Nagy. A couple months later, Hart added free agent Jack Morris. The once questionable rotation was now very formidable with the likes of Nagy, Martínez, Morris, and Mark Clark. The changes to the starting rotation allowed Nagy to drop back in the rotation and take off considerable pressure. Nagy went on to excel in his new role as a middle of the rotation starter.

The key free-agent pickups helped better shape a team of young potential all-stars who were ready to hit their stride. The clubhouse leader and fan favorite was catcher Sandy Alomar Jr. He was born into a family of baseball stars, and his brother Roberto was a Gold Glove second-baseman with the Toronto Blue Jays. Their father, Sandy Alomar Sr., grew proud, as both of his sons had reached the major leagues, following in his footsteps. Alomar came to Cleveland after the 1989 season in a trade where San Diego traded him, Baerga, and Chris James in return for All-Star outfielder Joe Carter. At the time, it was a controversial trade because Carter was a fan favorite in Cleveland, but Clevelanders accepted the move because Alomar was a highly touted two-time Minor League Player of the Year. Alomar didn't disappoint, and he quickly rewarded the Cleveland management's faith in him by winning the 1990 American League Rookie of the Year Award. He also managed to become the first rookie catcher to start for the 1990 All-Star Team, and he won a Golden Glove.

Alomar continued to amaze and improve as the seasons continued. He was selected to the All-Star Team again in 1991 and 1992. However, the remainder of his 1992 season was lost due to numerous injuries that kept the young sensation sidelined. Despite the injuries that plagued him, he was a dangerous hitter when healthy. When he wasn't knocking in runners at the plate, he was handling pitchers masterfully behind it. Alomar

Photo: Garry Gosky

Joe Carter was a key piece in the trade that brought in Carlos Baerga and Sandy Alomar Jr.

emerged as the outspoken leader of the team and worked well with any pitcher, who would become his battery mate of the game. Heading into the 1994 season, Alomar was even more excited, as he would have the chance to work with Martínez and Morris.

After he was traded to Cleveland in 1992, center fielder Kenny Lofton became the spark that lit the flame of the Indians red-hot offence for years to come. Lofton was raised by his grandmother in East Chicago, Indiana. He went to high school there and became an elite basketball player, earning a scholarship to the University of Arizona. He played for the legendary coach Lute Olsen, whose team reached the NCAA Final Four in 1988. This feat made Lofton one of only two men to appear in the Final Four and then, several years later, the MLB World Series. Lofton didn't even play college baseball until his junior year at Arizona. He didn't get much on-field experience, but the Houston Astros liked his speed and the potential they saw in him. They decided to select him in the 17th round of the 1988 MLB draft.

The Indians and Hart pulled off another steal when they traded for Lofton prior to the 1992 season. They sent backup catcher Eddie Taubensee and pitcher Willie Blair to the Astros. Lofton was yet another young prospect that Cleveland obtained with the hopes of becoming a decent player. What they got instead was a perennial All-Star. Lofton wasted little time in 1992 showing the Indians brass that their confidence in him was warranted because he hit for a .285 average while swiping 66 bases. The 66 stolen bases broke the American League Rookie record; it was also enough to break the franchise record previously set by Miguel Diloné.

In 1993, Lofton continued to excel. He stole 70 more bases, leading not only the team but also the league. He was hitting for average as well as stealing the opposition blind every time he reached base. He became a "five-tool player," regularly taking extra base hits and even home runs away while patrolling the Cleveland Municipal Stadium outfield. His leaping ability, combined with his speed, helped him become a Golden Glove winner in 1993. The award would be the first of four by the time his playing career ended many years later. With Golden Glove winners Alomar behind the plate, Lofton in center field, and Vizquel at shortstop, the Indians were rock-solid defensively up the middle.

Carlos Baerga was another key addition to the team acquired in the Joe Carter trade with San Diego. In 1985, the Padres had drafted Baerga out of high school when he was just 16 years old. In his initial season with the Cleveland Indians, Baerga played regularly at third base and did well when he had the chance. He hit for a .260 batting average and showed some power at the plate. Baerga continued to improve, and he solidified his position in the starting lineup as the full-time starting second-baseman in 1991. He average rose to .288, and he knocked in 20 home runs. The next year was a banner one for Baerga—he amassed 200 hits and finished the season with a .312 batting average. The fans fell in love with him because of his trademark smile and hustle. They remained behind him through some rough times for the team.

In 1993, Baerga again managed to reach the 200-hit mark in the final week of the season. He had to beg Hart to check him out of the hospital with an infection to get his 200th hit, and then he promptly checked back into the hospital when the game ended. That showed the passion Baerga had for his craft and also his dedication to his teammates and fans. The back-to-back 200-hit seasons were a rare feat. He was the first second-baseman to do it since Roger Hornsby in 1922. He made the All-Star Team in both the 1992 and 1993 seasons. The Indians were starting to amass plenty of young talent with Baerga, Alomar, and Lofton, all of whom reached their peak at the same time.

Baerga remembered his early years in Cleveland fondly and had these comments to share:

> *I was traded here as a 19-year-old from the San Diego Padres and never thought I would have the career with the Indians that I did. Thanks to God that my first manager, John McNamara, made me feel so good and taught me how to prepare myself and be a professional inside and outside of the field. It really helped me out to have someone who had confidence*

in me. The Indians gave me the opportunity to be here in the big leagues and that doesn't happen too often. I got to the big leagues young and had the chance to be a utility guy. I had the opportunity to come from the bench and prepared myself for that. Then they gave me the chance to play second base, and it was something special. We still had fans coming to the ballpark in the beginning when we were really bad. I loved hitting in the old ballpark even though the team was bad, because I felt I hit better in the old one than I did in the new one. Then we came to Jacobs Field and the fans loved it first, then the players loved it next. I remember the first game against Randy Johnson and having the ballpark packed. It truly was something special.

John Hart made the young players feel happy by giving them a multiyear contract. It gave us the chance to play and improve without worrying about the numbers, which took the pressure off of us. I was the first one to sign, then Kenny Lofton and Albert Belle. It was a commitment to the players, which allowed us to step up. It allowed us to have fun and put everything together to win games and do well. Then he brought in all the good free agents to further help us win. It was a winning recipe because we were so close when the strike set in. We were only one game back, so I knew we were going to the playoffs and had the confidence we were building from spring training on and we didn't want to lose it.

While Lofton and Baerga had been setting the table, it was power-hitting left-fielder Albert Belle who was reaping the benefits of knocking them all in. Belle had struggled with some serious personal problems early in his career, playing under his middle name, Joey Belle. He needed to get his life and career in order because he was to play a key role in the Indians' rebuilding project. Pitchers feared his intimidating presence and physical stature. When Belle overcame his personal problems, he became unstoppable. He had an intense glare that would strike fear into even the most seasoned of veterans who dared to face him. His power numbers increased yearly, as he became one of the most feared hitters in baseball. He hit 28 home runs in 1991, 34 in 1992, and a career high of 38 in 1993 with 129 RBI. Belle was just another weapon in the Indians' growing offensive arsenal.

Hart had done an amazing job assembling talent for Hargrove to manage. The 1994 roster was a work of beauty because it had come together with a little luck and plenty of skill. With the key factors in place, it left open a small crack in the door, just wide enough for two young hungry lions to come charging through it.

Photo: Garry Gosky

Mike Hargrove took over as manager of the rebuilding Indians.

Mark Lewis had been the established third-baseman, but few fans believed he would hold onto the job for much longer as the powerful, young Jim Thome nipped at his heels. Thome was a throwback player who ran laps before the game on the outfield grass and wore his socks up high on his pants. Thome pointed his bat to centerfield before every pitch, just like Roy Hobbes did in the movie *The Natural*. His worth ethic was unmatched, and it was only a matter of time before he overtook Lewis for the full-time starting spot at third base.

Thome grew up in Peoria, Illinois, and resembled a typical farm boy. He had massive arms and legs as well as a country grin on his face all of the time. He was a two-sport all-state athlete in basketball and baseball in high school. The Indians drafted him in the 13th round of the 1989 draft. Under the direction of future hitting coach and manager Charlie Manuel, Thome began to crush the ball in the minor leagues. He earned a name for himself by hitting everything in sight. Thome was called up to the big-league roster in September 1991, but he saw little playing time. Injuries kept him in the minor leagues throughout the 1992 season. In 1993, he showed his true potential by hitting an

International League best .332, knocking in 102 RBI along with 25 home runs. Thome's first starting season with the big league club came in 1992, and he was determined to make sure it wouldn't be his last. In fact, Thome would never again see the minor leagues apart from an injury-rehab start.

The final piece of the rebuilding puzzle was rookie right-fielder Manny Ramírez. The 22-year-old superstar was bursting with talent the second the Indians saw him playing at George Washington High School in New York City. He was selected as the 13th overall pick in the 1991 MLB Draft. He tore through the minor leagues in little time, emerging as one of the top prospects in baseball. In 1993, he was named Minor League Player of the Year by *Baseball America*. His minor league numbers were astronomical at the time he was called up: He was hitting 0.333 with 31 home runs and 115 RBIs between Double A and Triple A. Those statistics were almost identical to those of the eventual American League MVP Frank Thomas.

Photo: Garry Gosky

A young Carlos Baerga

Ramírez made his pro debut on September 2, 1993, by going hitless against the Minnesota Twins. All hope wasn't lost, however, because the very next day he hit two home runs and a double in legendary Yankee Stadium. This was an early sign of the power that the young man from the Dominican Republic possessed. Before his playing days were done, he went on to hit a total of 555 home runs.

Everything was in place to open the new ballpark, Jacobs Field, with a championship-contending team. They had the

Golden Gloves with Lofton, Vizquel, and Alomar, combined with the veteran leadership of Murray, Martínez, Morris, and Nagy. The young guns, Ramírez and Thome, blended together with the core of Belle and Baerga. This plentiful cornucopia of talent was under the direction of a sharp baseball mind in Hargrove. It would take each player working with his teammate to reach his highest. Hargrove described what it was like to have so much talent assembled on the team, combined with the excitement of moving into a beautiful new ballpark:

> *It is hard to put into words the depth of the excitement, because anytime someone has a passion for what they do, the stars start aligning toward the thing we had been building for a while to really take and be what we thought it would be. It made us real nervous but also very excited, too. The unknown was a little daunting, but it was a great time. The thing of it is that we started this thing out with the core players such as Baerga, Belle, Alomar, Lofton, Whitten, Clark, Nagy, Plunk, and guys like that. We had a mixture of veteran players in 1992 and 1993 that really taught our young kids how to win. Then we heard from a number of people around the league that they really liked our ball club and we had a good thing going. It was a perfect storm with the new ballpark. I really feel that if a person has talent and you feel good about who you're working with and where you're working for, that the talent really has a chance to take off. Our players enjoyed playing for John Hart and myself, and we had a good coaching staff. The brand-new ballpark was the ace of baseball at the time. It just amped everything up even more.*

The Cleveland Indians opened the Jacobs Field era with their first regular-season game on April 4, 1994. Because it was the day after Easter Sunday, many children around northeast Ohio were off from school and were able to watch it on TV. I was lucky enough to be one of those children. I fondly remember waking up extra-early that day and throwing a tennis ball off my garage door for hours. I was fielding ground balls and pop-ups as adrenaline and excitement for the new baseball season coursed through my veins. It seemed like a gift from God that we didn't have school that special day.

President Bill Clinton threw out the ceremonial first pitch in front of a sold-out crowd of 41,459 excited fans. The anticipation in the air was so thick it could be cut with a knife. The pitching matchup that day was Dennis Martínez versus the lanky left-hander Randy Johnson for the Seattle Mariners, who were managed by Lou Piniella and widely considered one of the best teams in the game. The Mariners had the league's most intimidating pitcher in Johnson combined with its best young hitter, Ken Griffey Jr. They were a very formidable foe to open against in the new ballpark.

Whether it was a case of nerves or just bad luck, after getting leadoff hitter Rich Amaral to ground out to Baerga to start the game, Dennis Martínez hit Edgar Martínez with a pitch. From there, Dennis Martínez issued back-to-back walks to Ken Griffey Jr. and Jay Buhner, which loaded the bases without allowing a single hit. Eric Anthony hit a sacrifice fly deep enough for Edgar Martínez to tag and score, giving Seattle the early lead. Tino Martinez flew out to Manny Ramírez in right field to end the inning.

Randy Johnson suffered from some of the same first-game nerves, walking two of the first three batters he faced. He worked his way out of the first inning jam by not giving up any runs or hits. Despite his early wildness, the tall lefty seemed to have his best stuff and it looked like it could be a long afternoon for the home team.

After a scoreless second inning, Seattle got back on the scoreboard with a solo home run by Eric Allen. It was the game's, and the stadium's, first official hit. It was a costly one for Dennis Martínez, who had already walked several batters, but he managed to pitch his way out of trouble until the home run. To make matters worse, it seemed the two-run lead was almost insurmountable—Johnson was keeping the Indians scoreless and hitless.

When Johnson took the mound to start the bottom of the eighth inning, the Indians had yet to earn a single hit. The fans and players were wondering if the worst would actually happen. When Alomar singled through the hole between short and third, fans gave a collective sigh of relief. Candy Maldonado had walked before Alomar, and suddenly the Indians had two on with no outs and their first legitimate scoring threat of the game. A few moments later, Johnson threw a wild pitch that allowed both men to advance.

Ramirez hammered the next pitch into deep left field for a two-run double to tie the game. In a matter of a few moments, the Indians went from being hitless to tying the game. It wasn't long after that when Ramirez exposed one of the few flaws in his game by getting picked off of second base. It ended the momentum, but not before the Indians evened the score and showed the magic that Jacobs Field would become known for.

The ninth inning proved to be uneventful when both teams failed to score. It was evident that this new ballpark was destined to provide exciting finishes, as game one went into extra innings, only increasing the drama.

José Mesa took the hill to start the 10th inning and quickly gave up a hit to Griffey. Jay Buhner laid down a beautiful bunt to move him into scoring position with only one out. Mike Hargrove decided to pull Mesa in favor of Derek Lilliquist. The move looked like it was the right decision when he forced Eric Anthony to pop out to first base. Tino Martinez drew a walk that forced Lilliquist to face Kevin Mitchell with two on and two out. Mitchell singled, allowing Griffey to score and give Seattle the lead at 3–2. Hargrove went back to his bullpen and Eric Plunk managed to get the final out.

Bobby Ayala pitched the bottom half of the frame by striking out Alomar. Ramirez drew the one-out walk, and Piniella decided to replace Ayala with Kevin King. Jim Thome replaced Mark Lewis and doubled to right field, advancing Wayne Kirby, who pitch ran for Ramirez, to third base. The Indians now had two men in scoring position with just one out,

Photo: Garry Gosky

Wayne Kirby was a key veteran to oversee the young talent.

giving them an excellent chance to win it. Piniella took advantage of the open base and walked Lofton to load them and create a force out at any base. Omar Vizquel ruined Piniella's plans when he sacrificed a ground ball out to score Kirby from third and, once again, tied the game. Carlos Baerga followed with a fly out to centerfield to end the inning, but not before the Indians had managed to tie the game at 3–3.

Eric Plunk had no problem mowing down the bottom half of the Seattle order, keeping the game tied into the bottom of the 11th inning. Then, King forced Belle to ground out to first before Eddie Murray came up and crushed a double. One batter later, Paul Sorrento sacrificed Murray over to the third base and put the winning run a mere 90 feet away. It was high drama after the intentional walk to Alomar brought Kirby to the plate with a chance to win. Kirby had been the Indians starting right fielder for several years before Hargrove and Hart chose to give his position to Ramirez. The crowd at Jacobs Field roared as Kirby singled a soft line drive into shallow left field to score Murray from third base and earn the Indians their first win in their beautiful new home.

The fans who were lucky enough to be at that game hold incredible memories that will never leave them. Shawn Gerboc, a die-hard Indians fan who grew up in North Olmsted, attended the opening game and shared these vivid memories:

> *I remember going with my mom and grandfather and remember feeling the buzz of the crowd as we first walked in. We had the same season-ticket location as the previous season at the old municipal stadium, right*

> *along the third-base line, behind the tarp, three rows up. I vividly remember how quiet the crowd was in the first few innings, as fans were awed by the new, beautiful ballpark. It took some adjusting for me to get used to such a cozy, small ballpark. I was so used to the giant municipal stadium. The buzz around the team was strong that year as the Indians made some big moves in the off-season acquiring Eddie Murray and Dennis Martínez in free agency. Watching Randy Johnson pitch a no-hitter into the seventh, I thought I might see the second opening-day no-hitter in baseball history (which is owned by Bob Feller). If I remember correctly, Sandy Alomar had our first hit and we were able to tie the game late. It was fitting that the game went into extra innings. What would the first game at the new ballpark be without a little free baseball? Finally, Wayne Kirby won it for us in the 11th and would pretty much set the tone for the Indians team of the late 1990s. That was the beginning of the comeback kids and two trips to the World Series. I think getting out of the old stadium really helped that team gel, as it was a more hitter-friendly ballpark. I will always miss the old stadium on the lake, but at the same time Jacobs Field needed to happen. Not only for the Cleveland Indians, but also for the city of Cleveland itself.*

Jeffrey Ickes, who is also from North Olmsted, witnessed the first game at Jacobs Field:

> *My grandfather got two tickets for opening day when I was in second grade. Our seats were right on first base, second level, a few rows up. I remember he got me a shirt that was more like a dress on me at the time that had the stadium on it. I wore the hell out of that shirt after that. I still have my ticket framed with the poster of opening day. It was the most memorable day for me as a Tribe fan.*

The Indians used the memorable opening-day victory as momentum to propel them to a hot start, winning six out of their first seven games. They finished April with a 13–9 record and appeared to be getting better each week. They got red hot in June by winning 10 games in a row. They had an impressive 51–33 record by the All-Star Game break, a record good enough to put them in a first-place tie in the newly formed American League Central Division.

The All-Star Game that season was played in Pittsburgh. Lofton and Belle came off the bench to play for the American League team. I remember watching proudly as they both took the field in the sharp blue uniforms representing our hometown team. We had two of the best young outfielders in baseball, and now baseball fans everywhere would finally get to see them shine.

The Indians remained hot after the All-Star Game break and looked to be unstoppable as they geared up for a playoff push. On August 10, 1994, the Cleveland Indians beat the Toronto Blue Jays 5–3 in front of more than 50,000 fans at the Toronto Skydome. The win gave them an impressive 66–47 record, only one game out of first place. Then, the worst fears of Cleveland fans occurred the next day when MLB players went on strike. The work stoppage was not resolved during the regular season and it ended up causing the rest of the season to be canceled. The baseball strike was a nightmare to all of Cleveland, because for the first time in years they had a great baseball team. But it also came to a premature end due to no fault of their own. Jerry Mires shared the excitement of the season and the disappointment because of the strike:

> *I remember following along and watching them win countless games. I also heard about the impeding strike and would read the sports paper every day for updates. The Indians were on such a roll and only one game back of first place. The newspaper writers were stating that it would end in a couple of days or a week. Then it just kept going and going until they canceled the season. I remember how awesome those times were until that point. It was different than in 1995, when people thought we would win; it was 1994 that caught everyone by surprise.*

Mike Hargrove also explained what the baseball strike meant for the team:

> *It was tough, and we knew it was coming. In reality, the last time we had an in-season strike was in the 1981 season, and when that happened and it was over, they declared first- and second-half winners, so we were hoping that may happen again if it was a short strike. I wanted us to finish ahead of the White Sox, so we really played and managed for that two-week period leading up to August 12 like it was the last game of the season. We were trying to make a big push to catch the White Sox, and we almost did it.*

The Indians had been on a roll since that dramatic opening day victory and never looked back. Four of their five starting pitchers had at least 10 wins. Dennis Martínez was 11–6 while Jack Morris held a record of 10–6. Charles Nagy was 10–8 and Mark Clark was rolling with a 10–3 record, and three of the starters had ERAs under 4.00.

The pitching wasn't the only thing going well; hitting was the best it had been in franchise history. Eight of the players had double-digit home runs, including Albert Belle, who led the team with 36. Belle was also batting .357 with 101 RBIs, strong numbers that would have contended, if not won, the batting title and MVP award if a full season would have been played. Lofton was batting a career high .349 with 60 stolen bases at the time of the work stoppage. Both young power hitters, Thome and Ramirez, were living up to their hype as well, with 20 and 17 home runs, respectively. Eddie Murray, one of the veteran hitters brought in to guide the lineup and clubhouse, didn't have the best batting average at .254, but his 17 home runs and 76 RBIs were exactly what the Indians needed from him.

Indians players were also recognized by the league and other baseball officials with Gold Glove recognitions. Lofton finished the season with the award and was the league leader in stolen bases. Omar Vizquel managed to win another Gold Glove. Carlos Baerga, who hit .314 with 80 RBIs, received the Silver Slugger award, as did teammate Albert Belle.

Photo: Garry Gosky

Omar Vizquel was one of the most popular Indians of all time.

The Indians had everything a great team needed. The only thing that could stop them was what they couldn't control. It was a terrible way to end a great season. It wasn't just the fans that were upset with the 1994 season ending prematurely because of the strike. John Hart shared his disappointment, saying, "We felt we had a team that was World Series–bound when we traded for Dave Winfield during the strike. When Bud Selig announced we weren't going to play anymore baseball, it was a very painful time." Fans could only hope that if and when play resumed, the Indians could somehow reflect the team they had witnessed that season. Little did anyone know that the following spring, summer, and fall would go down as one of the most memorable and best in baseball history.

Hart was correct when he said, "It was a very painful time," not only for the players but the fans as well. With the disappointment of seeing the promising season come to end, fans and players alike held out hope that the 1995 campaign would mirror the success of 1994. Everyone would soon find out that not only would 1995 match 1994, it would go above and beyond the previous season.

On April 2, 1995, baseball fans across North America breathed a loud sigh of relief when the MLB strike finally ended after 232 days. The player strike had eliminated the previous year's World Series and cast a dark shadow over baseball. When the strike ended, it not only meant baseball would start new in 1995, it also meant that the

Cleveland Indians would have a chance to prove that their 1994 season wasn't a fluke.

John Hart wasted no time improving the Indians by signing Orel Hershiser. This off-season addition improved the already stealth starting rotation. Hershiser was well respected throughout the league and was seen as the missing link that would take Cleveland to the playoffs. Drafted by the L.A. Dodgers in the 17th round of the 1979 draft, Hershiser made his pro debut in late 1983 as a member of the bullpen before eventually being promoted to starter midway through the following season.

In 1988, Hershiser had one of the most successful seasons in baseball history by pitching 59 straight scoreless innings, a record that has never been broken since and probably never will be. He led the league in wins with 23, innings pitched with 267, and complete games with 15. His 23–8 record with an ERA of 2.26 was good enough to earn the CY Young Award. His incredible season would finish brilliantly with his team winning the World Series with him capturing the MVP Award.

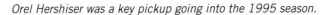

Orel Hershiser was a key pickup going into the 1995 season.

Photo: Garry Gosky

In 1990, Hershiser suffered a torn rotator cuff. Some experts felt that it was caused by his workload, which averaged 250 innings per season. He went on to miss considerable time that season and never returned to the form of the 1988 campaign. After the 1994 season, he was not re-signed by the Dodgers and became a free agent. Hart saw something in Hershiser and felt that the rewards far outweighed the risk. With Martínez and Nagy already in place, and the late-season addition of Ken Hill, the Indians rotation became one of the most talented and experienced in baseball.

By the time that the season began on April 27, 1995, the Indians were more than ready to pick up where they had left off in the previous season. They began the season with a blowout win in Texas against the Rangers by a score of 11–6. As they approached a critical series on Memorial Day with the Chicago White Sox, the Indians were rolling along with an 18–9 record. Many experts saw the White Sox as the division favorite, and they predicted that it would be just a matter of time before they caught up with the Indians for the Central Division lead. The Indians knew that a sweep of the White Sox would start to quiet the critics and show that they were a real threat to win the division. And that was exactly what they did, taking all four games from the White Sox and never looking back.

By June 30, the Indians had a 41–18 record and almost a double-digit lead on the Royals for first place in the division. Any doubts about their abilities had fully disappeared: The Indians appeared to be a runaway train that no one could stop. They had the perfect mix of clutch hitting with great starting pitching and a healthy bullpen anchored by former starter and first-time closer José Mesa. It was a roll of the dice to go with Mesa as the closer, but he quickly proved Hargrove to be a genius as he completed his first 38 saves in a row. Mesa was dominant and at times unhittable; it was a foregone conclusion that if they got to Mesa in the ninth, it was an automatic win.

As the final game of June approached, the Indians' veteran designated hitter Eddie Murray was on the verge of greatness. He was one

Sellouts were the norm for 455 straight games.

hit shy of reaching a career-defining 3,000 hits. This milestone in baseball is very rare, and when Murray singled off the Minnesota Twins in the Metrodome, he became a part of history. Dave Winfield, who was on the Indians bench that season, was also a member of the 3,000-hit club, making the moment even more special.

At the All-Star Game break, the red-hot Indians had accrued a 46–21 record with a staggering 12-game lead in the division. They were well represented at the midsummer classic All-Star Game at Coors Field, home of the Colorado Rockies. Baerga was starting at second base and Belle was voted in as the starting left fielder position. Sitting in the bullpen were Martínez and Mesa. Four Cleveland Indians on the roster was something almost unheard of just a few years prior. This was another sign that the Cleveland Indians were becoming one of the elite teams in baseball.

A few days later, on July 16, 1995, Manny Ramirez produced one of the most memorable moments in the rich history of Cleveland Indians baseball when he hit a majestic 12-inning, two-out home run off Dennis Eckersley. The Oakland Athletics closer was one of the greatest of all time, and the home run was forever immortalized when Eckersley stood on the mound and mouthed the word *wow* as Ramirez rounded the bases for the win. The Indians were making a habit of winning games on their last bat, and this one would go down as the most famous of all.

With the starting rotation performing well, the Indians traded for Ken Hill on July 27, 1995, to make the Indians rotation one of the best in baseball. The Indians sent David Bell and Rick Heiserman to St. Louis for the right-handed starter. He was a two-time, 16-game winner while pitching for St. Louis. The recent All-Star brought the added depth that the Cleveland pitching rotation needed.

It was Friday night, September 8, 1995, when, in the words of Tom Hamilton, "A season of dreams became a reality," with the Indians beating the Baltimore Orioles in front of a sold-out crowd at Jacobs Field to clinch the Central Division. It was their first playoff berth since 1954, and it ended a drought that had eclipsed most fans' entire lives. It was a moment that many fans believed they would never see, and one that defined a generation of die-hard fans.

The success of the Indians was a huge factor in bringing baseball fans back to the game after it had lost so much credibility during the strike. The fans needed a reason to fall back in love with the game, and the story of the Indians was great PR for the league. It was the ultimate Cinderella story of a team rebuilding from a perennial loser to becoming a winning powerhouse.

When the season ended, the Indians had won the division by an astronomical 30 games over the second place Kansas City Royals. They finished the year on a five-game winning streak that brought their final record to 100–44. They were the only team in American League history to win 100 games in a season that was shorter than 154 games. The dominance was not reserved to a few players either, but a good portion of the team. The entire roster put up career-high numbers in many areas. Belle finished the season with 50 home runs and 50 doubles, and finished second in voting for the American League MVP behind Boston Red Sox first-baseman Mo Vaughn. It was a vote that puzzled many—Belle's numbers far surpassed Vaughn's. It was apparent that the ill feelings Belle shared with the media factored into the voting.

Mesa, who was closing games for the first time in his career after years in the starting rotation and middle relief, went on to have a record-breaking season with 46 saves, 38 of which were consecutive. It was a streak that spelled doom for any opposing team looking for late-inning heroics. Mesa had gone from barely having a spot on the roster to being known as the most dominant closer in baseball.

Lofton had another strong season despite spending a little time banged up on the disabled list. He finished with a league-leading 54 stolen bases and 13 triples. His speed at the top of the lineup helped set the table for the rest of the order to knock him in.

In all, the Indians scored 840 runs in a strike-shortened season, which is a number most teams couldn't put up in a full season. Baerga, who had another strong season by hitting .314 with 15 home runs and 90 RBIs, was one of eight starters on the team that finished with a batting average over .300. Murray matched numbers he had during his prime by knocking in 21 home runs and 82 RBIs. Perhaps the brightest

José Mesa nailed down countless saves—except for the one that counted most.

Photo: Garry Gosky

of the stars on the team was Ramirez, as he once again proved to be one of the best young talents in baseball by hitting 31 home runs with 107 RBI. They were remarkable numbers for a second-year player. Thome joined in the fun by hitting 25 home runs with 73 RBIs. It was the best lineup in baseball and one that rivaled the 1927 Yankees in its dominance.

The starting rotation went hand-in-hand with the powerful lineup. The off-season addition of Hershiser paid off with him going 16–6 with a 3.87 ERA. Nagy finished with an identical record. Martínez held a 12–5 record with a low 3.08 ERA, including two shutouts. It was a strong rotation bolstered by a sharp bullpen. Young sensation Julián Tavárez became one of the best middle relief pitchers in baseball, compiling a 10–2 record with a low 2.44 ERA. The team also had left-handed specialist Paul Assenmacher to shut down some of the best lefty hitters in the game.

The 1995 season became known by many as a season of dreams as the Indians dominated the American League. Mike Hargrove, manager of this talented team, reflected on the positives and the challenges of coaching this extremely talented roster:

> *The 1995 season was shortened because of the strike, and we ended up winning 100 out of the 144 games, which is really hard to do. The season was unique because I don't think we ever lost more than three games in a row. We had a tremendous offensive ball club, so it was a magical season. Normally during a season, you will have your ups and downs with major fires to put out, but that year there weren't huge fires to put out. We had a new hero every night, so that made it a real fun season. The challenge was to keep the players focused the entire season. We had such a large lead, so the biggest challenge was keeping everyone focused on what we wanted to accomplish, and that was more than just getting to postseason but also winning a world championship. I had a lot of help with a great coaching staff and veteran leaders. The veteran*

players really did a nice job policing the clubhouse. They were guys who had been there before and were able to show our young kids how to win.

Carlos Baerga also recalled this magical season:

Everyone followed our team like we were the Yankees. We would beat anyone, and our confidence was so high. We won 100 times in only 144 games, and not too many people can do that. It was an unbelievable lineup, and we were living a dream. We were so cocky and felt like we couldn't be beat. Before our first playoff game against Roger Clemens, we were yelling at him from the dugout saying, "We are going to kill you tonight, you better be ready!" It was really a special time. I couldn't believe I got to hit third in that lineup for six years. At least six players from that lineup should go into the Hall of Fame. It was a very special lineup, and I got to hit third. It didn't matter the pitcher or the inning, we knew we could score. How many times we'd come back—it didn't matter. The Indians fans should be very proud of that team. I was very lucky to play with players of their caliber and players who cared about the game the way they did.

The 1995 American League championship was Cleveland's first in 41 years.

Photo: Garry Gosky

Don McKee, who grew up in North Olmsted, Ohio, and now lives in North Carolina, had these memories to share:

> *I was a junior in high school when the Indians made the 1995 playoffs. I remember buying tickets to the final nine games with a buddy. We purchased standing-room tickets and never sat further back than fifth row from the field. We sat and watched Belle crack his 50th home run on September 30 against KC. We would paint our faces and take the rapid down. The atmosphere was amazing and Sandy Alomar, one my favorite Indians during that era, played like a stud down the stretch. I remember the night we clinched, the late-night blast by Peña in game one of ALDS and the intense games against Seattle. I recall Slider falling and getting injured and making it to the World Series. The 1995 Indians are one of the greatest Indians clubs of my era! Go Tribe!*

Ken Carman, one of the top sports-radio talk-show hosts in Cleveland for CBS radio 92.3 The Fan, recalled those days fondly:

> *The team spoiled us during that stretch because of their massive success. People of our generation saw it done once and tend to think it is easy for them to duplicate it, even though we all know it is not. We had farm-grown guys mixed in with trades and free agents that led to a perfect storm. We acquired Hall of Famers by making skilled, but also lucky, moves that paid off. That is a very rare thing, for it all to come together like that. It is a tough thing to say, and I blame it on major league baseball, but it kind of spoiled me for a bit, because with the offense they had, I always thought it would be that way.*

Sports talk-show host and avid Cleveland fan Jerry Mires recalled the exciting 1995 season, too:

> *That season was crazy, and you just knew that the Indians were destined to win. They were so young and powerful. They were put together*

> *from top to bottom. Albert was coming into his prime as has he had his peak seasons in 1995 and 1996. You had guys as good as Manny Ramirez hitting seventh in the lineup—that is how stacked we were. That whole season was crazy; guys like Mesa with his save streak. They were just crushing everyone. It didn't matter where you were, you knew if they won or lost because we're going crazy for them blowing their horns as they were listening to it on their car radios. We had gotten kicked around by the other teams for so long, it was nice to have a winner. It was the first time in my life, since the 1989 Browns, that a Cleveland team had a real chance to win a world championship. You couldn't go anywhere without someone having a hat or shirt on supporting the team. I went to so many of those games just to be a part of it—I remember randomly in the middle of the afternoon making that decision to jump on the 79 bus to head downtown for a game. The playoffs were magical watching Tony Peña beat Boston and then the thrilling series against Seattle. I was 17 years old and remember it vividly. I remember staying up late watching those Indians playoff games, and it never dawned on me how much the national media was against Cleveland.*

The excitement of the fans was at an all-time high as the playoffs began with the Indians set to do battle with the American League East winners, the Boston Red Sox. Tribe fever had the fans in a frenzy during that time; Indians T-shirts, sweatshirts, and jerseys were being sold everywhere.

Game one of the Division I Series took place on October 3, 1995, in front of an enthused crowd at Jacobs Field. Not even a long rain delay before the game could damper the spirit of the fans. On the mound for Cleveland was veteran Dennis Martínez, his opposing pitcher was one of the greatest to ever play the game: Roger Clemens. It was the kind of matchup that baseball purists were excited to watch.

Boston scored first in the third inning on a two-run homer by John Valentin. Martínez had been pitching very well up to that point.

The early lead seemed much bigger than just two runs, as Clemens was shutting down the powerful Indians lineup and keeping them scoreless through five innings. Perhaps the damp weather was keeping the hot bats at bay. Whatever the issue, it was urgent that the Indians get on the board before it became too late.

The Indians batters started to heat up in the bottom of the sixth inning. Vizquel started the two-out rally when he drew a walk. Baerga followed with a single, which gave the Indians men on the corners with two outs. When Belle hit a two-out, two-run double to tie the game, Jacobs Field became unglued! It was a mammoth double for Belle that set the stage for Murray to knock him in with a single that put the Indians ahead 3–2. It was up to the Indians bullpen to hold onto the lead, which they did until the top of the eighth inning when Boston managed to rally and tie the game. Multiple rain delays mixed with a couple of lead changes meant that this game was headed for a possible all-night affair.

The game remained tied past midnight, as both teams entered the 11th inning. If the Indians were to earn their first playoff win in 47 years, they would have to battle from behind again. Tim Naehring hit a Jim Poole pitch over the wall in left field to give the Red Sox a 4–3 lead. Poole managed to get out of the rest of the inning not giving up any more runs, but the damage had been done.

Sportscaster Bob Costas, who was calling the game that night, said, "The last time Belle faced Aguilera, he homered." It was as if the moment was destined to happen. The words had just left Costas's mouth only seconds before Belle smashed a fastball from Aguilera over the wall to tie the game. Seconds after Belle rounded the bases, Boston's manager Kevin Kennedy stormed the field to protest. He demanded that Belle's bat be confiscated and taken in for inspection. It was his claim that Belle had been corking his bat and that the home run was not legitimate. A few moments later, Cleveland manager Mike Hargrove also stormed the field to argue with the umpire, who allowed the bat to be taken away. Hargrove explained what was going through his mind at that moment:

> *I have a real quick and bad temper—I get angry quick, but I can also get over things quick. That was one of those times that it was a real good thing that I was that far away from the dugout. If I were much closer, I would have been in there. I thought it was a real bush-league move—they knew that Albert wasn't using a corked bat. It was gamesmanship trying to avert Albert's attention, and it was just a chickenshit move, to tell you the truth, and I wanted to make sure Kevin knew that.*

The crowd was going nuts as Belle shot a look into the Red Sox's dugout and pointed to his bicep. It was a heated moment that showed the fight and heart of the team.

Later in the inning, Tony Peña came to the plate with two outs and two on base with a chance to win the game, but he grounded out to second. It was a golden chance for Peña to play the hero, but he failed to capitalize on it. It wouldn't be much longer until he received another chance at glory—this time cashing in.

Exactly five hours and one minute after the first pitch was thrown, with most of northeast Ohio fast asleep, Peña hit a 13th-inning, two-out, solo home run off of veteran pitcher Zane Smith deep into left field that gave the Cleveland Indians their first playoff win in nearly half a century. The image of the seldom-used backup catcher running around the bases with both arms up in the air in victory is one that will live in the memories of Cleveland fans forever. It was one down, two to go.

Hershiser tossed a game-two gem as the Indians rolled past the Red Sox 4–0 to take a two-game lead in the series. Boston countered with Erik Hanson, who pitched well himself, but a two-run double by Vizquel in the fifth proved to be too much for Boston to overcome. A two-run home run in the eighth by Murray was added insurance. It was a dominant win that gave the Indians full momentum as they headed into Boston for game three.

For game three, Tim Wakefield was the last line of defense for Boston as they hoped to avoid the sweep. The Fenway crowd was taken out of the game early when Thome hit a two-out, two-run home run, giving Cleveland the early lead. The bottom continued to fall out for Boston in the next inning: Thome once again did damage by drawing a bases-loaded walk, giving Cleveland a 3–0 lead. Boston managed to score in the fourth and draw back to within two runs before the Indians put the game out of reach with a five-run sixth inning. Sorrento hit an RBI single that was followed by an RBI double from Alomar. Vizquel joined the hit parade with a two-run single followed by an RBI double from Baerga. It gave Cleveland an 8–1 lead that would be more than enough to close out Boston and move on to the American League Championship Series against the Seattle Mariners.

It seemed as though the stars were lining up perfectly for the Indians to get an early jump on the Mariners, as they had swept Boston and were able to rest as the Mariners were engaged in a five-game battle with the New York Yankees. The series took every ounce out of Seattle's starting rotation, including having to use their ace pitcher Randy Johnson in extra innings relief to close out game five, making him unavailable in the first two games of the series against the Indians. Former Cleveland Indians general manager John Hart remembers winning the Boston series very well:

> *We sat on the tarmac for an hour and a half waiting to find out if we were going to New York or Seattle as their game five was ending. We didn't want to go to Seattle at first because we would have had to face Randy Johnson. Then in the ninth inning of that game, the Mariners had to bring in Randy Johnson in relief, so we started rooting for them. Then they won and were happy because we found out that we would face unknown Robby Walcott. At the time I said, "Get the reports out because we were going to light this kid up!"*

Baseball commissioner Bud Selig, in his delusional logic, decided on a playoff format that actually gave Seattle the home-field advantage and allowed the series to open up in Seattle. Despite the fact they had to open on the road, the Indians remained confident as they prepared to face the unknown pitcher, Bob Wolcott. Cleveland loaded the bases in the first inning on three straight walks. With Belle coming to the plate, it looked as though game one was on the verge of a possible blowout before one out was even made. Then Wolcott shocked everyone by promptly striking out Belle, forcing Murray to pop out, and getting Thome out on a hard hit ball, allowing him to get out of the inning unharmed.

The failure of the Indians to score would prove costly in the bottom of the second when Mike Blowers put Seattle on the scoreboard at 2–0 on a two-run home run. Martínez was pitching well, but he left the pitch up and Blowers took it out of the ballpark. Thome was able to knock in an RBI single in the top of the third, putting the Indians back in the game. Belle hit a solo home run off Wolcott in the top of the seventh, and just like that, the game was tied. The tie would not last for very long, however, as Jay Buhner hit a one-out double to get the Seattle rally going in the bottom of the seventh. Two batters later, Luis Sojo hit another double off Martínez, giving Seattle a 3–2 lead that they would hold onto for the game-one win.

Game two was a pitching matchup between veteran pitchers Hershiser and Belcher that remained a pitcher's duel until the top of the fifth when Baerga broke the scoreless tie with a two-run single. In the top of the sixth, Ramirez hit a solo home run and Alomar hit an RBI triple that increased the lead to 4–0. Ken Griffey Jr. then hit a solo home run in the bottom half of the sixth to put Seattle on the board. Ramirez hit his second home run of the game in the top of the eighth, increasing the lead to 5–1. The Mariners managed to score again in the ninth, but it was too little too late, as the Indians won 5–2.

Game three brought the American League Cy Young Award winner Randy Johnson to face Cleveland at Jacobs Field. Seattle quickly provided the giant pitcher with a two-run lead by scoring in both the second and third innings off Nagy. Cleveland was able to rally for a run in the bottom half of the fourth when Lofton continued to be a thorn in Johnson's side with a leadoff triple. Moments later, Vizquel sacrificed Lofton in with a long fly ball that cut the lead in half. The score remained 2–1 until the bottom half of the eighth when Lofton singled and drove in pinch runner Wayne Kirby to tie the game. Lofton was wreaking havoc on Seattle's normally unflappable Johnson.

Hargrove called upon his strong Indians bullpen as the game entered extra innings. Seattle caught the Indians off-guard, however, and managed to tag them for 3 runs in the top half of the 11th when Eric Plunk gave up a three-run home run to Jay Buhner. The blow was too devastating to overcome; the Mariners held on for the 5–2 victory, retaking the lead in the series.

It was a devastating loss for the Indians, but one that was character building as they came out stronger the next night in game four. If the Indians were to climb back up in the series, they would have to do it shorthanded—both Belle and Alomar were out of the lineup with injuries. The Mariners would send Andy Benes to the mound against Ken Hill for the Indians.

The Indians wasted no time jumping on Benes in the bottom half of the first inning as Baerga hit a sacrifice ground out that put Cleveland ahead 1–0. Murray, who was batting cleanup because of the injury to Belle, followed with a two-run home run that put Cleveland in the lead, 3–0. One inning later, Lofton hit a sacrifice fly to increase the lead to 4–0. The next inning, Thome hit another two-run home run to increase the lead to 6–0 and end all doubt for the outcome of the game.

Hill was mowing down Seattle hitters one-by-one, and it looked apparent that the series would soon be even. In the seventh inning, Vizquel hit an RBI double that increased the lead to 7–0. The Mariners were not able to score a single run and Hill picked up his first playoff win as a Cleveland Indian. The only negative of the night for Cleveland was their beloved mascot, Slider, taking a tumble off the outfield wall and twisting an ankle.

With the series tied at two games apiece, it was time for the pivotal game five at Jacobs Field. Hargrove decided to skip Martínez's scheduled start in favor of the hot-handed Hershiser. It was a gutsy move, but one that Hargrove was confident would work based on Hershiser's excellent playoff history.

Facing the Indians for game five was the Mariners veteran pitcher Chris Bosio. The game had all the makings of a baseball classic and did not disappoint. The Indians jumped on Bosio in the first inning when Vizquel reached on an error. Baerga followed with a single, giving the Indians and early two on with only one out. Belle then struck out, which made Murray coming to bat even more dramatic. Murray came through with a two-out RBI single that put Cleveland ahead, 1–0.

Hershiser managed to hang on to the lead until the top of the third when Griffey hit an RBI ground rule double to tie the game. Seattle scored again in the fifth to take the lead after an ill-timed error, 2–1. With the pressure mounting, Thome stepped up in the bottom of the sixth and smashed a two-run home run deep into the right-field stands of Jacobs Field, giving the Indians a dramatic 3–2 lead. The home run also knocked Bosio from the game. In the top of the seventh, the Mariners had the top of their order coming up to face the Indians bullpen. Indians relief pitcher Julián Tavárez managed to get one out, but not before getting himself into a bit of trouble, allowing two runners to reach base. Hargrove wasted no time pulling Tavárez in favor of Assenmacher, his left-handed specialist, to face the two best hitters in the Seattle lineup. Assenmacher showed he was up for the test as he set down both Griffey and Buhner with beautiful back-to-back strikeouts. It made two of the best hitters in baseball look clueless with an excellent display of off-speed breaking-ball pitches. A few innings later, Mesa closed the game out in the ninth, and the Cleveland Indians were only one win away from going to the World Series.

Cleveland traveled back to Seattle for game six in the raucous Seattle Kingdome. The date was October 17, 1995, and the Cleveland Indians were only nine innings away from returning to the World Series for the first time since 1954. Standing in their way was the 6-foot-10-inch pitching giant Randy Johnson, a.k.a. "The Big Unit." Johnson was the most feared pitcher in all of baseball and an eventual five-time

Cy Young Award winner. He appeared in 10 All-Star games before his playing days were over and was known for having a wicked slider and untouchable fastball; he excelled against left-handed hitters.

Taking the mound for the Indians was veteran ace Martínez, who had a lot to prove after being bumped from his regular start in gave five. Seattle had a "refuse to lose" attitude for months, overcoming a large deficit in the Western Division, behind Anaheim, to capture the division win in a one-game, sudden-death playoff. The team was used to having their back against the wall and played their best when they were in a must-win situation. It would be the job of the crafty right-handed veteran Martínez to shut them down for good and punch his team's ticket to the World Series.

How did the Indians get ready for this critical game six? Hargrove shared what was going through his mind leading up to the series:

> *You don't have to tell guys in that situation too much because they are fully aware of the magnitude of the situation. They knew what was going on, so we didn't have to prepare them for too much. We had played top pitchers well all year long, so I wasn't really worried about us not being able to get to Randy. I was more worried about shutting down their great offensive ball club.*

Baerga recalled the pregame strategy and how the team decided to address Johnson:

> *We had a meeting before the game and decided we needed to score runs by bunting the ball and making them crazy. We wanted to get him pissed off at us. We had to force him to make mistakes and not wait for the big home run. The little things would be important for us to win. We told Kenny to steal bases and bunt on him because we needed to get Johnson crazy. It was so loud that night that we needed to put in earplugs on top of having to face a giant on the mound. It was crucial to win that game because it was going to be tough to have to come back and face them for game seven if we didn't. It turned out to be one of*

> *my biggest games because I went three-for-three against him and hit a home run, so it is something I will never forget.*

The game remained scoreless through the first four innings as it lived up to the promised pitcher's duel. Álvaro Espinoza reached base on a one-out error by Joey Cora, Seattle's second-baseman who had been having an incredible defensive series up until that point. Espinosa was able to advance to second base on the throwing error, and the Indians had a man in scoring position with only one out. Peña flied out to medium-deep center field for the second out. This brought Johnson's nemesis, Lofton, up to bat at yet another crucial situation. Lofton was the one left-handed hitter that seemed to have Johnson's number, as time and time again he got the best of the tall pitcher. With two outs and the game scoreless, it was a now-or-never moment that Lofton didn't fail to capitalize on. He hit a hard line drive to short left field that dropped in for a hit and scored the game's first run. Lofton had gotten the best of Johnson once again and had put the Indians on top in the process. The frustration on Johnson's face was evident, and it was clear that Lofton was inside Johnson's head.

Two more scoreless innings went by, and the Indians were clinging to a 1–0 lead as they entered the top of the eighth inning. Peña continued his postseason heroics by leading off with a double to deep right field. Pinch runner Rubén Amaro was then inserted in the game to replace Peña on the base paths. Lofton continued to play mind games with Johnson as he bunted to the right of the mound where Johnson was unable to field the ball in time to throw Lofton out. The Indians now had runners on first and third with no outs. Lofton continued to wreak havoc as he stole second base, which put two men in scoring position with no outs. Johnson, who was clearly rattled from Lofton's antics on the base paths and his ability to get big hits off him all series long, threw the next pitch wild and past catcher Dan Wilson. As Amaro strolled home on the wild pitch, Johnson slowly walked to home plate with little-to-no urgency; he didn't even notice that Lofton was flying by third base and heading for home. By the time Johnson realized what was going on, it was too late—Lofton flew past him to score the second run of the play. It was a backbreaking moment for Johnson and Seattle, because the heart and hustle of Lofton had singlehandedly given Cleveland a 3–0 lead late in the game.

Vizquel took the next Johnson pitch to deep left field before it was tracked down just in front of the warning track for the first out. It would be the last out recorded by Johnson, as Baerga came to bat and smacked a solo home run over the wall to put Cleveland ahead, 4–0, chasing Johnson from the game in the process.

As Johnson left the mound and headed for the showers, homes and bars across northeast Ohio were going wild with excitement. The fans could sense that they were very close to seeing their beloved Indians capture a pennant for the first time in 41 years. They had jumped on the best pitcher in baseball and had all the momentum to close out the victory. It silenced the loud crowd in Seattle.

Tavárez showed his relief pitching dominance by shutting down all three batters that he faced in the bottom of the eighth. The Cleveland Indians were only three outs away from the win. Cleveland fans everywhere held their breath as Mesa took the mound in the bottom half of the ninth inning. For more years than anyone would care to remember, the Indians had been the joke of baseball. There had even been movies, such as the baseball spoof *Major League*, poking fun at the long losing history the city had endured. Mesa was only three outs away from ending all the jokes and putting Cleveland back on the sports world map once again.

Mesa began the bottom of the ninth by forcing Griffey to ground out to Baerga for the first out. Edgar Martínez, who was having a stellar series, struck out and brought the Indians just one out away from the World Series. The Indians would have to wait a little longer as Mesa walked Tino Martinez to extend the drama one more batter. Buhner swung at the 0–1 fastball from Mesa and hit it on the ground to Thome at third base. Thome fielded the ball cleanly and threw it across the diamond to first base to record the final out and send Cleveland fans into a frenzy. I can still recall jumping up and down with excitement in my living room with my brother. I was 14 years old but felt like a little boy on Christmas morning. The players mobbed Mesa on the pitcher's mound and celebrated wildly. Hargrove shared his feelings on that day when the Indians brought the pennant home to Cleveland:

> *I will never forget when Jim Thome caught that ball to win the division earlier in the season. I don't think that it really struck me that we were actually going to the World Series until I had showered and was walking to the buses. It hit me as I was walking to the bus that we were actually going to the World Series. It was a real sobering and exhilarating moment, and also pretty cool!*

General manager John Hart also remembered the celebration in Seattle fondly:

> *Carlos Baerga and my wife danced down the hallway in Seattle after the series win. It was a great night with Dennis Martínez beating Randy Johnson and we won the American League pennant. When we won the pennant that night, it was one of the best-pitched ballgames I have ever seen. Martínez was fabulous and slowed the game down doing what he did. I remember going down to the locker room and saw all the guys we traded for and young players that came up together. It was a great group. Then I looked over and saw all the veterans like Orel, Eddie, Dennis, and Peña. I looked at this group of guys that were finally going to a World Series in Cleveland, and I sat over in the corner and I cried like a baby. We really were going to the World Series, and it was a very special time.*

It truly was a season of dreams that became a reality for fans across northeast Ohio. So many fans had suffered through decades of losing baseball in the hopes that one day their beloved Indians would finally turn things around. That day had finally arrived, and it felt better than anyone could have imagined!

Like a true team of champions, the Indians won with help from the top to the bottom of their lineup and pitching. Each player contributed and rose above an early deficit to win the American League Championship. Any memory of empty stadium games and losing seasons at Municipal Stadium had disappeared, and the Cleveland Indians were now known as the champions of the American League.

Dan Graney, of Westlake, Ohio, CEO of Clock and Tickers, Inc., has been a die-hard fan of the Cleveland Indians his entire life and shared these memories of the Indians' winning season:

> *Where do I start? Albert Belle's grand slam off Angels star closer Lee Smith. Manny Ramirez's walk-off homer off Oakland star closer Dennis Eckersley, where Eckersley went, "Wow!" Eddie Murray getting his 3,000th hit against the Twins at the Metrodome. Belle hitting 50 homers and 50 doubles. José Mesa recording 46 out of 48 saves, winning 100 ball games in a strike-shortened season. Starting the playoffs with Tony Peña's walk-off homer off Boston reliever Zane Smith. Oddly being defeated by Bob Wolcott to begin the ALCS in Seattle. Dennis Martínez outpitching Cy Young winner Randy Johnson in game six to send the Tribe to the World Series . . . and if only the umpire's strike zone wasn't the size of a five-lane highway for Atlanta pitchers in the World Series that year. What a season it was!*

It was a special time indeed. For nearly 50 years, Cleveland sports fans had to sit back and watch other teams celebrate, but not this year, not this team. It took a starting rotation of four Cy Young–caliber starters in Atlanta to finally defeat Cleveland, but not before they treated all of their fans to one of the most memorable seasons in Cleveland Indians baseball history.

Two years later, with a revamped roster, the Cleveland Indians returned to the fall classic. It would go down as one of the most exciting World Series of all time. Cleveland fans everywhere wondered if this time the last game would end in victory.

Expectations were high heading into the 1996 season for the Cleveland Indians. They made it to the World Series the prior season for this first time in 41 years, losing to the highly talented Atlanta Braves in six closely contested games.

They had almost the entire starting lineup coming back with the exception of first-baseman Paul Sorrento, who had left for Seattle. Sorrento was replaced by a returning Indian from years earlier, Julio Franco. It was a fairly lateral move—Sorrento's and Franco's 1996 numbers were close, with Sorrento having the slight edge in power.

While the majority of the roster continued with their dominant ways, Murray and Baerga seemed to be struggling. In a surprising move, Hart dealt Murray to the Baltimore Orioles halfway through the season. In return for Murray, the Indians received pitcher Kent Mercker. It was a surprising move, but nothing compared to what Hart was set to do just eight days later.

On July 29, 1996, Hart made a trade that broke the hearts of many, if not all, Cleveland Indians fans: He sent fan favorites Baerga and Espinoza to the New York Mets in exchange for shortstop José Vizcaíno and second-baseman Jeff Kent. It sent shockwaves throughout Cleveland. Baerga was struggling badly, but not many fans expected the sudden trade.

In the summer of 2013, during his introduction weekend into the Indians Hall of Fame, Hart reflected back on this trade:

> *It was the hardest trade I ever had to make. Carlos was a defining player in an earlier trade and was one of the first guys that was bought into Cleveland when we wanted to do multiyear contracts. He was such a large part of the team and such a leader. He was the happiest player in our locker room and was great. His first five years in the big leagues drew comparisons to Roger Hornsby. I loved my players, but I had to take that hat off and make moves for the best of the organization. It was painful because of the relationship that I had with Carlos and still have to this day.*

Carlos Baerga was a core player in the organization for many years, and the news shocked him as well as his many legions of fans. He discussed how hard it was to be traded at that time:

> *In the beginning it was very hard because I didn't understand why I was traded. We had a very good record and were headed to the playoffs again. I was hurt in the playoffs the year before when I had hurt my ankle. I was never healthy and the decision was hard to take because I was happy here and the captain of the team. It was something that took me a couple of years to forget about. I understand it better now. I had lost my concentration for the game and preparation for the game. Things happen for a reason in life, and I'm more mature now and able to talk to my son about it now. I explained to him what happened to me and also tell a lot of young players to be careful. When you put on a uniform, you represent an entire organization, so you have to be cautious of what you do outside of the field. Sometimes you may lose your job because you lose that focus.*

The Indians went on to win the Central Division again in 1996, but never seemed to recapture the magic of 1995. With the newcomers never quite fitting in and poor pitching, the Indians got upset in the first round of the playoffs by the upstart Baltimore Orioles. It was an early end to a season that led the Indians organization to have to face numerous off-season questions.

On October 28, 1996, power-hitting left-fielder Albert Belle became a free agent. Most fans assumed that it would only be a matter of time before Belle re-signed with the Indians. In the first of many signings to come (baseball is still a business to many players), Belle betrayed his hometown fans and signed with the team's rival, the Chicago White Sox. He joined perennial All-Star Frank Thomas, and,with the new power duo in place, many in the media declared the White Sox the new team to beat.

With Belle gone, the Indians needed to replace his power in the lineup and searched for a trade to do so. Hart found his trade partner with the San Francisco Giants, who were looking to improve their defense. On November 13, 1996, Hart sent Vizcaíno, Tavárez, and Kent to the Giants for power-hitting veteran and third-baseman Matt Williams. Williams had been a two-sport athlete at Carson High School in Nevada. He had a strong arm and played quarterback for their football team. He attended UNLV on a baseball scholarship and excelled. He was later drafted by the San Francisco Giants in the first round of the 1986 draft as their third overall pick.

Williams quickly became one of the best athletes on the Giants roster, excelling in the field and at the plate. He was good enough to make the National All-Star Team in 1990, 1994, 1995, and 1996. He led the majors in home runs in 1994 by hitting 43 in only 112 games during a strike-shortened season. Many felt that is if the season had gone the full length he could have broken the home run record of 61 set by Roger Maris. His power matched his teammate Barry Bonds, as they became one of the most feared combinations in all of baseball. Along with his power-hitting swing, Williams also brought three Gold Glove Awards with him. His fielding had been good enough to win the award in 1991, 1993, and 1994. However, his power numbers had slumped over the previous two seasons, and the Giants were willing to part with him. Williams would make it his mission to turn his numbers back around in 1997 with the Cleveland Indians.

A couple days after trading for Matt Williams, the Indians decided to part ways with two veterans when both Peña and Martínez were granted free agency. They were replaced a few weeks later with veteran catcher Pat Borders, who had been a two-time World Series winner with Toronto. The Indians also improved their bullpen by signing veteran setup man Mike Jackson. The Indians front office closed out the 1996 calendar year by signing another veteran and second-baseman, Tony Fernández.

Williams's signing forced third-baseman Jim Thome to learn a new position: first base. Thome's power numbers were too good to remove him from the everyday lineup and he was young enough to learn a new position. Thome again proved how much of a team player he was by welcoming the new challenge.

The biggest move took place just a week before the new season was set to begin. On March 25, 1997, Hart once again shocked Indians fans when he traded away perennial All-Star and fan favorite Kenny Lofton, along with reliever Alan Embree, to the Atlanta Braves. In return, the Braves sent power-hitting outfielder David Justice along with speedy leadoff-hitting centerfielder Marquis Grissom. It was a gutsy move by Hart, as the team would now have two-thirds of its outfield changed. For the infield, only Vizquel was returning to his normal position as shortstop.

The addition of Justice was met with a mild reception by the Cleveland fans, as the memory of him hitting the winning home run for the Braves in the 1995 World Series was still fresh in their minds. Despite the sour memories, he was a talented player that would combine with Williams, Thome, and Ramirez to keep the lineup potent with power. Justice began his career with the Atlanta Braves, where he won the 1990 National League Rookie of the Year Award. He was a huge part of the Braves surge from "worst to first" in 1991. They appeared in back-to-back World Series, albeit losing both times to the Minnesota Twins and Toronto Blue Jays. He made the National League All-Star Team in 1993 and 1994. Justice received a Silver Slugger Award in 1993 and was a constant source of power in the Atlanta Braves lineup. His 1996 season was cut short in May due to an injured shoulder. He loved his time with the Braves and it came as a shock to him when he was traded to the Cleveland Indians. He had a bit of a chip on his shoulder and looked for his time in Cleveland to prove his former team wrong for giving up on him too soon.

Grissom grew up in Atlanta before leaving to play college baseball at Florida A&M University. The Montreal Expos drafted him in 1988 with the 76th overall pick. As an Expo, Grissom excelled at stealing bases and led the league in both 1991 and 1992. In 1993, as the rest of the National League started to realize his talent, he was voted to his first

All-Star Game. He would repeat that honor in 1994. He enjoyed two more solid years of batting and fielding after being traded to Atlanta in 1995. He also brought four Gold Glove Awards with him to Cleveland. His speed and incredible defense was seen as the perfect replacement for the departing Lofton.

Hargrove shared how he handled all of the player changes to mold the Indians into a contender:

> *Players of that caliber make it somewhat easier. It wasn't like we traded away Kenny Lofton and brought in Joe Blow. We thought Grissom and Justice were dynamite players in their own right. We knew it was coming because we had talked about a possible trade earlier in spring training, so when it did happen I wasn't surprised. It was one of those things that you learn to live with. In baseball, the more things stay the same the more they change. I felt like that with the ball club we have and the hitters we brought back, that we would be all right.*

With the additions of Justice, Grissom, Williams, and Fernández, the Indians were set to contend for their third straight Central Division title. With the emergence of Ramirez and Thome, combined with the young Brian Giles, the Indians had the talent to do it. Mix in the veteran leadership of Vizquel and Alomar, and it was hard to find any weak spot, top to bottom, in the lineup.

The season began on the road in Oakland against the Athletics, where Indians fans had to stay up late to see their team win the season opener in a shootout, 9–7. Despite the opening night victory, it took them a quarter of the season to find the team chemistry needed to contend. To the surprise of many, they were 18–20 on May 16 after losing to Roger Clemens and the Toronto Blue Jays in the Skydome. To be just a few games under .500 at that point in the season was a huge step back from the early winning records of the three previous seasons. The Indians finally started to find their stride after that loss when they went on to win the next six games. It was their longest winning streak of the early season and a sign that the team was finally starting to gel. It came at a perfect time, because they went on to beat the Chicago White Sox in their first meeting of the year at Comiskey Park. They held Belle to just one hit in his first game against his former team. The Indians finished the month of May with a modest 27–24 record, but in the weak Central Division it was more than enough to contend. The pitching had been inconsistent so far, outside of the top three starters: Orel Hershiser, Charles Nagy, and Chad Ogea. It would be a move made in June, however, that would alter the rest of the season and almost change the course of history.

Jaret Wright grew up in Anaheim, California, as the son of major league pitcher Clyde Wright. He had baseball in his blood, which led to a good amateur career at Katella High School. He was drafted by the Cleveland Indians with the 10th overall pick in the 1994 amateur draft. Wright rose quickly through the ranks of the Indians farm system and in 1996 was mentioned as one of baseball's top prospects by *Baseball America* magazine. The Indians badly needed help with their starting rotation and made the call to bring Wright up to the major league roster in June 1997. On June 24, in front of a sold-out crowd at Jacobs Field, he made his first major league start and earned the victory with a 10–5 win over the Minnesota Twins. It was Wright's first win of eight that season. Wright was the missing piece in the rotation that the Indians would need to make another serious run at the division.

At the All-Star Break, the Indians had reached a season high of eight games over .500 at 44–36. They were catching fire at the right time and looked to have a strong second half of the season. The midsummer classic that year would be held at Jacobs Field. It was a spotlight for Cleveland: "The Jake" was widely considered one of the nicest ballparks in baseball. The excitement over having the All-Star Game in Cleveland gave the city an extra reason to puff out its chest.

The Indians' hottest player was Sandy Alomar Jr. He was in the middle of a 30-game hitting streak and was on pace to surpass all of his career-high numbers. Sure enough, he added to his great season with an outstanding performance in the All-Star Game. He was one of three members of the Indians to make the American League All-Star Team, along with Thome and Justice. Belle was also on the American League roster for the White Sox, and he had received loud boos from the hometown crowd when his name was called. Lofton made his return to Cleveland that night as a member of the National League All-Star Team and, unlike Belle, he received some of the loudest cheers of the evening.

The ballgame was close when Alomar came to the plate in the bottom of the seventh inning. The game was tied at one run apiece and the American League had a man on base. If there were any doubts about Sandy having a special season, they were quickly erased when he hit a fastball thrown by Shawn Estes over the fence to give the American League a 3–1 lead. They would hold on to win, and Alomar was later named game MVP.

The Indians rode the wave of momentum from the All-Star Game to win their first five of seven games following the break. They stayed consistent the rest of the way and finished the season in first place with a record of 86–75. It wasn't the usual dominant season, but it was enough to get them back into the playoffs. The additions of Justice and Williams had paid off. Justice batted .329 with 33 home runs and

Sandy Alomar won the 1997 All-Star game as part of his magical season.

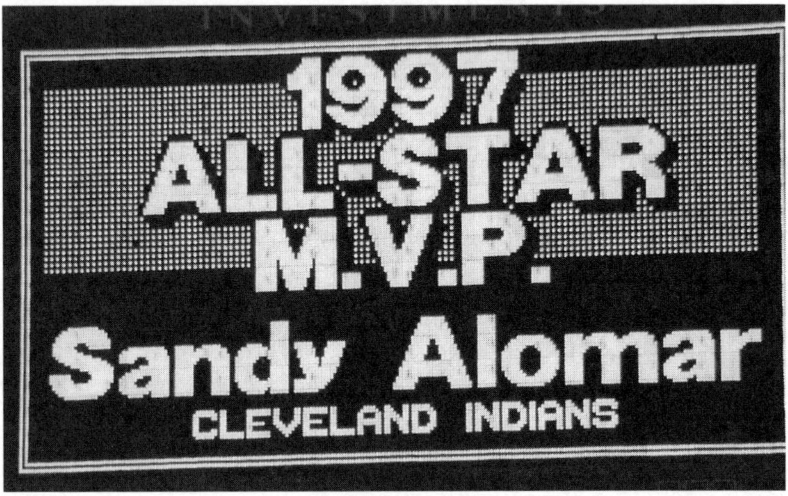

Photo: Garry Gosky

101 RBIs. It was good enough to earn him a Silver Slugger Award. Williams also looked strong, batting .263 with 32 home runs and 105 RBIs. Thome hit a career-high 40 home runs with 102 RBIs. Ramirez joined the hit parade with 26 home runs and 88 RBIs. Alomar had his best season, finishing with a .324 batting average and 21 home runs while driving in 83 RBIs. The starting pitching that remained a question mark all season came together to finish with a modest record. Nagy had 15 wins and Hershiser finished with 14. Wright, who only pitched half the season, finished with 8 wins and took fifth place on the Rookie of the Year voting. Other pitching hopefuls, such as John Smiley and Albie Lopez, never remained consistent and fell out of favor early.

Local sports fans reactions to the season were vivid, as always. Jerry Mires recalled that season fondly:

> *I think Marquis Grissom was much underrated and a big pickup in the David Justice move. That is when the Indians starting to move into mercenary mode, just signing guys at every chance to get the right pieces. Guys like Matt Williams, who came to town to play third, which moved Thome to first base. It was such a fun season because we were underdogs. In 1997 we were magical, with guys like Sandy Alomar hitting the home run in the All-Star Game and many more moments like that. Jaret Wright coming out of nowhere to throw smoke and get on a hot streak. Even guys like Bip Roberts coming up huge until the very end. Veterans like Tony Fernández playing great until the last play. They just kept pulling the upsets in the playoffs until game seven of the World Series. We had no business winning the World Series in 1995 because Atlanta was ready. However, in 1997 we should have won, and there is no one person to blame. There were so many elements that came into play with that game seven loss that we can't pinpoint one person. I knew the minute Mesa didn't finish the game that that was it. I remember feeling the pressure in 1995 as a fan because we were supposed to win, but in 1997 it was a lot more fun because we didn't have that pressure.*

One of the biggest question marks of the 1997 season was the role of closer. Due to legal problems, Mesa missed the start of the season and finished with only 16 saves. His replacement, Mike Jackson, did well in the closer's role and was able to save 15 games. It seemed as though everything was in place to be competitive going into the playoffs. A first-round matchup with the defending World Series Champions, the New York Yankees, was waiting.

The 1997 season was different than years past because the Indians won the division but didn't dominate the league. The season record was the lowest of all division winners heading into the postseason. Hargrove explained how the team felt like the underdogs before heading into the playoffs:

> *I think we most likely did. I felt that no one was picking us to do anything. We had always played well when we had to in years past, and the tougher the competition the tougher we played. There were a lot of rough spots on the road that season, and we didn't find our identity until late in the season at Anaheim. It was Jim Thome's birthday, so all the players got together and decided that they would pull their socks up high to honor him. We won real handily, so we decided to do it again and got on a roll, and that was the rallying point of that season and brought that team together. They jelled after that and became good.*

Game one of the division series in New York couldn't have begun any better in the first inning. The Indians were able to score on David Cone, who was normally close to unhittable when pitching against them. The Tribe's midseason pickup, Bip Roberts, reached on a walk and then quickly stole second base. Vizquel laid down a beautiful sacrifice bunt to move Roberts to third. Ramirez hit a line drive single to centerfield that scored Roberts and put Cleveland on top. Thome followed Ramirez's single with one of his own, and they had two on base with only one out. Justice hit into a fielder's choice, which got Thome out at second base, but Ramirez advanced to third. The normally accurate Cone showed his playoff jitters by throwing a wild pitch against

Williams, which allowed Ramirez to score from third, making it 2–0. Cone continued to look shaky and hit Williams with a pitch, putting him on first base and advancing Justice to second. The red-hot Alomar continued his amazing season by belting a Cone fastball over the wall in left field to give the Indians a 5–0 lead. Cone rebounded to get Giles to fly out to end the inning, but the damage had been done.

Hershiser set down the Yankees lineup in order in the bottom of the first, and it looked as though the night would belong to Cleveland. The Yankees slowly started to hit their way back in the game by scoring a run in the second, fourth, and fifth innings. The Indians had also scored in the top half of the fourth.

The Yankees came to bat in the bottom of the sixth, trailing 6–3. Eric Plunk had replaced Hershiser late in the fifth inning and came out to start the bottom half of the sixth. It didn't take long for Plunk to completely ruin the quality start of Hershiser. After getting Chad Curtis to foul out, he gave up a single to Wade Boggs. Plunk managed to get Joe Girardi to ground out, and it looked as though it would be a routine inning despite the one-base runner. Rey Sanchez had a different idea, singling off Plunk to score Boggs, cutting the lead to 6–4.

What followed the Sanchez RBI single can only be described as a nightmare for the Indians and their fans. The Yankees hit three straight home runs off Plunk by Tim Raines, Derek Jeter, and Paul O'Neill to take a commanding 8–6 lead. The Indians were demoralized and never recovered, losing the game by that same score.

Game two at Yankee Stadium in the Bronx took on a feeling of desperation for the Indians. Down one game to zero, they knew they couldn't afford to lose. They turned to their rookie sensation, Jaret Wright, who quickly made everyone question the decision to start him by walking the bases loaded in the bottom of the first. The Yankees would make him pay with a two-run double by Tino Martinez, followed by an RBI sacrifice fly by Charlie Hayes. Before the fans in Yankee Stadium could digest their first hot dogs, the hometown team had spotted starting pitcher Andy Pettitte with a three-run lead.

The Indians knew from their own experience in game one that no lead is safe when playing October baseball. Wright had settled down and starting mowing down Yankees hitters in order for the next couple of innings. The Indians still trailed 3–0 when they went up to bat in the top half of the fourth inning, but something in the air was about to change drastically. After Pettitte forced Roberts to line out to center field to begin the inning, he allowed a single to Vizquel, who then advanced to second on a throwing error. Pettitte rebounded by striking out Ramirez before walking Williams. With two on and two out, Justice hit a single that gave Cleveland its first run. Alomar and Thome followed with singles of their own, and the game was tied 3–3. Fernández followed suit and hit a two-run double that put Cleveland ahead by a score of 5–3. One inning later, Williams hit a two-run home run and increased the Cleveland lead to 7–3.

While the Cleveland bats were coming alive, Wright was silencing the Yankees bats. After a shaky first inning, he rebounded to throw five scoreless innings, striking out five and only allowing two more hits. Wright showed incredible mental toughness and assured manager Mike Hargrove that he would be ready if called upon again. Mesa took the mound a little earlier than normal when he came on in relief with one out in the eighth inning with a 7–3 lead. The Yankees proceeded to make things interesting by scoring on Mesa in the eighth and then again in the ninth on a home run by Derek Jeter. But Mesa and the Indians managed to hold on for the 7–5 victory to even the series. Hargrove explained how important a come-from-behind win was for the team, saying, "We lost a lot of game ones, but the one thing is that a team feeds on a history. I'm talking about the history of the team dating back to the 1920s. All the players on the ball club realized the Indians as a whole were, really, a pretty good ball club. I think that what we had done in the recent history of 1995 helped keep our focus and realize that it was just one game."

The series moved to Cleveland for game three and noted Indians killer, David Wells, took the mound for the Yankees. It was a quiet Saturday night for Indians fans as the Yankees used a four-run fourth inning to take a 6–1 lead and never looked back. Wells was dominant and Nagy couldn't get out of the fourth inning. It wasn't looking good for Cleveland.

Game four shaped up to be a battle of two veteran playoff heroes from the 1980s: Orel Hershiser against Dwight Gooden. The Yankees jumped on Hershiser in the first by scoring two runs with clutch hits by Jeter and O'Neill, who continued to have an amazing series. The Indians cut the lead in half with a solo home run by Justice in the second inning. Both pitchers then settled down and there wasn't any movement in the score, as it remained 2–1 heading into the bottom of the eighth. The Indians were down to their last six outs and facing Mariano Rivera, one of the greatest closers of all time. Rivera wasted no time in striking out Justice and forcing Williams to fly out. Only four outs away from eliminating Cleveland from the playoffs, Rivera had to face a man who was having a season of destiny. Alomar stepped up to the plate, and it was almost as if no other hitter in all of baseball was more qualified for that moment than him. Alomar continued his dream season by crushing a fastball over the fence in right field to tie the game.

Jackson took the mound in the ninth and set down the Yankees lineup in order. It was up to Ramiro Mendoza to try to hold down the Indians hitters and send the game into extra innings. Grissom led off with a single. Roberts sacrificed Grissom over to second with a bunt, which brought Vizquel to the plate with a chance to win it, who wasted no time hitting a single off of Mendoza that had enough steam on it to roll past Jeter in shallow center field, allowing the speedy Grissom to score from second base and win the game.

It was high drama heading into game five as manager Mike Hargrove once again rolled the dice and started Wright. It was a gutsy move to start a rookie in such a high-profile game, but Hargrove had faith in Wright after he shut down the Yankees following a shaky start in game two. Hargrove looked back at his decision, saying, "Jaret was the hardest thrower we had on the ball club. He didn't have a lot of pitches, but he pitched well in New York in a tough spot.

I just felt that he was a tremendous competitor, and I'm not saying that someone else wasn't, but he just had a knack to really bear down and focus, which gave him that pinpoint concentration to be as good as he should be and even a little bit better in those situations."

Wright proved Hargrove's faith well founded, as he pitched four consecutive scoreless innings to start the game. Meanwhile, the Indians were doing well against Pettitte. They used singles by Grissom and Roberts to set the table for a two-run double by Ramirez. Williams followed the Ramirez double with an RBI single, giving the Indians a 3–0 lead. One inning later in the fourth, Fernández hit a sacrifice fly that stretched the Indians lead to four runs.

The Yankees slowly climbed their way back into the game and managed to score three runs and cut the lead to 4–3 heading into the ninth. Cleveland Indians fans took a deep breath as Mesa took the mound in the top of the ninth. He forced Raines and the red-hot Jeter to ground out and get two quick outs. O'Neill continued to be a thorn in the Indians side by hitting a two-out double and keeping the game alive. Williams smashed a Mesa fastball to deep left center field that looked like it might leave the park before softly landing into Giles's glove and sending the Indians back to the American League Championship series.

Up next for the Tribe would be the American League Eastern Division Champions, the Baltimore Orioles. This was a perfect chance to get revenge on the team that had beaten them the previous year in the playoffs. It would be a tall task, as Baltimore was loaded with veteran talent and excellent pitching. The series would begin in Baltimore because the Orioles had the better regular-season record.

Game one proved to be a pitcher's duel, with Baltimore starter Scott Erickson pitching a four-hit shutout. Chad Ogea did a good job as well, giving up only three runs, but it was three too many as Baltimore took a one-game lead in the series.

Nagy took the mound for game two hoping to even up the series. The Indians gave him the early run support he would need by scoring two off of Baltimore veteran starter Jimmy Key in the first inning.

Ramirez's two-run home run gave Nagy the early lead. The Cleveland lead would not last long, however, as Cal Ripken Jr. hit his own two-run home run to tie the game. The game would remain tied in a tight pitcher's duel until the bottom of the sixth when Mike Bordick hit a two-run single off of Nagy, giving Baltimore the 4–2 lead and knocking Nagy from the game. The Cleveland bullpen, comprised of Alvin Moorman, Jeff Juden, Paul Assenmacher, and Mike Jackson, held the Orioles scoreless and kept the score at 4–2 heading into the eighth.

Armando Benítez, one of the best relief men in baseball, took the mound for the top of the eighth inning. This normally would have spelled doom for most teams. However, The Indians were not most teams and actually had good success in the past against Benítez. The table was set for high drama and Benítez would not disappoint. Benítez managed to strike out two of the first four batters he faced to start the inning. The problem for him was that the other two drew walks and brought out Grissom, the go-ahead runner, to the plate. Benítez continued to have horrible luck against Indians batters as Grissom crushed his pitch over the wall for a three-run go-ahead home run. Suddenly, after two games of futile hitting, the Indians held a 5–4 lead and were only six outs away from evening up the series before heading back home for game three. Jackson and Mesa did exactly that, and the series was tied. Cleveland dodged a dangerous bullet and held all the momentum coming back home for game three. The Baltimore Orioles were loaded with veteran talent both on the mound and in the lineup, so a two-game lead may have been too much for Cleveland to overcome. The previous year had already proven that.

Jacobs Field was packed on a sunny Saturday afternoon to watch one of the greatest pitched games in baseball-playoff history. Orel Hershiser and Mike Mussina used the shadows of the setting sun against opposing batters all game long, and the game remained scoreless through six and a half innings. The Indians finally broke through against Mussina in the bottom of the seventh inning. Williams's single to centerfield was good enough to score Thome and give Cleveland a 1–0 lead. Mussina followed by getting two quick ground outs, and after seven innings, he and Hershiser had combined for a remarkable 22 strikeouts and only one earned run.

Mesa took the mound in the top of the ninth with the Indians clinging to a 1–0 lead. He immediately gave up a leadoff single to Chris Hoiles. Two batters later, Brady Anderson hit a fly ball that Grissom somehow lost in the lights and the ball fell in for a double, allowing the tying run to score. Just one game earlier, Grissom was the hero. Now, just a few days later, he was in position to be the goat.

The game remained tied 1–1 heading into the bottom of the 12th inning when Randy Myers took the mound for Baltimore and struck out Giles to start the inning. Grissom, who seemed to be in the middle of any crucial situation, came up to bat and managed to draw a walk. Fernández followed the Grissom walk with a single to right field, putting the winning run just 90 feet away. With Grissom on third and only one out, Hargrove called for Vizquel to lay down a bunt in the hopes of sacrificing Grissom home to score. Vizquel attempted to lay down the bunt on the next pitch and the ball missed his bat, but it also missed catcher Lenny Webster's glove. The alert Grissom, who was already halfway down the line, came home to score uncontested. It was a highly controversial call, but it gave the Indians the win and a 2–1 lead in the series. Baltimore manager Davey Johnson and Webster argued soundly, but it was too little too late. One of the finest-pitched games in playoff history had ended on a fluke play, but it also gave the Tribe the win!

A pivotal game four took place in Cleveland with the young Wright on the mound. Despite getting some early run support from a two-run Alomar home run, Wright struggled to remain consistent and fell behind 5–2 after only three innings. Geneva, Ohio, native Brian Anderson was called on by Hargrove to keep the game close. Cleveland would attempt to mount a comeback against Baltimore pitcher Scott Erickson, who had previously shut them down in game one. Ramirez hit a solo home run with one out in the bottom of the fifth to bring the Indians to within a couple of runs. Thome and Justice followed with back-to-back singles. After a Williams strikeout, Alomar hit an RBI single to score Thome. Baltimore relief pitcher Arthur Rhodes then walked Giles before throwing a wild pitch, which allowed Justice to score from third and tie the game. As Justice scored, Webster lost track of the ball after colliding with the umpire. In the middle of the mass confusion, Alomar was able to race home and score to take the lead. It was another wild play in a series that had been filled with them.

The Indians had a 7–5 lead to try to hold onto it for the second half of the game. The Indians bullpen looked sharp, only giving up one run and handing Mesa a 7–6 lead to start the ninth. Mesa, who had blown the save the prior day, looked shaky again as he took the mound. He walked Roberto Alomar to start the inning and then gave up a single to Gerónimo Berroa, which allowed Roberto to advance to third base with still no outs. Mesa recovered to strike out Eric Davis before letting up the game-tying single to Rafael Palmeiro. Mesa had blown two saves in two days—it was a bad omen of what was to come a few short weeks later.

The game remained tied as Mesa was able to get out of the inning without giving up any more runs. Ramirez led off the bottom of the ninth inning with a walk and was sacrifice-bunted over to second by pinch-hitter Kevin Seitzer. Veteran pitcher and former Cleveland Indians teammate Jesse Orosco forced Justice to fly out for the second out before Johnson pulled him for Benítez. With first base open, Benítez gave Williams the free pass and decided to pitch to Alomar. Benítez's previous record against Cleveland, combined with the magical season Alomar was having, ensured that no one was surprised when Alomar hit the game-winning single to score Ramirez and give Cleveland the 3–1 series lead.

The Indians brought a commanding 3–1 series lead into game five with the hopes of clinching the series in front of their home crowd. Baltimore pitchers Scott Kamieniecki and Jimmy Key put a stop to any celebration plans the Indians may have had with a shutout through eight innings. Ogea fell victim to no offensive support for his second straight start, and the Indians ended up losing 4–2. It was a crucial loss, because it meant the series would return to Camden Yards in Baltimore for the next game.

Game six took place Wednesday, October 15, 1997, on a sunny afternoon in Baltimore. The fans in attendance and watching at home viewed a classic; for the second straight start, Mussina was untouchable. Luckily for Cleveland, so was their ace, Nagy. Through 10 innings, the game remained scoreless and Cleveland managed only two hits. With Cleveland preparing to bat in the top of the 11th, Baltimore reliever Benítez jogged in from the bullpen to pitch. Benítez looked to shake off his past playoff-game demons as he put away the first two Cleveland hitters with ease.

From here, what the history books will tell you is that Fernández came to bat in a scoreless game with two outs in the bottom of the 11th to face Benítez. The intertwining of stories that go along with that sentence can last for miles. Fernández was only playing that day because Roberts, the scheduled starting second-baseman, was a late pregame scratch when he hurt his thumb in batting practice on a ball that Fernández hit. Some people may call it coincidence, but others will call it simply baseball destiny. In a finish that was right out of a Hollywood script, Fernández hit a Benítez fastball over the wall in left field to give the Indians the lead. That was all they needed, as Mesa closed it out in the ninth and sent Cleveland back to the World Series. Hargrove explained what happened in batting practice of game six that led to Roberts to not play, giving Fernández the start that led to his eventual series clinching home run:

> *I always felt that when you get in those situations—that you indicate to whatever degree that you can't go—then it's best we don't have you on the field. Bip came to me in the World Series that year and said that he had flu-like symptoms and I told him that he wasn't playing. I know it pissed him off, but if you don't want out of the game then don't tell me you're sick. Because all you're doing is saying that you don't have a*

lot of confidence in your ability to do your job and you're looking for an excuse. In those situations, we don't need people like that around.

The Florida Marlins were an expansion team that came into the Major League in 1993. Most fans outside of Miami didn't pay much attention to them, as the Marlins rarely gave them any reason to. Just prior to the 1997 season, the Marlins loaded up their lineup with some high-priced, free-agent talent to go along with a little bit of their homegrown talent. For the first time in their short team history, they became a viable threat in the National League. To the surprise of many, they made the playoffs and swept the San Francisco Giants in the first round before knocking off the defending National League Champions, the Atlanta Braves, to advance to the World Series.

The national media was against this series, believing it would result in very poor ratings. What they got in place of poor ratings was a classic seven-game series that people still talk about years later. The two teams had contrasting styles, but both had made playoff runs as the underdog, and one of the teams was bound to win it all.

The Marlins possessed the needed tools to win the World Series, and it started at the top with their savvy manager, Jim Leyland. He had been at the helm of the Pittsburgh Pirates years earlier when they made their postseason runs. Leyland was a respected manager who was then capable of handling the versatile Marlins team. The Marlins' starting rotation boasted veterans such as Kevin Brown and Al Leiter, along with young sensation and sentimental favorite Liván Hernández. The lineup consisted of power hitter Gary Sheffield, who was an original Marlin. Bobby Bonilla was a power hitter who came with Leyland from Pittsburgh. Moisés Alou came from playing for his dad in Montreal and was considered a five-tool player. Jeff Conine was another crowd favorite and Marlin team original who had been traded to the Marlins in their original season. Mixed in with the seasoned veterans were young talents like Craig Counsell, Edgar Rentería, and Charles Johnson. It was clear that the Florida Marlins had come far since their days as an expansion team.

Game one of the World Series took place on a hot Saturday night in Miami. Hershiser had built a reputation of being a postseason ace. It came as a surprise and a disappointment to Cleveland fans that Hershiser had his worst playoff outing, giving up seven runs in only five innings. The worst blows were back-to-back home runs from Alou and Johnson. The Indians battled back with solo home runs from Ramirez and Thome, but it was too little too late and the Indians dropped game one, 7–4.

Almost as bad as having to watch the Indians lose was Costas's constant chatter about Florida's starting pitcher. Hernández's story of being a Cuban defector and making a life for himself was inspirational, but Costas and the staff at NBC talked about it ad nauseam—almost to the point of taking attention away from the actual game.

Being down one game was a familiar place for the Indians, as they had lost both game ones in the lead-up playoff series. Game two would be an even greater challenge as they faced the Marlin's ace pitcher, Kevin Brown. Ogea took the hill for the Tribe, pitching well in the ALCS despite his 0–2 playoff record. Ogea allowed only one run in the first inning of the game and then nothing after that, looking sharp all night long. Timely hitting, combined with Alomar's two-run home run, gave Cleveland the 6–1 victory and sent the tied series back to Jacobs Field.

Frigid air greeted both teams as they arrived in Cleveland for game three. With the temperature just above freezing, it remains one of the coldest World Series games in history. The elements should have favored starting pitchers Nagy and Leiter, but the results were anything but favorable for either.

Nagy allowed a first-inning solo home run to Sheffield that would set the tone for the rest of the night. The Indians scored two runs in the bottom of the inning on back-to-back RBI singles by Williams and Alomar to take the lead at 2–1. A Sheffield walk with the bases loaded tied the game 2–2 in the top of the third. In the top of the fourth, Darren Daulton hit a solo home run off of Nagy and Florida retook the lead, 3–2. Florida handed Leiter the lead as he took the mound in the bottom half of the fourth inning. Leiter wasted no time allowing Cleveland to tie the game by walking four of the first six batters he faced. Ramirez followed the walks with a bases-loaded two-run single to put Cleveland ahead, 5–3. The scoring was far from done, though—in the next inning, Thome slammed a two-run home run to make it a 7–3 Cleveland lead.

Nagy continued to struggle despite being given a four-run lead. The Marlins used a two-run home run by Jim Eisenreich to climb back into the game in the top half of the sixth. One inning later, timely hitting by Edgar Rentería and Gary Sheffield allowed Florida to tie the game. Cleveland fans were freezing, but the Marlins' bats were on fire.

After a scoreless eighth inning, bewildered relief pitcher Eric Plunk took the mound to start the ninth in the hopes of holding the Marlins bats silent for another inning. Unfortunately, what unfolded was a series of mistakes and blunders committed by the Indians that led to a seven-run inning for Florida. It was walks, intentional walks, errors, and wild pitches that spelled doom for the Tribe. The Indians managed to score four runs of their own in the bottom half of the ninth before losing the game 14–11. Hargrove reflected on what happened that led to the Indians loss: "Your job as a manager is to prepare for the worst and hope for the best, and sometimes no matter who you have playing things just get out of your control. It was just one of those things. Both teams played really hard and really well, and it was a nail-biter all the way through."

The Indians had let one get away in game three and vowed to play sharper in game four the next evening. Hargrove once again turned to his rookie sensation Wright to try and even the series. He rewarded Hargrove's faith in him by tossing a scoreless first inning. A two-run home run by Ramirez off of Florida's starting pitcher Tony Saunders gave Cleveland a 2–0 lead. Alomar hit an RBI double a few batters later, and the Indians jumped out to a quick 3–0 lead after one inning. A couple innings later, RBI singles by Alomar, Fernández, and Justice expanded the Cleveland lead to 6–0. Wright was cruising along and gave up just three runs through six innings. He received plenty of run support, capped by a two-run home run by Williams in the eighth that finished the scoring with the Indians on top 10–3. It was a dominant win that evened the series heading into what would be a pivotal game five. Hargrove explained how it was important to give Wright an early lead in his first World Series start: "It's much easier to play ahead than it is from behind because you can be more aggressive. So it's really important when you have a young kid on the mound because when you beat the other team by putting more pressure on them then they do you. Anytime you can get a lead and put the pressure on the opposition, it gives you a chance to bury them."

Game five was a rematch of Hershiser versus Hernández, and again Bob Costas felt it was necessary to talk about Hernández's epic journey to America for the majority of the game. Costas even went as far to say that his mother was snuck in from Cuba just for the game, only to be released back on a journey halfway through the game. It seemed as though NBC struggled to say anything good about Cleveland throughout the series, angering many fans.

The Marlins raced out to a quick 2–1 lead against Hershiser heading into the bottom of the third. The red-hot Alomar turned the tide back in Cleveland's favor, as he smashed a three-run home run to put them on top 4–2. Things stayed that way until the bottom fell out for Hershiser in the top half of the sixth inning, when he gave up a three-run home run to Alou. Later in the inning, Plunk relieved Hershiser and promptly gave up a bases-loaded walk to increase the Florida lead to 6–4.

Hernández held the Indians lineup in check through eight innings and did not allow them to score again. The Marlins scored two more insurance runs and held an 8–4 lead heading into the bottom of the ninth. Jose Mesa gave up one of the runs in the top of the ninth and continued to look shaky throughout the entire playoff run. The Indians fought hard and rallied for three runs in the bottom half of the ninth to draw within one run. Florida closer Robb Nen was walking the tightrope as he gave up RBI singles to Thome and Justice, but he managed to hold on and secure the 8–7 win for the Marlins. The series was headed back to Florida with the Marlins having two chances to win it all.

All the pressure was mounted squarely on the shoulders of Cleveland's starting pitcher for game six. Ogea was matched up against the highly touted Marlin starter Kevin Brown. Some of the media did not give Ogea a chance of coming out the victor. What the media and others didn't count on was the heart shown by Ogea as he went out and pitched a gem.

Ogea kept the Florida batters silent throughout most of the game, allowing only one run over five innings. Ogea was contributing not only on the mound but also at the plate as he drove in the first two runs of the game with a two-run single in the top half of the second inning. Hargrove shared why he thought Ogea was so effective in game six: "Chad was a good athlete and competitor despite not being able to throw the ball 95 mph. He was more so 89 to 91 with a nasty changeup. Florida was a pretty good fastball-hitting ball club, so it was his changeup and his competitive nature that helped him play so well. He also turned out to be our best hitter in the lineup that evening. It was just one of those things that played to his strengths."

Cleveland was holding on to a 4–1 lead heading into the bottom of the ninth, thanks to a pair of RBI sacrifice flies by Ramirez. Despite

Chad Ogea had an incredible 1997 postseason.

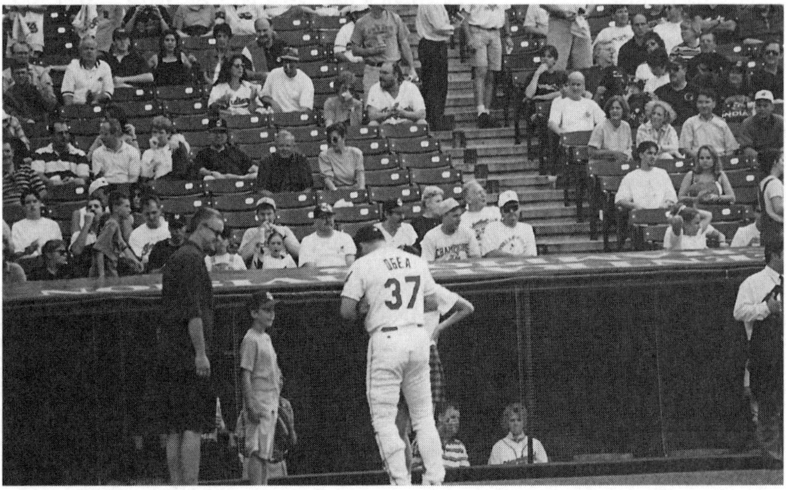

Photo: Garry Gosky

a triple, Mesa was able to hold the Marlins scoreless, and the series became tied.

Game seven was set for Sunday, October 26, 1997, at Pro Player Stadium in Miami. Hargrove hoped to celebrate his birthday with a World Series Championship win that evening. The fans of Cleveland wished for a miserable 49-year run without a World Series Championship to finally end. Hargrove shared what he was thinking prior to the start of game seven: "Again, there is nothing to say, you play so many games starting in the middle of February and by then it was October 26, which was my birthday. So there is not a whole lot you can say that they are ready to listen to—they are ready to play. We had a short meeting before and pitchers meeting and hitters meetings so they knew what they had to do. They knew it was game seven and the importance of it."

The hopes of everyone would rest on the shoulders of Wright. Hargrove was not only skipping Nagy's spot in the rotation but also pitching Wright on short rest. "That was a tough decision," Hargrove explained. "Charles Nagy was one of my all-time favorite players. I just felt that every time we asked Jaret to pitch in a crucial game, he did a great job. I just felt like it gave us our best chance to win." Hargrove told Nagy personally that he wasn't starting the game. "It was really hard because of my own personal feelings for him and because during the season he had been one of our best pitchers. It was a very difficult decision, but Charlie, despite not being too happy with it, understood and accepted it."

Wright and Leiter both held their opposing lineups scoreless through the first two innings. Cleveland got things started in the third when Thome walked and Grissom followed with a single. Wright laid down a perfect sacrifice bunt and moved both runners into scoring position with only one out. Vizquel failed to score the runners when he popped out to the shortstop. The pressure was on starting second basemen Fernández as he came to the plate with two in scoring position with two outs. Fernández was a savvy veteran and came up big in the clutch by hitting a two-run single that gave the Indians a 2–0 lead. Thanks in large part to a great pitching effort by Wright, the 2–0 lead stood until the bottom of the seventh inning when Bobby Bonilla smashed a solo home run to cut the lead in half. Hargrove justified his decision in keeping Wright into the sixth inning: "He was still throwing quite well and it was just one bad pitch. It was a first-pitch changeup that he left over the plate, and Bobby crushed it. I knew that both Jaret and Sandy thought Bobby was looking for a first-pitch changeup, but it just didn't work out." Wright went more than six innings only giving up one run. It was more than anyone in Cleveland could have asked for. Hargrove went into a bit more detail about the bullpen setup with Jackson leading into Mesa: "We rode Mike Jackson really hard, and my pitching coach Mark Wiley walked around and talked to our relievers with a little note card. He kept a card with him asking them how much they have thrown and how much they had left going into that night. Mark said that Jackson stated he only had one hitter left in him. So I brought him in the eighth and went to Mesa in the ninth." The Marlins pitchers had been sharp as well, holding the Indians to only two runs heading into the ninth inning.

The Indians would need an insurance run because Mesa had been shaky in the postseason and a one-run lead hardly seemed safe. They almost got their wish, as two men reached base in the top half of the ninth. With only one out, Alomar had a chance to score as he raced home on a ground ball hit to the shortstop, but for some reason Alomar chose not to slide and was thrown out at home. It may not have seemed like a big mistake at the time, but only minutes later the inability to score that run became enormous. Hargrove disclosed that he never considered having a pinch runner for Alomar, saying, "Sandy ran pretty well and was our best catcher. He was a large part of the team, and for me, there was no reason to pull him from the game. Not in the seventh game of the series with a one-run lead.

Many stories have been told about the mental condition of Mesa as he took the mound to try to save the game in the bottom of the ninth—and none of these stories are flattering. On paper, it looked like a foregone conclusion that Mesa would get the save and

Cleveland would finally get that long-awaited championship parade. After all, Mesa had been one of the most dominant closers in the game for three straight seasons. As Cleveland fans held their breath, Mesa bounced his first warm-up pitch 2 feet in front of home plate, and it was all downhill from there.

Alou continued his amazing series by hitting a line-drive single to start the inning. The next batter, Bonilla, failed to capitalize and struck out. It looked for a moment that Mesa was only two outs away from giving the Indians the World Championship title. Tragically for Cleveland fans, the Indians would never get any closer. Johnson hit a line-drive single to right field, which allowed Alou to advance to third base with only one out. Mesa needed a strikeout or double play to keep the lead. He was unable to get either as Craig Counsell hit a long sacrifice fly ball to right field, allowing Alou to tag from third and score. The game was tied and Mesa had blown his third playoff save in a matter of weeks. The game's momentum shifted squarely to Florida, and the air was completely taken out of Cleveland's sails.

It was only appropriate that Nagy would be the one to come out of the bullpen to face the Marlins in the bottom of the 11th. Nagy had suffered through so many lousy years as the Cleveland team rebuilt while continually fighting to stay positive about the team. Nagy was one of the most beloved Indians of the 1990s. Sadly for Nagy, on this evening he wasn't just pitching against the Marlins, he was pitching against destiny.

Bonilla led off the bottom half of the inning with a single. Up next, Gregg Zaun failed to execute the bunt and popped out to Nagy. It looked like maybe the Indians were about to catch a break when destiny reared its ugly head yet again. Counsell hit a tailor-made double-play ground ball toward Fernández. The Indians were seconds away from getting out of the jam when Fernández let it roll between his legs. At that one moment, it seemed as if time stood still. Fernández had built a reputation as a solid defensive player, and this error was almost unthinkable.

The error was costly, allowing Bonilla to advance to third base with only one out. Hargrove had no choice but to call for an intention walk to Eisenreich to load the bases and create a forced out at any base. Fernández had a chance at redemption as he fielded a ground ball hit by Devon White and threw out Bonilla at home for the second out. Costas, on the NBC broadcast, accurately said, "And that, ladies and gentlemen, is what it means to be a professional." Fernández had redeemed himself for the moment, and the Indians were one out away from extending the game. That one out would never materialize: Rentería hit a soft line drive over the glove of Nagy and through the hole at shortstop to win the game. If things had ended differently in the inning, Hargrove would have had Nagy come out again for the next inning. It was one of the most painful ways a team could lose a World Series. Hargrove revealed what he said to the team when the game was over: "I told them that I was very proud of them and that we had gone a lot farther than anyone thought we would—the usual things you say to people in that situation. It was such a tough situation that nothing you say is going to make it any better. I let them know I was proud of them and that they played a great ball club. The Marlins were loaded." However, Hargrove doesn't dwell too much on this pivotal game:

> *I don't think about it that often. I had a guy ask me about it about a month after the series was over. He asked me how long it took me to get over it, and I told him as soon as I got over it I would let him know. Then, about a month ago, someone else asked me and I repeated it: "As soon as I get over it, I'll let you know." It's been 16 years. It's easier not to think about it because I'm like anyone else. I start playing "What if?" I ask myself, "What if Mesa had thrown the fastball in like we wanted or thrown the slider down and away?" I have no clue why he was so scared of throwing his fastball, I really don't. I know Omar came out and blasted him in his book, but he had saved so many important games for us in the past, including the ALCS clincher by striking out Roberto Alomar.*

Hart also revealed his the disappointment with the game-seven loss:

> *I had dinner with Mike the other night and we both mentioned how we have never went back and watched game seven. Time does heal it, and I think it may have been more painful for Mike, but it was still painful for me as well. When we lost game five in 1997, it was a terrible game to lose because we wanted to go back to Florida up 3–2 because we had Chad Ogea facing Kevin Brown. I remember after Ogea had a great game and we won, I walked onto the roof at the Fawn Blue hotel later that night and thought, "This is game seven." I remember 1995 was a great experience and we had a great team, but I had to come to grips with winning or losing. We had done everything we could do and just had to go play the game. Then you turn the ball over to Jose Mesa, who had saved so many games and we wouldn't have gotten there without him, but it ended up tied. Before Mesa blew the save, they called us out of the stands because it was major league protocol for the wining team's owner and GM to be in the locker room, so we watched the rest of the game in Grover's office. It was painful to watch the rest of the game in the bowels of Joe Robbie Stadium as our team eventually lost. I was devastated, but Dick said to me that we gave it our best. Then he waited and greeted each player as they came in from the field. He told each player he was proud of them and that we would get them next year.*

It was an amazing postseason with plenty of incredible moments for the Indians and the fans. Still, despite the greatness, questions remain. Alomar had a career-best season, yet people still wonder why he didn't slide in the top of the ninth. Hargrove took a team with the fourth-best record of American League playoff teams and got them two outs from winning it all, yet people want to second-guess him for sticking with Mesa. Fernández hit the game-winning home run in the ALCS clincher, as well as drove in the only two runs by the Indians in game seven, yet people want to crucify him for missing one ground ball. If anyone deserved the blame it would be Mesa. In this case, however, even Mesa can't take full blame. It's impossible to pinpoint a single player, coach, or moment to blame the loss on—it was simply destiny. Cleveland Indians baseball has a destiny of its own, and that is to win multiple championships. It is only a matter of time when it will happen. With the fan base supporting them, it will be an incredible moment when it finally does happen.

In the cruelest of ironies, the Florida Marlins' ownership dismantled the team shortly after the World Series win. Hernández was awarded the series MVP, even though both Alou and Sheffield had MVP numbers—they simply lacked the dramatic backstory that Hernández carried with him.

CBS sports-radio talk host Ken Carman, of 92.3 The Fan in Cleveland, was a little boy growing up in Perry during the 1997 series. He had these comments to share:

> *In 1997, I thought, well it's okay because we will be back in 1998 or 1999 and it will eventually happen. I remember game one of that World Series. I was sitting at a Canton McKinley versus Warren Harding football game at Stambaugh Stadium in Youngstown with my late Uncle Jack. The guys in front of us were even saying that the Indians didn't have to worry about winning this year, but rather trying to repeat the following season. Florida won the game and I remember them showing the score on the scoreboard and people being shocked at the result. It was a terrible evening, to be honest with you. During game seven, my dad tried sending me to bed, but I could hear my mom in the next room getting upset at what was happening. I remember the players in the dugout crying; it was awful. It has gotten so much harder as the years have gone on and having to look back at it. We realize now how lucky we were as kids because the teams were so good. The probability of the team being built like that again is very slim. The less I think about it the better, because now as an adult I appreciate certain things differently, and this one just gets harder with time.*

Vic Travagliante, a colleague of Carman's at 92.3 The Fan, had these memories to share of the excitement of Jacobs Field during the 1990s:

Jacobs Field was rocking. It was an event every time I had the opportunity to go to a game. There were 455 straight sellouts, and I was lucky enough to be a part of 50 to 60 of those. If you got tickets that day, you would go to school so excited. If it was during the summer, then you would wake up extra-early and play catch with your buddy in the front or backyard. It really was something that you got excited about for a number of years, the two World Series runs in 1995 and 1997 being the major highlights of that run. I remember the players and games vividly, including sitting in Independence Middle School when they would make certain announcements about achievements with the team. I remember being in a team meeting that was stopped so they could announce that the Indians had made the playoffs. It was a huge part of my growing up—I even had all the fitted hats. I remember collecting the World Series items, including the stuff you would get at McDonald's. It was the first and last time that I got a taste of a winning baseball franchise that I set my day around.

John Hart also described the atmosphere in Cleveland during the heyday of the 1990s Indians:

It was a very festive atmosphere. We had a great club that was never out of it despite falling behind early. We had a great bullpen despite not having great starting pitching. We had a tremendous and versatile offense that would come back late in games often to win. There was such a buzz downtown filled with excitement from the fans. It was just an era of excitement surrounding such a special and talented group of players that we had here.

The people of Cleveland continue to love Mike Hargrove to this very day. He explained why he has stayed in Cleveland:

> *I was born and raised in panhandle Texas, and the people I was raised with and raised by were strong, independent-minded people not afraid to share their opinions; I liked being around people like that, who are not afraid to face what is ahead of them. The people around here remind me of them. They are well-rounded and good-hearted people. We raised our kids here and made great friends. It was an easy decision to stay because Cleveland has always been so good to us and we felt comfortable here. Cleveland has gotten a black eye around the country for so long, but you talk to people who come in with preconceived notions and then they come to the city and realize how great it is and discover that it is a good place to live and raise children.*

It was clear to me after speaking with both Hart and Hargrove that the game-seven loss will hurt for a long time to come. However, it wasn't from any lack of strategy, hustle, or hard work. It was a great group of ballplayers and a fine class of people. In the end, one may never know what could have happened if Alomar had slid or if Fernández hadn't committed the error. Destiny is a harsh mistress, and the Indians sadly found that out in the cruelest of ways. Sometimes in baseball, as in life, the ball just doesn't bounce the right way. But maybe, just maybe, next time it will.

CHAPTER EIGHT

Chico

St. Ignatius High School, a private college-preparatory institution in Cleveland, is an all-male Roman Catholic school that has produced many fine student athletes. Built in 1891 at 1911 W. 30th St., the school remains standing more than 120 years later. St. Ignatius is not only a Cleveland landmark, it was added to the National Register of Historic Places in 1974.

The school imposes strict standards on its students so they can achieve academic and athletic goals that prepare them for success in college and in life. The United States Department of Education has recognized it as a Blue Ribbon School several times.

St. Ignatius has won state titles in multiple sports programs, including wrestling, hockey, baseball, golf, track and field, soccer, basketball, and, most notably, football. It is regarded as a top-notch school for young athletes wanting to excel at both sports and academics. *Student Sport Magazine* named its football program the "High School Team of the 1990s." The St. Ignatius Wildcats have achieved 11 Division I state titles along with three national titles; they are respected not only in northeast Ohio but also nationwide. A number of athletes who came through the football program have gone on to careers in various pro sports. Most notable among them have been LeCharles Bentley, Jack Corrigan, Larry Dolan, Anthony Gonzalez, Mike Hegan, Brian Hoyer, Chris Hovan, Matt Kata, Oliver Luck, and Dave Ragone. The school also graduated a gold medalist, Timothy Mack, who won the pole vault in the 1990 Olympics.

Chuck "Chico" Kyle, who took over the football program in 1983, is a St. Ignatius alumnus. As a student in the late 1960s, he played football, lining up each week at halfback. His desire and skill led him to John Carroll University in University Heights, Ohio, where he continued to play until injuring his shoulder. In 1973, Kyle returned to the school he loved and began teaching English. *USA Today* named him "Coach of the Year" in 1989 and 1993. He led the St. Ignatius Wildcats to 11 state titles from 1988 to 2011.

His is a run of dominance never seen before in Ohio high school football, and one that very few expect to see again. What has made Kyle such a leader on and off the field is the mutual respect shown by anyone who has ever come into contact with him. He treats people with class, which makes him a great ambassador for the school, the religion, and the football program. Kyle was asked to coach the first-ever United States First Junior National Football team in 2009. He led the team to an unbeaten record, and they competed in the International Federation of America Football Junior World Championship.

Kyle has been the head football coach (as well as the track coach) at St. Ignatius for more than 30 years and has never taken a season off. He could have chosen to coach any northeast Ohio college, but he has turned down several offers in order to continue his work with the youth at St. Ignatius. Kyle has commanded and received respect from student athletes and fellow coaches. The words his players and assistant coaches have said about him are perhaps the greatest of his achievements.

St. Ignatius 2001 graduate Chris Meder made these comments concerning to his playing days under Coach Kyle:

> *My memories of St. Ignatius football go as far back as I can remember. My dad is a graduate of St. Ignatius, class of 1972, and he took my brother and me to countless games. Along with my dad, my uncle and my brother also attended the school. One of my uncles was also a Jesuit*

> *there. St. Ignatius and football was and still is a huge part of our family. I remember telling my dad as early as the age of 10 that I would play for them someday.*
>
> *I started at St. Ignatius in the fall of 1997 and joined the football team. I was thrilled knowing that soon enough I would be playing for coach "Chico" Kyle. When I became a junior, I was on the varsity team and was playing under Coach Kyle. I played both my junior and senior years. I was never a starter, but that never made me feel any less a part of the team. The team was like a family, and Coach Kyle made it that way. He had a tremendous ability to motivate players, whether they were starters or third string. He made each kid on the team aware that they played a special role in making the team better each week. He had a knack for preparing our team every week for the game. He made each week, no matter the opponent, significant in the sense that it was a key to our ultimate goal: a state championship. He was a teacher first, and he brought that mentality to the field day in and day out. Anytime he had the opportunity to relate football to academics, he did. He always stressed the importance of doing well in school.*
>
> *I will never forget Coach Kyle's pregame speeches. Most games he gave great motivational speeches that would end in a roar from the team, but in December of 1999 at the Division I State Title game, he gave a pregame speech that sent chills down my spine. He made us believe that we would win the game and that we were the best, deserving to hoist that trophy. It made me think back to all of the great teams that played before me. It made me think back to the 1988 State Championship team, the one that started the dynasty, and what he must have said to them. He made us believe, and we won!*

In addition, I met with the play-by-play man for their weekly radio broadcasts, Ed Daugherty. He took over the job in 2007 after hosting the pregame and halftime show since 2002. Although he graduated from rival high school St. Edwards, his respect for St. Ignatius became

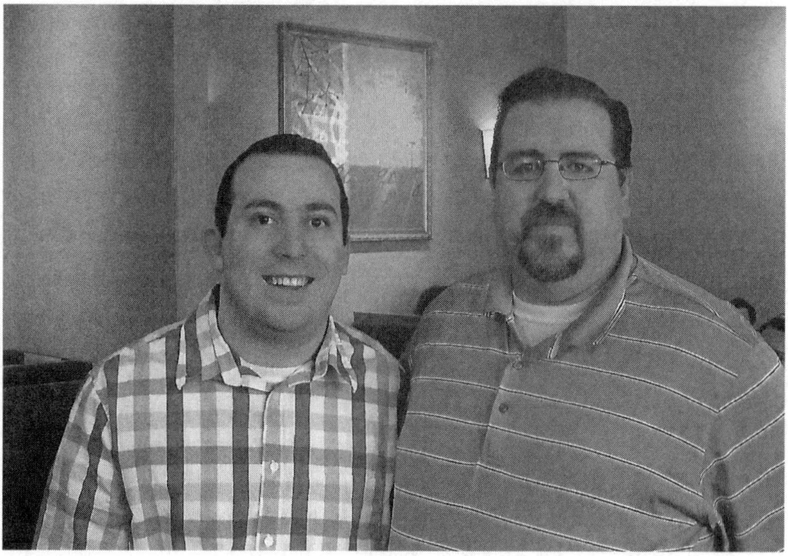

The author with Ed Daugherty (right), the voice of St. Ignatius football

clear when speaking with him. A graduate of Xavier University in Cincinnati, Ed is well educated, with various intelligent viewpoints on the school and sports program.

Ed grew up listening to legendary announcers like Al Michaels, Gib Shanley, Nev Chandler, and Joe Tait. He has fond memories of listening to the radio with his father and wanting to be on a radio show someday. His mother took pictures as he pretended to be a broadcaster like Bob Costas and Brent Musburger. He even went as far as commenting on friendly wiffle ball games in the backyard. I had the chance to meet "the man with the golden pipes," and he was gracious enough to grant me the following interview.

Vince: What is your impression of Coach Kyle and the school?

Ed: I think overall the person and the coach blend together, and that's what makes him one of the most successful coaches in Ohio. It is because football is secondary to him. When you talk to former students and players, they will tell you that he was a better English teacher than a football coach. He is somebody that truly lives by the standards that he sets, as he has high expectations for himself and his players. That doesn't mean that he is overbearing or grouchy, because every coach gets that way. They are going to have the time when they get frustrated because they know that you can do better. That is a key that his players and classmates say makes him a good leader. He has always had that desire to get to the next level. It can be a student who has a C grade average in English to have a desire to learn about Chaucer and the other classes of English literature, and all of a sudden he has an A-minus in the class. He can have an offensive lineman or receiver or a defensive back who, through certain ways, he can talk to in film breakdown or get on him at practice to challenge him to be better. He will challenge them to become more committed in all areas, and that has led to average players becoming all-state. He lives by the St. Ignatius motto of "Men for Others." He is truly committed to the school and is what the school truly stands for. He had been with the school for nearly 50 years, going back to his time as a student there. His stability in the program is what draws people to the school because they know he is not going anywhere. He has had other opportunities to coach at the college level and turned them down because he was where he wanted to be. With Coach, you know what you're going to get: a humble man who is willing to teach. He will tell you that each one of the state championships mean the same because each one was different. People see that he is committed to the program, and this has led numerous generations of families to come to the school.

Vince: In your time calling games, have there been several that stand out to you that show the fighting spirit of the program along with the leadership skills of Coach Kyle?

Ed: There are several that really stand out for me. The two state-championship games are the easiest to recall because they had some of the biggest impact. Much like players, broadcasters don't know when they will get to go back and take part in a state-title game. With it being Division I, it is always the last game that gets played in Ohio every year. I did the lead in 2008 and 2011. The 2008 game was extra-special because it was the first time that had been back since 2001. I think that those games stand out the most as well as the playoff game in 2011 against St. Ed's. That game had gone back and forth, and at the time it was the most significant game in the history of the storied rivalry. It was decided on the final kick of the game, after several turnovers led to a climactic conclusion. I could never forget the game in 2009 at home against Clayton North Mount High School. They were down 20–0 within minutes of the start of the game. They managed to get a quick score before the half to cut into the lead. Jake Ryan, who currently plays at Michigan, had an unbelievable series in the second half as he sacked the quarterback, which led to a fumble and touchdown. They came all the way back and held a 27–20 lead late in the fourth quarter before going on to win. [The 2012] game against Mentor that ended up 57–56 was a wild one. If you tuned out when Mentor took the lead with 4 minutes to go by a score of 35–28, you missed eight touchdowns. All of a sudden, the Ignatius team comes down the field and scores to send it into overtime at 35 apiece. It ended up being a triple-overtime thriller.

Vince: What do you see as the future of St. Ignatius football under Chuck Kyle to be?

Ed: I think some of the changes they're making in the OHSA will affect how they are winning championships. In terms of drawing kids to the school to play, I don't think there will ever be a problem, if and when Coach Kyle decides to retire. Right now he is 20 wins behind Augie Bossu, the legendary coach from Benedictine. In terms of total wins, he currently has 301 and is closing in on Bossu. Coach Kyle began his teaching career almost 40 years ago, so he is into teaching. He is 60 years old now and, in terms of a personal setting, I'm sure retirement is on the horizon. It doesn't mean anything; he may coach until he is 80. I don't feel that he is all about the record, however. I think his progression would be a couple more years until he is truly content to retire; I can see that happening three to five years from now. There are some coaches in the system that have been with him a long time and may get promoted or they may bring in someone else. Whomever they choose to bring in to replace him will have a St. Ignatius tie.

Vince: Would Coach Kyle retiring affect the ability for the school to bring in top-notch players?

Ed: You're always going to get players—people I talk to say as much—because they want to play football for a winner, they want to play there to continue the tradition of the family. Many current players have fathers and uncles who played there, and it is pure tradition. There is a tradition and a legacy there that kids want to be a part of, and fathers want their sons to carry it on. You often hear that St. Ignatius and St. Ed's recruit kids, but that is not the truth. Most of these children came from Catholic private grade schools. The elements that are associated with St. Ignatius go far beyond football.

Vince: The Hoyer family was a product of the public school system, and Brian Hoyer has gone on to a career in the National Football League after spending time under Coach Kyle at St. Ignatius. During his time there, he accomplished a winning record of 16–7 as a two-year starting quarterback. From there, he went on to a fine career at Michigan State before eventually being signed by the New England Patriots as an undrafted free agent. His career eventually led to him becoming the starting quarterback of his hometown team, the Cleveland Browns. What were some of the factors that brought him to the school and the coaching he received there that led to the great success afterwards?

Ed: His father and brother went to St. Ignatius, so it's the legacy again and the networking that can go on. It is almost like graduating from a small college because now you are in this club when you start. You have that association and connection with the alumni, it helps you in your future professional life even more so than it would help you in your athletic life. That is a reason why kids still flock to Ignatius. Even in a down economy, the school still has over 1,500 students in it, with nearly 800 of them playing some kind of athletics. Between the freshman, junior varsity, and varsity, there are over 200 students that play football. They like playing for Chuck Kyle, but they also like the school and the tradition. The pillars on which the school stands are in line with Chuck—they go hand-in-hand. I think the reason is because the coaching staff hasn't changed in 40 years. St. Ed's is trying to get there, but they never will if they keep changing coaches. You can't win five state titles in one year; it is the one-year-at-a-time approach that Ignatius takes that helps them continue to dominate.

Vince: You've mentioned words like *legacy, tradition,* and *dynasty.* Can you give us an example of a tradition St. Ignatius has that keeps the kids coming back?

Ed: One of my favorite traditions is the Thanksgiving Day practice every time they have a game Thanksgiving weekend. Most times the game is either a state-playoff semifinal or even a championship game, depending on how the calendar falls. They have a practice Thanksgiving morning, a light walk-through with some timing drills. The alumni return to watch and other students come to support. If you want to know why so many kids come to Ignatius, take them to a Thanksgiving Day practice. The wives and girlfriends of the current coaching staff hand out breakfast sandwiches, coffee, and doughnuts. The older players come back, and it is a reunion-type setting. There is also a speaker who will come back and give them a pep talk—most times a former player or student of the school, whether it's Jack Corrigan or LeCharles Bentley—and the effect on the players is always great. It is about that sense of community which keeps the enrollment up and the desire to attend.

Vince: The motto of the school is "Men for Others." Can you explain what that means to you and the students?

Ed: You see that on the football field during the Thanksgiving practice among other times throughout the school. They may win at football, but they are not a football factory. They are not Huntington Prep in basketball, where they bring in kids from all over the country to win basketball games. It is the legacy and sense of community, again, that brings students to the school.

With Coach Kyle leading the program, it is likely that St. Ignatius will continue to dominate for years to come. It is a school that not only preaches winning on the field but, more importantly, winning in life through the Holy Spirit.

CHAPTER NINE

In the Booth

Cleveland is known as a city of sports lovers, and it's only natural that the local sports talk-radio shows often become heated with calls from enthusiastic fans. No matter what the issue, the fans often feel that their opinion is the only correct one. It is further proof that Cleveland fans are always dialed into what the hot sports topic is—and never short on opinion.

The most popular station for sports fans to tune into for the latest news is ESPN 850 WKNR on the AM dial. It was purchased by Good Karma Broadcasting in February 2007, and then-new CEO Craig Karmazin was smart enough to keep the biggest talents on the station in place while adding several new talents along the way.

One of the very best at ESPN 850 is Kenny Roda. A favorite in the Cleveland market for over 20 years, he is a passionate sports fan who will never ride the fence or back away from the opinion that he feels is right. He has served several roles at the station, including hosting the hottest afternoon drive-time talk show for several years. Whether alone or when sharing a two-man booth, Kenny truly has the charisma and knowledge to be a mainstay in the Cleveland radio market for a very long time.

Kenny grew up in Springdale, Pennsylvania, a small town of 3,500 people just minutes outside of Pittsburgh. A self-admitted sports junkie, he grew up not only playing sports every chance he got but also listening to sports talk on the radio with his dad. He has fond memories of listening to Pittsburgh Pirates radio play-by-play man Bob Prince, who was called "The Gunner" because of his rapid-fire delivery. It was Prince's style that helped a young Roda fall in love with radio; he enjoyed Prince's game call so much that he would listen to his call even when the game was on television. Prince's influence planted the sports-broadcasting seed in Roda that would grow into an incredible on-air radio career.

Kenny played basketball in high school and was recruited by a few Division I and ll colleges. His dream of playing professional ball took a hit prior to his sophomore year at Baldwin Wallace College in Berea, Ohio. He had gotten hurt, and Bob Laurie came in from Tennessee to take Kenny's spot at point guard. Laurie was a star athlete in high school at Cathedral Latin in Ohio prior to playing college ball. The move allowed Roda to follow his second love—broadcasting—as he joined the radio station at Baldwin Wallace, WBWC 88.3 FM, and starting calling football, baseball, and basketball games. It was further proof that everything happens for a reason. Fans of Cleveland radio are thankful today that Kenny's basketball career didn't pan out and that his radio career most certainly did.

I had the honor and privilege of speaking with Kenny Roda in July 2013 regarding his role in the ever-changing world of Cleveland sports media. It was an exciting interview for me because of the great respect I had for the skills of this longtime radio personality. Kenny was gracious to take time away from chasing the lead story of NBA free agent Andrew Bynum coming to Cleveland long enough to grant me the interview.

Vince: Can you describe some of the pressures and joys of hosting an afternoon drive-time show in such a passionate sports radio market?

Kenny: Stay credible and keep people tuning in to hear valid information along with your opinion. As a talk-show host, you cannot ride the fence; you have to take a stance. I tell people that I train at WKNR that they must

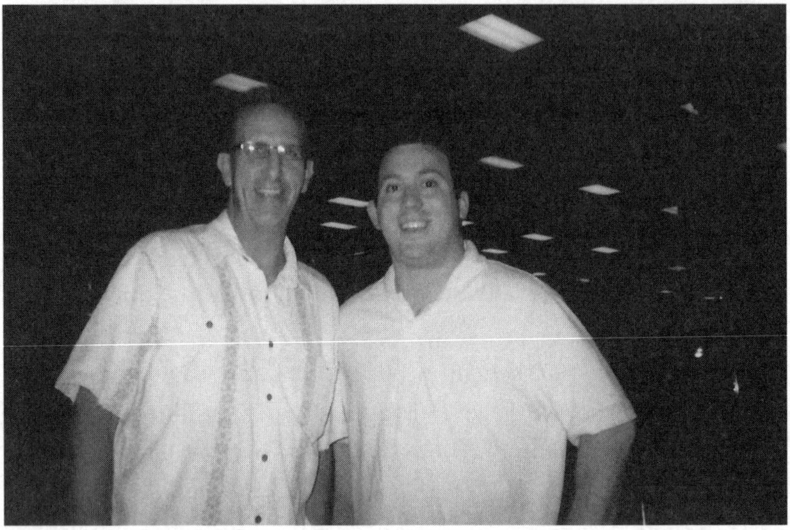

Vince with Cleveland's number-one sports-radio host, Kenny Roda (left)

always pick a side and stand by it. If you waffle too much, then you won't get a reaction from the listeners. Along with being credible and picking a side, you always want to be entertaining, so it's crucial to combine those three things. You want to keep your audience informed, entertained, and coming back for more. I have never been a shock-jock kind of guy. Some will say things just to get a reaction; I do not believe in that approach. Plenty of guys in radio have made a career out of that, but that's just not my style. If I'm making an argument, I'm doing so because I truly believe it based on my experiences [and what] I have gathered from sources. You always want to be right. You want to be the first one to break a story, but you want to make sure it's right.

Vince: Is there certain people in the industry you mold yourself after?

Kenny: The late, great professor Geoff Sindelar. Pete Franklin may be the godfather of sports talk radio in Cleveland, but a very close second was Geoff Sindelar. He had the most influence on me because I did updates for his show for a number of years. He took me under his wing and gave me solid advice, and we became very close friends. He was taken from this world far too soon, and I miss conversations with him. He would call me out of the blue and loved to talk fantasy sports. He taught me so much about the preparation of the radio business. He taught me what it took to be a good talk-show host; he's number one on my list.

Vince: How do you feel about Cleveland sports fans?

Kenny: I want them to experience what it means and feels like to win a Super Bowl. They deserve that because they are the most loyal fans in the world. Think of everything they have been through. They deserve a winner because of the loyalty and passion they show toward their sports teams. I think the Browns are overdue to turn this thing around.

Vince: What are some of your favorite memories of your career thus far in Cleveland?

Kenny: The 2002 NCAA season National Championship game, in January 2003 in Arizona, covering the Ohio State Buckeyes title win. I was down on the field literally 10 yards away from where that flag was thrown. I was 5 yards away from where Tressell and Krenzel met to draw up the fourth-down play. It was the greatest sporting event I have been too. In 1995 and 1997, it was great to cover both trips to the World Series by the Cleveland Indians. The city was electric and the atmosphere was incredible in the ballpark. We were doing pre- and postgame shows in the area between Quicken Loans Arena and Progressive Field.

[I also have] memories like Tony Peña hitting the home run for the first playoff game win and staying after to do the postgame show until 4 a.m. And I remember the devastating postgame shows in 1995 and 1997, after they lost both series. I'm a basketball junkie and enjoyed the NBA Finals in Cleveland in 2007. I'm hoping the Cavs can get it done again here in the next couple of years. I just love the game of basketball and getting to cover the NBA. I also enjoyed covering both the MLB and NBA All-Star Games that came to Cleveland in 1997, and being involved in things like the NBA's 50 greatest players who were announced at the game. I also got to sit next to Roger Clemens at the MLB All-Star Game during the home-run derby. I remember he had leaned into some gum and asked me to remove it from his jersey. Sandy Alomar, who was the game's MVP, was nice enough to give me one of his batting gloves. It was an incredible experience.

Vince: What is one of the biggest names you have interviewed?

Kenny: I did a phone interview with Tiger Woods. He does not grant many radio interviews, and it took us a year and a half to line it up with his agent, Mark Steinberg. My producer, Scooter Reese, and I worked very hard to pull that off.

Vince: How would you want your fans to remember you if you were to walk away from broadcasting for good tomorrow?

Kenny: The best thing that fans can say about me is that they didn't want to miss one of [my] shows because [I] was passionate. I would hope that I was entertaining, honest, and informative enough to keep them coming back for more. I try to give the fans as much honesty as I can, with as many facts as I can, while also being entertaining. The fans know that by listening to my show, they're going to get the most informative sports talk out there.

Vince: Do you have any final words for your fans?

Kenny: I want them to know that I appreciate them. We may not always agree and it's great to "agree to disagree" because it makes for great radio and conversation. I want them to know just how much I truly appreciate them. They truly are the most loyal fans around. They are not only loyal to their sports team, but also to their sports talk and our station, WKNR. I have been there 21 years and I wouldn't have been without the support of their fans. I want to say thank you to them because I have enjoyed the ride so far. I hope it continues for many more years because I'm not ready to retire, but if I did I would want them to say I was a passionate sports talk host who kept it real.

A few weeks after speaking with Kenny Roda, I had the privilege of talking with his on-air colleague at 850 ESPN, Greg Brinda. Greg has been in the industry for 34 years and has been with the station since its beginning more than 20 years ago. He can be heard daily on their afternoon drive-time show with his cohost, Bruce Hooley. It is one of the most popular afternoon shows on either side of the dial.

Greg grew up in Cleveland as an only child and spent much time listening to talk radio with his dad. Talk radio provided a second voice, which Greg felt replaced not having a sibling. As he grew older, he began to have a fascination with weather and even considered going to school to become a meteorologist, but he took physics his senior year at St. Ignatius, and two weeks into the class he was completely lost.

Because a working knowledge of physics is vital to a career in meteorology, he decided he needed a different career path.

Mass media caught Greg's attention when he attended Kent State University. He was lucky enough to get a broadcasting job right out of college and has been entertaining sports fans in Cleveland ever since. He began his radio career in August 1978 and hasn't looked back. He has been on every type and time of show on WKNR, including weekend shows and Indians postgame shows. He has excelled in every role. I was able to ask him a few questions regarding his passion for the job and also the key to his success.

Vince: You've hosted every show that WKNR has had to offer its listeners. What are some of the challenges and also the rewards that come with your time on the air in multiple roles?

Greg: It's a challenge, but it's also vital to make it informative and entertaining every day. Sometimes we have to think outside of the box as to what will make people listen and keep listening. I think we could get involved in the breakdown of games when needed in postgame shows, but also the everyday talk shows where you have to be more creative and keep things entertaining. It takes a lot more than the knowledge of just sport, but also the knowledge of everyday life. You have to figure out what people will react to. Sometimes you think you have a really good subject and people won't even react to it, so you always have to have other things to go back on if your main thing doesn't click with the audience. The reward is at the end of the day when you know if you have done a good show. When people have responded and, in your mind, the show has flown by. I have done three-hour shows that felt like 15 minutes—those are the best. I have also done three-hour shows that felt like 10 hours—those are the worst. My goal is to eliminate the bad shows and have nothing but good shows that feel like 15 minutes. If you can do that then you have accomplished a lot.

Vince: In the 35 years that you have been covering Cleveland sports, what are some of your favorite moments?

Greg: When the Indians made it to the postseason in 1995 and the entire great run of Indians teams. I never wanted those days to end, even though I knew they would end one day. I also enjoyed covering the Browns of the mid-1980s because they were in the playoffs every year with Bernie Kosar. The team made it to the AFC championship game three out of four years. Covering the Cavs during the Lenny Wilkens era was fun because they were such a great group of human beings. They were always in the hunt for the playoffs. Finally, the LeBron era. There was nothing like expecting to be in the post-season every single year. We got spoiled by that a little bit, but it meant that we would be on national television every day and we were relevant.

Vince: In 2000, you were inducted into the broadcasting Hall of Fame in honor of your years of hard work and sacrifice. What did it feel like to receive such a prestigious honor?

Greg: I was inducted with a great class of people such as Bill Randle and Mike Douglass, and just to be in the same room as those people was incredible and breathtaking. I took a step back and realized that the reason I was there was because I really worked hard and thought outside of the box. I think going above and beyond and even working for free all helped me figure out what I had to do.

Vince: If you were to walk away from broadcasting tomorrow, how would you want the fans to remember you?

Greg: I would want them to remember that I was passionate about my job and that I really cared. I tried hard to entertain them without compromising what I really believe in. I never wanted to be one of those people in the business that only say something to get a reaction; I could never do that. When I say something on the air, I truly mean it. It is how I say it that will get people to react, and that is something that you learn over time. I never compromised my integrity and was passionate with my views while working hard at my craft. In the world of radio, I was told that a quarter of the people like you, a quarter of the people don't like you, and the rest have never heard of you. It is humbling, but also true. No matter who you are, there are going to be people who like you and those who don't. I love a good argument when someone has a good take and is willing to bring something totally opposite but has a great point because it makes for great radio. I just want them to enjoy the conversation and keep listening. I think at the end of the day, I have served them well and have never cheated the audience.

One of ESPN 850's brightest young stars is Emmett Golden. He started behind the scenes working as an intern but quickly rose to cohost three different shows. He currently hosts *The Golden Boyz,* the drive-home show broadcast on 850 every Monday through Friday. Emmett is the star of the show, but he has not gotten this far without years of hard work and sacrifice. He is not only a good coworker but also a great and proud father. Emmett is the picture of class and everything right about sports talk radio. I was able to catch up with him and, despite his very busy schedule, he made sure to set aside time to speak with me because, once again, Emmett made sure to put the fans first and his own time second. I couldn't have been luckier than to share a few minutes with this incredible human being.

Vince: Growing up, was there anyone in the sports media that you really enjoyed watching and even looked up to?

Emmett: No, not really. The funny thing is I used to hate listening to sports talk growing up. My dad would listen to KNR and I would beg him to turn it off. I remember hearing Brinda in the car and thinking, "I couldn't care less about what this guy is talking about," not knowing he would be a friend and a mentor to me years later. Right before I decided to pursue this, I loved listening to Dan Patrick. I thought it would be cool if I could be like Seton. [Patrick "Seton" O'Connor is one of Dan Patrick's producers.] I just thought he added some fun to a show that was pretty good already.

Vince: Why did you decide to get into radio? Who helped you with that decision and encouraged you?

Emmett: I had a long talk with my wife, Kameela, about finding a career. I was happy to just have a job, but she really pushed me to find something I was good at that I would enjoy dedicating my life to. My entire family encouraged me. Everyone thought it was cool that I set a pretty big goal and that I was going after it.

Vince: Can you describe your first job in radio? Including the year and station?

Emmett: I started as an intern at WKNR in 2009. Basically, I had to do all the stuff that sucked. The awesome thing was I got to be around guys like Kenny Roda, Michael Reghi, Tony Rizzo, and Greg Brinda. So I made sure to develop relationships with those guys and pick their brains. I learned a TON of stuff during my internship. I also got to meet LeCharles Bentley and Jerod Cherry, two guys that ended up being really good friends of mine.

Vince: People, including myself, loved the show *Three Deep* with you, Will Burge, Jerod Cherry, and T. J. Zuppe. Why did you guys mesh so well?

Emmett: That's easy—we were friends before we started doing that show. So it felt like we were just hanging out for 2 hours every night. When I worked with any of those guys, we were the same with the mikes on as we were with the mikes off (minus the cursing by Will, T. J., and me). We had fun every day. We didn't have to try to have fun, it just happened, and I think that's why people liked the show so much.

Vince: Can you describe some of your responsibilities as a producer for several shows on WKNR?

Emmett: Coming up with topics, elements, segments, and everything in between. I still have a long way to go as a producer. Being a good producer is hard, and I'm working my butt off to improve every day.

Vince: How do you mange to keep the show so fresh?

Emmett: It's tough. I try to keep an eye on social media to see what people are talking about. I follow almost 1,300 people on Twitter for that reason alone. We need to know what our listeners want to talk about. I always want something that's not sports related as a part of each show. Some people hate it and tell me to stick to sports, but I believe that just because you're a sports fan doesn't mean that you want talk batting averages all day. Throwing something in about a viral video or some crazy story helps keep the show fun and fresh.

Vince: What is the biggest challenge of your job on the radio, and also your biggest reward?

Emmett: The biggest challenge is finding the hot button every day. Sometimes it's easy: A Monday after a Browns game is a no-brainer, but in July on a random Wednesday, it can be tough. The biggest reward is making my family proud of me. To see my wife, sons, sisters, brother, aunts, uncles, and cousins all with a smile on their face because I get to tell the world what I think about sports is the best feeling ever!

Vince: What are one or two of your favorite moments covering sports in northeast Ohio?

Emmett: My favorite moment was being in Ann Arbor for OSU–Michigan during Luke Fickell's year as the Ohio State head coach. I know how Ohio feels about its teams, but to see it from the other side was awesome. The atmosphere was breathtaking. That is easily my favorite moment. Second favorite was when I was covering the Cavs. I had never gotten a chance to introduce myself to then-coach Mike Brown. During a postgame press conference, I asked him a question and he said, "Well, Emmett, . . ." and answered the question. I thought it was cool that he knew my name without me telling him. I'm sure Cavs PR gave him a heads-up as to who everyone was that covered the team, but I thought that was pretty cool.

Vince: What do you feel are the virtues and skills anyone thinking of getting into sports media needs to have?

Emmett: You have to be a hard worker and you better be patient. The beginning of the process is the hardest. You don't make much money, the hours aren't the greatest, and it can put a strain on your family life. You have to be able to get through that. Once that's over, it's awesome, but it's tough when you're just starting out.

Vince: Can you see yourself doing this the rest of your life? Are there any obstacles you would someday love to tackle and achieve new heights?

Emmett: Absolutely! I've paid my dues, so I ain't going nowhere! As for something I'd love to tackle, I think doing some TV would be cool.

Vince: Who in radio has been your favorite person to cohost with? Who is that one person you have never cohosted with but would love too?

Emmett: It's way too hard to pick just one. My favorites are Roda, LeCharles, Jerod, Will, T. J., Brinda, Munch [Mark Bishop], and [Michael] Reghi, just to name a few. As for someone I haven't worked with but would love to, it's a tie between Andre Knott and Ken Carman. Andre and I are friends, so it would be a ball to work with him. Ken does a really good job, and I think it would be fun to work with him.

Vince: If you could only talk one sport, which one would it be?

Emmett: Basketball. *Love* basketball. I grew up a really big Cavs fan and I just enjoy the movement of a basketball game, if that makes any sense.

Vince: Finally, you have become a household name among sports fans in Cleveland. What does that mean to you that so many people count on you to get us through a stretch of our workday and, for some people, the drive home from work?

Emmett: First of all, I appreciate it greatly! But honestly, I think it's weird. I don't really do anything special. When someone comes up to me and says "Hi," I'm blown away because I feel like I'm just a dude that works in the media, so why would anyone want to meet me? But it does feel good to know that people find me entertaining.

ESPN 850 WKNR airs the highest rated sports talk show every weekday from 9 a.m. to 1 p.m. Local sports-broadcasting legend Tony Rizzo and his young and highly talented partner, Aaron Goldhammer, host *The Really Big Show*. The show focuses mainly on local sports issues but has several segments each week about non-sports-related issues that are very entertaining as well. They also bring in top names from around the nation to give their opinion or knowledge on the pressing topic of the day. The show has grown so much in popularity that it has moved from its original 2-hour time slot to 4 full hours.

Tony Rizzo had entertained fans on the radio for many years on WHK 1420 AM. He was also the WJW–TV 8 sports anchor for more than 14 years. He was already a popular name among Cleveland sports fans when he was asked to be a part of ESPN 850. His partner was an unknown in the market and had to prove early on that he had what it took to make it in Cleveland sports radio.

Aaron grew up in Denver in a home of big sports fans. His dad was a big fan of the minor league baseball teams that played in Denver until 1993, when the Colorado Rockies were created as an expansion team. His mom loved watching tennis. It was clear early on that a passion for sports was also in his blood. He was fortunate to grow up during the John Elway era of the Denver Broncos. It was hard for Goldhammer not to get swept up in "Elway Mania," one of his first sports-fan memories being Elway's game-winning drive to beat the Cleveland Browns in the 1986–87 AFC championship game. (Unfortunately, this is a memory that most of his listeners find to be quite painful.) Aaron's love of Elway continued to grow as he watched the All-Pro quarterback reach the Super Bowl three times, getting crushed in each one. He continued to be a fan when Elway won back-to-back Super Bowls, ending his brilliant football career.

Aaron also had a love for the NBA's Denver Nuggets. Growing up, the Nuggets weren't always good, but they did manage to reach the conference finals on a couple of rare occasions. He always stuck by the Nuggets, which showed that he was a loyal fan. Even at 3 years old, he had such a strong knowledge of the team that one time, while with his parents at an Italian restaurant, he spotted legendary Denver Nuggets trainer Robert "Chopper" Travaglini before anyone else even noticed the trainer being there. Sports in Denver was a big part of his life and helped shape the culture of his childhood.

Aaron attended New York University, spending an amazing four years in that environment. There was so much going on in New York City that he made the smart move to get into broadcasting, despite not being 100 percent sure that a career in broadcasting would even happen. It was important for him to get a diverse education, which NYU clearly offered, and he was smart enough not to pigeonhole himself in case the broadcasting choice didn't work out. He did a lot of work on college radio doing sports updates; he also spent time broadcasting college basketball. NYU opened the doors to incredible internship opportunities for him. With his experience interning at two of the biggest sports-radio stations in Denver on his resume, he earned the opportunity to work in radio at Madison Square Garden. He spent a summer producing games for the New York Liberty of the WNBA; his coworkers were so impressed by his ability that he was kept on that fall to help produce games for the New York Knicks' Spanish-language broadcast. Being at the arena every night working with top producers was an incredible opportunity for him to improve his skills.

After his time at MSG, Aaron applied for a position at a small radio station in Beaver Dam, Wisconsin, for Good Karma Broadcasting. The previous intern from MSG, Evan Cohen, was already at the station, and Aaron quickly hit it off with both Cohen and company CEO Craig Karmazin during the interview process. He was offered the job and moved from New York to Beaver Dam to begin his professional career. He was smart enough to know that the best way to start in broadcasting was in a small market where you can afford to make mistakes and allow your talent to grow. He spent 18 months at the station covering high school sports as well as performing such duties as running the board. He got to cover big-league sports such as the Green Bay Packers and Wisconsin Badgers. It was hard for him being a big-city kid living in a small town, but he made the most of his opportunity as he learned from his teammates and worked for a great company. It wasn't much longer until Good Karma Broadcasting bought a couple of stations in the Cleveland market. Karmazin asked Aaron to move to Cleveland to help get the station off the ground. It was a big step, but one that he had the skills to take.

Aaron started his first day in Cleveland cutting down trees near the 1540 transmitter to help the station get better reception. There were times where he sat in an abandoned church on the east side of Cleveland with mittens on to run the board for 1540. He was working with really smart and great people to help build the station from scratch. Aaron will tell you that it was a pleasure to do the wide variety of duties because the CEO and even the owner of the company were right there with him, working hard to make the product a winner.

The hard work paid off when Karmazin called him into the office to let him know that they had purchased WKNR—the biggest sports talk-radio station in town. From there, Aaron was able to learn from some of the best talents in the business, including Steve Dole, Jason Gibbs, Kenny Roda, and Greg Brinda.

I recently had the chance to speak with Aaron regarding his position on the show and what has made him one of the most talented figures in sports talk radio today.

Vince: With your ability to be truthful and state the facts, as opposed to pandering to what the fans want to hear, you have earned a lot of respect among your fans and peers. With that being said, what do you find to be the biggest challenge of your job?

Aaron: One of the first things my partner Tony Rizzo told me was that we were going to be ourselves on the show. In general, even though our fans might not identify with me the way they do with Tony, it's that "yin and yang" that naturally exists between Tony and me that people find interesting about the show. We also have great help from Casey Kulas, who finds the right topics and notes to bring out and puts Tony and me in a great position to connect at our best. Trying to do that every day and find four hours of top-notch content is one of the hardest things about my job because you don't want any of your segments to slip or any moment to lack the needed energy. We have to keep the positive momentum going forward for every second we are on the radio. When you're on the radio every day, you have to be able to turn that switch on no matter what else may be going on in your personal or professional life. It is also vital and a daily challenge to keep the show fresh and current. For us it never stops: There is always the next game, the next show. It doesn't matter if it is Christmas or Yom Kippur, sports never stops. It is a constant challenge for me to do the best show every single day.

Vince: What are a couple of your favorite moments from your time in Cleveland thus far?

Aaron: I was really proud of how our station handled coverage of "The Decision." It was an amazing story to cover from start to finish, despite the fact it didn't turn out how we hoped it would. As a team, we all had a role, and my teammates did their role incredibly well. We were able to be there for our fans and that is something that gets lost in the process of trying to make advertisers and station management happy. In the end, our primary responsibility is to service our fans by keeping them as informed and entertained as possible. I'm also very proud of the day we broke the story that the Browns were getting sold to Jimmy Haslam. I was woken up by a phone call from Kenny Roda at 6:30 a.m. letting me know the Browns were about to be sold. I then communicated it to Tony and spoke with Bruce Hooley and Greg Brinda. We all worked together to make that happen. I always think it's really satisfying when you can a have a real, true team win. It is really cool to be on a team, because we are talking about sports all the time and you cannot win unless you do so as a team. I think we have an amazing team on *The Really Big Show* and also ESPN 850 WKNR, and we are at our best when we are a team. Those big days wouldn't have happened without everybody chipping in with their bit of effort. It reminded me why I'm here and love this job so much.

Vince: How would you describe the Cleveland sports fan?

Aaron: Passionate, die-hard, persistent, hopeful, and strong believers in their teams. Cleveland sports fans *always* believe in their teams. Every year on the first day of spring training, we have people talking World Series. There is that positive buzz on the first day of training camp every year, despite the Browns' lackluster record since returning to the NFL. People still have that persistent hope in their teams that never stops. I also believe that Cleveland Sports fans are one giant family. Sports are a lot about family, with your mom and dad passing it down to you to pass along to your kids. They show the love of their teams with the history behind them. I know that was important to me to have that connection with my dad, and one day I hope to pass that along to my kids. Cleveland sports fans all have these shared experiences of pain. There is no way that Cleveland fans could get through the shared painful experiences without all the other local sports fans. Because you have that family, you feel like you can get through it while waiting for the day when a team breaks through and wins a championship so you can all celebrate together.

Vince: If you were to walk away from broadcasting tomorrow, how would you want your fans to remember you?

Aaron: I do this job because it is one of my life's passions and I can't see a time where I wouldn't want to do this. I don't do it because it is just a job: I do it because I really love it. Even though I wasn't one of them, I have a tremendous amount of respect for how knowledgeable and passionate the Cleveland fan base is. I would want people to remember the fact that for six years our team has had so much fun. We try to make each other laugh for four hours every day. There are times on the show when I laugh harder than I ever have in my life. During those times when we are smiling, I feel like it was all worth it for me. I hope people can remember times when they were listening to us and we put a smile on their face, maybe in a time when something wasn't going great for them. The thing that people say to me that means the most is when they explain how they have a job they really don't like and our show makes their day better. Those are the kind of moments I want people to remember from us more than anything else."

It was a pleasure speaking with Aaron Goldhammer and learning more about what made him the host that he is today. He shows a great work ethic and passion for his job. It is clear to anyone who has heard him on the air or had the pleasure to work with him that he is one of Cleveland's Finest!

A former member of *The Really Big Show* and one of the bright young stars who left WKNR to start working in television is Gene Winters. Gene is the current producer for the most popular show on Sports Time Ohio, *Drennan Live*. Bruce Drennan, a longtime broadcasting legend in the Cleveland market, hosts the show, but it is Gene who works tirelessly every single day to keep the show entertaining and new. It is a call-in show, but Gene also books studio guests as well as phone-call guests. He also has to be prepared at a moment's notice to move the show to various locations depending on what is going on in Cleveland sports. Winters has seen it all and worked on both sides of the glass. I had the chance to speak with Gene and discover how he has adapted to the world of Cleveland sports

Photo: Garry Gosky

Vince with Ashley Collins and Gene Winters, the producers of Drennan Live

media so well, and to ask about some of his fondest memories in this exciting business.

Vince: Growing up, was there anyone in the sports media that you really enjoyed watching and even looked up to?

Gene: Casey Coleman. The family was always watching Fox 8, so Casey was my sports guy. I always loved his highlights and rounding first and heading home. I'll never forget, I was doing a Browns postgame at KNR and the Sunday following his death the Browns won in overtime over KC (in 2006, I believe). I also liked the WUAB sports-extra crew growing up because they always had 15-minute blocks for sports.

Vince: Why did you decide to get into radio/sports media? Who helped you with that decision and encouraged you?

Gene: Family, of course, but it was more of an unknown for everyone since no one in the family or that we knew worked in this field. Couple others include my TV-production teacher at Mentor High School, Mr. Scott Kawalki, and all my old bosses who let me work the drive-through at Burger King.

Vince: Can you describe your first job in radio? Including the year and station?

Gene: As an intern in 2000, I worked at [WASN] 1330 in Youngstown and I played commercials during an afternoon high school football show, took a nap, and then did the same thing during a live broadcast of the football game of the week. For all that hard work, I did a postgame show on Fridays reading scores for the games in the Valley. No pay, but some local restaurant brought chicken wings and I thought that was the greatest thing. My first paid job came as a morning board operator at WKNR in April 2001. I worked 6 to 9 a.m. for the Greg Brinda show, Monday through Friday. On Fridays, I'd work the morning, then come back to work the overnight shift from 10 p.m. to 6 a.m.

Vince: People, including myself, loved the show you did with Bruce Drennan on WKNR. Why do you feel you guys had such good mojo with one another?

Gene: It was the trust factor. He believed in me. I knew what he wanted to execute, and the rest was history. The biggest misconception about the time together at KNR, I wasn't his main producer; I was the board operator for the show. Josh Sabo was, and we even had another kid for a hot minute, Adam something, that was second in command. Adam eventually went away, leaving Josh as the producer and me as number two but still the board operator. That was definitely a reason we are still together today and have lasted this long. At KNR, I didn't have to deal with off-the-air or early-morning Bruce—that was all Josh, and there is a place upstairs for

The late Casey Coleman (pictured with his father, longtime Boston Red Sox broadcaster Ken Coleman) was the voice of Cleveland sports for many years.

Photo: Garry Gosky

him. Bruce and I clicked because we speak the same language. I eventually knew what he was thinking before he did. I knew what buttons I could push and ultimately it came down to everyone wanting to put on the best show possible. Another reason: We both love baseball.

Vince: Can you describe some of your responsibilities as a producer for several shows on WKNR?

Gene: The main job is putting on the best show possible. How? With interesting guests or timely guests that help improve that day's show. Printing stories and selling the host on that topic from all the sports that affect the Cleveland teams or that the sports world is talking about. Listening to endless press conferences or locker room interviews to find sound bites that help improve the show. Working with other producers to avoid booking the same guest. Dealing with sales for sponsored elements or, in radio, remote broadcasts from locations around northeast Ohio.

Vince: Why did you make the transition from radio to TV?

Gene: Two reasons. First, at the time SportsTime Ohio approached me to join them [to produce *All Bets Are Off*], WKNR was going through an ownership change and I wasn't sure where I stood. Second, if you count the time I was an intern at KNR to the time I left [2000 through April 2007], I felt I did everything I could there and was ready for a different opportunity and challenge. I worked my way from intern to board op to producer to weekend host and, eventually, two seasons as a Browns postgame host. The challenge of taking a radio show and putting on an entertaining TV show was interesting to me, and joining Bruce again and being the man [main producer] made the choice a little easier.

Vince: How do you mange to keep the show so fresh?

Gene: It's Cleveland. They provide content every day without trying. Being a championship-starved city, and with all the turnover due to bad seasons, the content or freshness isn't hard to find.

Vince: What is the biggest challenge of your job? What is your biggest reward?

Gene: Bruce! I need him to be on his A-game everyday. I know I can sell him on ideas or topics every day, but the challenge is placing the stories in the correct spots of the show, finding the right guests, and not being afraid to blow up a planned show to go into another direction at any time. The challenge of changing a show last minute is not upsetting a guest who was currently booked, finding a new guest in a short amount of time, and getting the callers to follow along instead of going with their original agenda, but if it works, it's very rewarding.

Vince: What are one or two of your favorite moments covering sports in northeast Ohio?

Gene: My first year at SportsTime Ohio, 2007. The Cavaliers made the NBA Finals (LeBron had that great game in Detroit), the Indians clinched Central, knocked out the Yankees in the ALDS (closing Yankee Stadium with a loss) having a 3–1 lead against Boston in the ALCS before blowing it, the Browns going 10–6 before Jim Sorgi couldn't win a game to sneak them in, and OSU football and basketball was in the mix or close to it.

Vince: Who is your all-time favorite guest?

Gene: Joe Tait. One, because he's a legend, and two, the relationship he and Bruce have going way back to calling games. Larry Bird would be in that mix, as well as Casey Blake and Paul Byrd.

Vince: What do you feel are the virtues and skills anyone thinking of getting into sports media needs to have?

Gene: Get ready to work a lot and get paid very little. Power naps will become your friend.

Vince: Can you see yourself doing this the rest of your life? Are there any obstacles you would someday love to tackle and achieve new heights?

Gene: Yes! I've been doing this since 2001, so no going back now! Only thing that can stop me would be computers or automation that would replace actual workers. I'd eventually like to become a suit and have control to make programing decisions.

Vince: Who in radio has been your favorite person to work with? Who is that one person you have never worked with but would love too?

Gene: Can't pick just one, and Drennan would be the obvious choice, but I always enjoy my time with Jim Donovan. All the old KNR guys will hold a special spot, including Rizzo, who I was with for a couple months. A number of former producers in my early KNR days, when they had a stable of talent and didn't realize what they had: Andre Knott; Josh Sabo; Scott Smoot; Neal Bender; my first producer, Casey Kulas; Seth Stager; and many more I'm forgetting. I would have loved to work with Gib Shanley and Nev Chandler.

Vince: If you could talk only one sport, which one would it be?

Gene: Simple . . . BASEBALL.

In late 2011, sports talk in Cleveland moved to the FM side of the dial with the addition of the sports-talk station WKRK 92.3 The Fan. One of its best and brightest is weeknight show host Ken Carman. He grew up in Perry, Ohio, as a huge sports fan. He looked up to his favorite athletes: Larry Nance, Mark Price, and even Michael Jordan. (He admits that it was tough to root against Jordan when he played the Cavaliers, but he always had to stay loyal to his hometown team.) When football season came around, he would cheer for Michael Dean Perry. He watched football games with his buddy Eric and always rooted passionately for the orange and brown. Ken's loyalty took a hit when they let go of Bernie Kosar. When it came to baseball, he became a fan of Albert Belle and was disheartened the day Belle left Cleveland. He can recall watching Belle in the minors as he played near his home in Canton. Ken's love of Kenny Lofton was so strong that he asked his mother, who worked at a sporting-goods store, to buy him cleats exactly like the ones Lofton wore. He went to a bunch of minor league games and saw many of the great Indians of the 1990s develop. It instilled an incredible passion for Cleveland sports in him from that young age.

I contacted the station in the hopes to secure an interview with Ken. I was excited when my phone rang shortly after and he was on the other line, eager to schedule an interview with me. He was nice enough to travel to meet me almost an hour from his home on a weeknight. It was the first sign of many that Ken was a class act.

Vince: Thank you for joining me this evening.

Ken: You're very welcome, It's my pleasure to be here.

Vince: You grew up near Akron and had the privilege of seeing many Indians greats before they reached the majors as they played their minor league ball in Canton/Akron. Do you have any memories of those times that stand out to you?

Ken: Watching the players that would go on to the majors and play for the Indians who become some of my favorites was incredible. One such story was when I met Bartolo Colón. He had two beautiful women with him as he stood outside this brand-new black-and-gold Lexus. I was in amazement of the women as I stood there holding out my hat, as my father encouraged me to try and get the signature. He was wearing a huge gold chain with black jeans and a black shirt as he stood next to these amazing women. It was just an awe-striking sight that led me to believe that he was already on the path of greatness.

Vince: I have been listening to sports talk radio my entire life, and I can say with confidence that you are one of the best I have ever heard. It is clear to the fans that listen to you that you sound intelligent and confident with what you are expressing. Many have called you a natural on the microphone. Is this something that you wanted to do your whole life?

Ken: When I was 11 years old, reading the sports paper in study hall, I remember someone near me had a radio on sports talk that diverted my attention. I would listen to it from that day on with the likes of Kenny Roda, Jim Rome, and many others. I loved *Mornings With Bruce Drennan* to the point that I would wake for school and even on snow days not go back to bed because I wanted to hear his show. I would be shoveling the snow with my headphones on to keep listening to Drennan. I just loved him as a kid. I never called into a show, I just really liked it. My initial thought in high school was to try my hand out at being a sports writer. I ended up taking a speech class and one of the assignments was to do a fake radio show. My teacher thought I was good at it and recommended that I try that instead.

Vince: What steps did you take to follow this newfound talent?

Ken: I attended the University of Akron to major in broadcasting, with a fall-back notion of becoming a teacher if it didn't work out. It's kind of a scary thought—no one should have becoming a teacher as their fallback plan. You have it or you don't when it comes to broadcasting. It's a lot more than just turning on a microphone. If I realized early on that I didn't have it, then I would have majored in something else. I liked the school a lot, I really did!

Vince: How much did it help working for the college radio station?

Ken: It wasn't like some of the other ones when you would just spin records. Mr. Beck, the supervisor, and Mr. Hoffman, on the television side of things, ran a tight ship. It was hard to get in and you had to write three papers about why you wanted to do it and go through several classes. Then, if they said you could, only then were you allowed in the group. They did well to get me prepared for my future endeavors. We would do a 3-hour sports show every Sunday, and if you were bad at it, they would make adjustments and even threats. They wouldn't hesitate to cut you down to an hour or even a recorded hour. I thought to even have airtime that we really had to take it seriously. We had to kick out a couple of guys that fooled around during it; we wanted to take it seriously. I really enjoyed it and couldn't see myself doing anything else.

Vince: In this market of such passionate fans, how does it help you to be from northeast Ohio originally when it comes to relating to the voice of the Cleveland fan?

Ken: We have a mix of fans both young and old, positive and negative. We have people who have seen it all and tend to be skeptical if we can ever win a championship in this town. This is a town that can take a joke pretty well, but does not want to be laughed at. We have a chip on our shoulder for a good reason. It's a shame that in today's society so many people look down on the hard work that this town was built on. The Cleveland fan base is a family. I have been everywhere on the east coast and people can talk about the arts and other such things, but Cleveland is a great city filled with real people. It is a city where the vast majority of people can look at themselves in the mirror and know exactly who they are. They know who their parents are and who they believe in when it comes to the teams they believe in, like the members of their family. They truly intend to make the right decisions and have the problems to deal with like everyone else.

Vince: What is it like to have so many people close to you listen to you on the radio?

Ken: It is a blessing and a curse at the same time because it makes you that much more nervous. My mom and dad listen, my family listens, my friends listen. It isn't that long ago that I was in high school, so a lot of high school friends listen. With Facebook and Twitter, it becomes a small world and not everyone is always going to be a fan. There will be some people who may say some very mean-spirited stuff. It has to be that right mix. Every single word counts when everyone is listening. There are a lot of good things about this town that others don't want to recognize. I think at some point it will build back up and show its strength again. Other towns have had it and still do worse than us, both in the sports and economic world. Cleveland is a city on the rise. It is my job to be honest with the fans about our positives but also our negatives. There are many on the national level who fail to highlight anything positive for Cleveland. The people who live here stay and try to make it better; they just don't pack up and move. It could be rainy and cloudy, but our fans remain loyal as they stick with it and do whatever they can to help things improve.

Vince: If for any reason you were to walk away from broadcasting tomorrow, how would you want the fans to remember you?

Ken: Every single second I was on air I never took it for granted. It has never been a job! You can get stuck in a bad time slot when you're not feeling good and a lot of guys can forget that. I have had the pleasure of not knowing guys like that. I have been lucky for every single second that I have been given, and it is hard not to get emotional over something like that. I think about my parents and the sacrifices they made. I think about my wife and the sacrifices she had to make. She moved here from Youngstown to be here with me. She had a lot of Youngstown pride and for her to move here was a big deal for me. It is a job, but not really. It can end at any time—the station can switch formats or if you get a new boss that doesn't care for you. It is something to never take for granted. It is amazing to be able to say what you want to say and people actually listen. The long and short of it is that it is a blessing, every single second of it. It is a dream and I'm grateful for every second of it. No matter where I go from here, I always want to be that same person my family knew me as. It is nerve-racking sometimes because my family made some heavy sacrifices for me to do what I do. That is something I carry with me every day.

Vince: Who are the people you know in the industry that you try to mold yourself after?

Ken: I have met several Hall of Fame athletes and never been nervous, but when I meet some of the legends in our industry, I do get nervous because of the respect I have for them. I remember meeting John Telich and reflecting back to watching him and Casey Coleman during Friday-night touchdown for high school football. I was terrified to meet guys like Joe Tait and Jim Donovan because of how much I liked watching them. You want to do it the way they do it because they have been around for so many years and paved the way. Even though people may not always agree with those guys, they will still remember them for being great at what they did. It is something that I always shoot for and hope I can get there one day.

Vince: It has been my pleasure to speak with you, as again you have proved why you are such a class act and beloved by so many fans. On behalf of all of us, I want to say thank you and good luck!

Ken: I want to thank all of you as well. It has been my pleasure and a dream that I'm thankful to have daily.

The top-rated show on 92.3 The Fan is currently the *Kiley & Booms* morning show. While Kevin Kiley and Chuck Booms are both veterans of the booth, the show is produced by a man who is emerging as one of the biggest players on the scene. Joseph "JG" Spooner is no stranger to hard work, dedication, and a drive to succeed that few people in the industry possess. Still in his first decade on Cleveland radio, he has a long way to go, but he has a work ethic to make big things happen. JG sat down with me recently to discuss his meteoric rise in the Cleveland media spotlight.

Vince: Growing up, was there anyone in radio you looked up to and who inspired you to get into the business one day?

JG: I always admired and aspired to be Joe Tait. I have been a die-hard Cavaliers fan and basketball fan in general since birth, and to me no one did it better than Joe. I wanted to be able to paint a picture with my words the way he did and bring people into the game who couldn't physically be there.

Vince: After making the choice to have a career in sports media broadcasting, what path did you take to make your dream happen and what people helped you out along the way?

JG: I got a real late start and, to be honest, it was my wife, Jessica, who was the person who not only pushed me to follow my dream of pursuing a broadcasting career but was instrumental in me seeing it all the way through. That, coupled with the support of my parents, was all I needed to cross the finish line.

Vince: What was your first job in radio?

JG: I was the sports director for Big Horn Mountain Radio in Buffalo, Wyoming, and was also the morning drive host on their country station, KIX 92.9 (KLGT).

Vince: How did you end up with 92.3 The Fan?

JG: I had been out of touch with the Cleveland media scene since I had been out west for nearly three years before taking a job as morning drive host on KISS 106.9 (WKZA) in New York. I got off the air one day and received a phone call from Andy Roth, who is now my boss, telling me about CBS Radio's launch of The Fan and, after a brief phone call, I sent him a demo and was offered the opportunity of a lifetime—the chance to talk sports in my hometown on The Fan.

Vince: As the producer of the highly rated *Kiley & Booms* morning show, you have the heavy responsibility of booking the show that most people count on to put them in a good mood on the way to work. How do you handle such a heavy task?

JG: It's not easy, that's for sure, and it truly is a 24-hour job in today's age of social media and instant information. Kevin and Chuck are two completely different personalities with two completely different skill sets and strengths. I try to take those and bring them to a harmonious meeting point we like to call "controlled chaos" and a show that is truly about its own mistakes.

Vince: And, on a personal note, what time do you have to get up in the morning to get your day started so early? Do you do most of your show prep at night?

JG: I talk to Chuck multiple times each night about what is going on in the world of sports and what he is hottest on for the next day. Then I talk to Kevin when I get into work and help blend his thoughts with what Chuck and I talked about the night before. I don't have a healthy sleep schedule, that is for sure. I usually go to bed around 11 p.m., I try to catch as many of the day's games as I can, and then my alarm goes off at 3 a.m. On a lazy day, I might snooze it until 3:30.

Vince: What is the biggest challenge you face in your job? What are some of the biggest rewards of your hard work paying off?

JG: I think the biggest challenge every day is taking two polar-opposite people and personalities and trying to find a common ground that breeds humor, entertainment, and information. The biggest rewards come from the fans of the show—it might be on social media, might be when they stop me at the store or out on the town—but when someone says that they enjoy the show or that we make their morning a little more enjoyable or that they could share a laugh with their son or daughter, that is all the reward anyone could ask for.

Vince: What segments of the show do you feel the fans most relate to, and why?

JG: I think the most popular segment on our show is the "Idiot Pop Quiz," hands-down. But to be honest, I think people relate to the show as a whole, not one particular segment. I think it is the blend of Kevin, Chuck, and me. We span a huge age range, multiple lifestyles (Kev has grown kids, I have a young child, Chuck never had kids) and a wide range of social interests. How could you not relate to one of us?

Vince: Recently, you took part in a charity event at the zoo. You have a very busy schedule but took time for this event, which shows a lot about your character. Why do you feel giving back is so important?

JG: Without the people who listen, our fans, we would literally be *nothing*. Plus I just think it's important to give back when you can. I am incredibly fortunate to be in the position I am in and I *never* take a day off for granted. I am incredibly humble and grateful to be where I am, and anytime I can say thank you and give back, I do it.

Vince: Before your career in sports radio comes to an end one day, what goals do you have that you would like to achieve?

JG: I have achieved goal number one, which was to one day be back doing radio or TV in my hometown, and i am lucky enough to do both. the huge goal or dream would one day to be Joe Tait, Fred McLeod, etc.

Vince: At this point, do you have any career-defining moments you have been part of and are extra-proud of?

JG: It was a scary leap to take when I switched careers and took my wife, Jessica, who was pregnant at the time, clear across the country to Wyoming. I didn't even know if I would be any good at this or if I would fall flat on my face and be back to square one within weeks. I think I am proud of the fact that I set a record in the Wyoming Association of Broadcasters that still stands today by winning five WAB Awards in a single calendar year. No one had ever won more than two in a calendar year previously. And of those awards, I won Best Radio Show and Best Play by Play. I feel like that validated my career move and proved that I made the right choice for my family.

Vince: Finally, what message do you have for the Cleveland fans that have supported you and your show?

JG: Thank you, honestly, from the bottom of my heart. You are the reason we grind every day and wake up at unthinkable hours to put together an entertaining, informative, and funny show. If I could thank each one of you individually, I would.

Another one of the up-and-coming young men on the microphone is Vic Travagliante. He is currently a CBS Sports update anchor and an occasional host on 92.3 The Fan. Vic, who is on the verge of huge things in the broadcasting industry, possesses determination and an amazing work ethic.

Vic grew up a die-hard Cleveland sports fan in both Independence and Richfield, Ohio. He came from amazing pedigree in the music and broadcasting industry, being related to Kid Leo from WMMS. His brother, Chris, is in the music industry, having been on tour with NSYNC, The

Backstreet Boys, Paul McCartney, U2, Cher, Britney Spears, Janet Jackson, Jay Z, and many more. His grandfather, Elmer, was a radio sports broadcaster many years ago. He even took part in broadcasting during the World Series runs of the Cleveland Indians of 1948 and 1954. His other grandfather, Larry, worked as a cameraman for several local television stations. He was lucky to have all of them in his life because they provided great inspiration and plenty of encouragement.

Vic will be the first to remind young people looking to get into broadcasting that they must stay dedicated and prepare to make huge sacrifices. If you want it badly enough, then you have to be willing to work hard. This is a motto that he lives daily. He has had to miss birthdays and holidays to fulfill his dream. Simply to get the experience, he once drove nine hours to call a college basketball game for free. He will remind young prospects to be ready for hard times but that it will be worth it if they continue to work hard.

Vic went to Revere High School in Richfield, Ohio, where he played varsity basketball and ran track. He followed his desire to be in broadcasting when he attended the University of Findlay. He also continued to play basketball there and became part of a dynasty. His college team won four straight conference championships, including the 2009 National Championship. Vic has preserved his family values and, combined with his excellent work ethic, has earned the respect of both his peers and Cleveland sports fans. He took time out of his busy schedule to grant me the following interview.

Vince: Vic, thank you for taking the time out to speak with me about your experiences growing up as a die-hard Cleveland sports fan, as well as your current profession, which has made you a prominent voice on the current Cleveland sports scene.

Vic: Thank you for having me.

Vince: Growing up living in Richfield, what are your earliest memories of the Cleveland Cavaliers as a young boy during the Lenny Wilkens's era?

Vic: Some of my fondest memories were shared with my grandfather and four older brothers as we watched the games together. It didn't matter if it was the regular season or playoffs, no matter the day, or at whose family member house we were at, we watched the games together. The Cavs of that generation always make me think of family and the time we spent together watching the games. I remember one game that I attended with my mother and we were sitting in a suite. I remember Austin Carr coming up to me and handing me a Cavaliers duffel bag filled with candy. Those are some of my favorite memories of things not done on the court but more of me spending time with my family watching the games and coming together. Craig Ehlo is my favorite basketball player of all time. I always loved watching him play. The one thing that stands out in my mind is obviously "the shot," as Michael Jordan hit in on Craig Ehlo. Later on, I ended up working for Ed Kostyack, in the city of Independence, who was and still is the Cavs clock operator. He told me some good stories about watching Jordan play and some clock issues of starting it too late or too soon.

Vince: Were you a baseball fan as a child?

Vic: I used to be a huge baseball fan as a kid. I would sit in front of the television and fill out scorecards for every single game in those large scorebooks. I would put them in boxes when I was done, and I believe my mom still has a few of them. I would fill them up so fast that my mom would have to go to the store and buy more on a regular basis. I would also go outside in my backyard and paint the square on the red barn white and pretend to be Orel Hershiser or Dennis Martínez and pitch to this square box. I would throw the ball, then run up and grab it after it hit the barn so I could throw it again. When they started to become good, I wasn't even 10 yet—I was born in 1985. This was the first time that I had a team that was winning. If you go back to that time, the Browns were coming off of several losing seasons, and I was too young to remember their run of the late 1980s. The Cavs were around but not nearly as good as they had been. The Indians became the crown jewel of the city.

Vince: With your history as an athlete, does that give you a different perspective on sports today?

Vic: With myself and my wife being athletes, as well as knowing people who have played on the professional level or at the high college level, such as Aaron Craft, who is a friend of our family, it is a reminder that there is no guarantee for next year. That result of the finals gave me an insight of how few and far between great teams and chances to win championships truly can be. It is hard to win and keep a team together. So when that team is winning, it is crucial that the whole city jumps on those teams' back with support. We should embrace whatever team it is because it is very hard to win a championship. The Cavs loss of 2007, along with the Indians getting close later that fall in the playoffs against Boston, shows it is very hard to be a competitive team and stay competitive. I really believe with the fan base in Cleveland that if there is another winner that everyone needs to get together and give them all the support they possibly can.

Vince: You're currently on the radio with 92.3 FM The Fan, one of the hot, new sports radio stations in town. How does your history as a die-hard fan benefit or hinder your role in the media and give you the perspective others not originally from here but broadcasting in this market may not have?

Vic: I think it may give me the advantage over some; however, we have so many talented people working on air at the station as hosts and update guys. The only thing I ever wanted to do as a kid, if I was ever to get into sports broadcasting, was come back to Cleveland and cover our teams. That was my main goal because I grew up here and loved all of our teams. I wear all the teams on my sleeve in support. The Browns are king in my heart; I get so emotionally invested in the games that I sometimes throw a foam brick at my television. I tend to show more emotion watching the Cleveland Browns on a Sunday then I did at my wedding. That is just the way it is because I'm deeply rooted in Cleveland. For me to come back with CBS, a huge broadcasting company, to this city is something I have to pinch myself sometimes because it's all I ever wanted to do. I'm very grateful that CBS gave me this wonderful opportunity.

Vince: Does all of that help you relate to Cleveland fans?

Vic: I can relate to Cleveland fans because I'm one and will always be one. When the Browns lose, I won't sugarcoat anything because I want the same answers all the fans want. The same if I'm covering the Cavs because again I want all the same answers the fans want. At the end of the day, I'm not a media member: I'm a Cleveland sports fan that just happens to work in the media. It is funny because I have the platform to speak and express my feelings that a typical Cleveland fan wouldn't have. What someone talks to their boss at the water cooler about is something that I get to talk about with the entire city. That is what makes it fun for me because I basically get paid to be a Cleveland sports fan. It was a dream job growing up, and I'm just glad I got to achieve it.

Vince: Thank you for your time today. It was a pleasure to speak with someone so passionate and knowledgeable. Cleveland sports fans will be lucky to have you around for many years to come.

Vic: Thank you.

While some radio shows can at times be repetitive, *The Sports Fix*, hosted by Jerry Mires, makes the most of the chance to captivate listeners every time it goes on the air. For several years, *The Sports Fix* could be heard on WHK 1420 AM on Saturday nights. It has since moved permanently to a daily online format.

The Sports Fix has done an incredible job of reaching out to all the local Cleveland sports teams and their fans, including the Lake Erie Monsters of the AHL. Jerry passionately covers every sports topic with both knowledge and a fresh feel, and has brought the show from its small beginnings to more than 15,000 followers on Facebook.

As host, Jerry calls it right down the middle and never makes his callers feel insignificant. He listens to his callers and lets them express themselves, which can sometimes be a strange concept for other radio sports talk hosts. He is the only sports show host in town that will allow a first-time author to come on his show and talk about a book they wrote related to sports. He doesn't demand money from fans or anything ridiculous, if he feels the cause is good he will show his full support. He is also the only host in Cleveland sports talk that hosts and produces his own show. On certain days, he can be seen running the board and taking the calls all the while keeping up with his hosting duties.

Jerry grew up with sports being a dominant force in his home. His great-uncle, Abe, is known in Browns history as "the man in the brown suit." Abe worked for the Browns most of his life. He started off catching the balls after extra points and field goals in the days before there were nets to capture the ball after it went through the post. (He earned his nickname because he would wear a brown suit when he was catching the balls.)

Jerry attended Cleveland city schools as a boy before graduating from Lincoln West High School, where he played football. He attended Baldwin Wallace University before venturing into a successful pro-wrestling career, performing under the name J-Rocc and earning a loyal local fan base. Years later, Jerry would follow his heart back to Cleveland sports and pursue a career in broadcasting. In 2007, he graduated from the Ohio School of Broadcasting and got a job with WHK.

Jerry began his career as a board operator before quickly learning commercial and show production. He was handed the reins of *The Sports Fix* by program director Joe Sweeny and started as the show's producer before becoming a host upon the death of regular host Victor Cortes in 2010. After two years with several cohosts, Jerry became the solo host in 2012. He was more than capable of hosting the show by himself, and because of his skills, the fan base quickly grew.

Since late 2011, Jerry has also served as the afternoon drive-time news anchor on WHK and traffic reporter on both WHK and WFHM 95.5 The Fish. While in college, he had an internship as the assistant producer for *The Brian and Joe Morning Show* on WMVX 106.5 FM. He was fortunate enough to spend nearly a year working under Brian Fowler and Joe Cronauer, two legends in Cleveland radio. To this day, Jerry still uses the skills that he learned during his internship.

Jerry gives plenty of credit to Joe Sweeny for seeing his potential and giving him lots of opportunities to advance his career. Sweeny saw what Mires wanted to do and gave him as much opportunity as he could. He entrusted Jerry with *The Sports Fix* and then helped him land the news-anchor position, which allowed Jerry to truly begin his sports-radio career.

I had the privilege of meeting Jerry and sitting in on several of his shows. His crew was professional and run like a well-oiled machine. He took time out of his busy schedule to sit down with me and be interviewed on his own memories as a die-hard Cleveland sports fan and his current work in broadcast media.

Vince: Thank you for joining me today. It is an honor to speak with you.

Jerry: It's my pleasure to be here.

Vince: You grew up as an avid sports fan surrounded by a family of Cleveland loyalists. What was it like being surrounded by so many Cleveland sports enthusiasts?

Jerry: It wasn't a choice where I come from, as my Dad was the biggest fan of them all. I can't relate to kids today that root for other teams that are not Cleveland teams because that wasn't an option in my family. If you wanted to wear a baseball cap in my house, the only choice was the Indians—there was never any other option. My dad told me about watching Jim Brown actually playing, not just video like I have to tell my children, but actually being there to see it live. He was downtown during the 1948 World Series as well, and it was that kind of stuff that was embedded into me at a young age. I didn't realize until I grew up how hardcore my dad was. He would be wearing one of those mesh Indians hats in the 1970s and 1980s when the team stunk; there was no wavering with my dad, and that is a real fan. I was out there as a kid going to Browns games in the freezing cold and eating dog biscuits. From the day I was born, I was a sports fan!

Vince: What does it mean to you to be a Cleveland sports fan?

Jerry: It means I'm tough; it means I'm a legit, bad mama-jama. It takes courage to be a Cleveland sports fan. I hate to say it, but a lot of them are fair-weather fans. They love to tell you they are Cleveland fans when something good happens, but they are the first ones to tell the Cleveland jokes and join in on the bandwagon when things are bad. When the Dolans aren't spending money and the Indians are only winning 60 games, but the Dolans are making money because of the revenue sharing in baseball, I believe as a fan you have the right to feel you are getting ripped off. It stinks because no one wants to be a loser. Being a sports fan with the media around here is tough because these guys make up a story out of nothing or just keep talking about the same things daily. Being a fan ties me back to my dad and family things. I remember the Earnest Byner fumble game; my dad had a huge party with his friends in our basement. Meanwhile, my brothers and I built a huge fort with blankets in our room to form a tent and watch the game in there. You could hear my dad and his friends yelling from downstairs. I remember at halftime we were getting crushed and I remember the noise of anger downstairs. Then watching the TV as Byner is crossing the goal line and being devastated when the announcers confirmed the fumble. Then, we got the safety and I started thinking again that we might still have a chance. It was the first time I cried watching sports. The year before, I remember getting angry, as I was sure the field goal did not go in. I went to St. Rocco's and the city was so Browns crazy that they even allowed us to wear Browns gear those weeks instead of our uniforms. We would tape the newspaper to our windows because they had dog bones with the Browns on them.

Vince: Two of the main sports radio stations in town have several on-air personalities that aren't even from here. What advantage does it give you hosting *The Sports Fix* as someone who grew up here and is a true die-hard fan?

Jerry: I can feel their pain because I lived it actively. I'm not trying to say that people not from here can't understand it either, but I do think it makes it different. I know the feeling and the hot buttons to how people are going to react to the things I say because I have been a Cleveland fan—good, bad, and ugly. I think that is a huge part of what motivates me.

Vince: Why did you choose to get into sports talk radio?

Jerry: I chose to get into it because of my Dad. I listened to sports talk radio my whole life with him, including before and after the games. I remember calling into the Triv show one day after school and waiting to speak, only to get too nervous and hang up when it became my turn to speak. I remember hearing the people talk with the passion they had, and my Dad was always into it. He would also listen to the Indians games any chance he got.

Vince: You mentioned the relationship with your dad. Now that you have two sons who are big sports fans, would it be better now to watch your team win a championship because you would get to share it with them?

Jerry: To a point, yes, but things are so different now and it drives me nuts. I don't look at sports the same anymore. There are a lot of things about sports in 2013 that I just don't like. I don't like the economics of it. We can talk about dollar amounts in the millions about sports, but we can't figure out how to fund schools. How can our country be in so much debt yet we have all of this money that gets paid to athletes?

Vince: Do you have a solution as to how sports can help the country's massive debt?

Jerry: You can take every athlete in every sport and pay them 50 percent of what they currently make and they would still be rich. Take that 50 percent and put it in a pile, then give it back to the economy. If we just did this for one season, the debt would disappear. A person who makes 20 million dollars would still be rich if they were making 5 million dollars. One athlete, one year times hundreds of athletes—the numbers are enormous.

Vince: I want to thank you again for spending time with me, as I know you are very busy. What would you like sports fans of Cleveland who know you and have heard your show to say about you when you're done one day? What impact do you hope to leave on them?

Jerry: Hopefully they would say I was entertaining—that is the goal. Our listeners know that I keep it real. Just because I'm on the air doesn't make me always right. That is the one thing that I'm really proud of. I don't care what the popular opinion is—if I don't agree with it, I will say it. I will stand up for what I believe in. When everyone else in town on the radio is running for cover, I will show loyalty to myself in what I believe. I don't call people stupid or demean people's opinions. I love to have discussions with people who have the opposite opinion of me. I'm interested in the psyche of the average person, and I like the art of conversation. I want people to say I was real, loyal, passionate, entertaining, and represented Cleveland well.

Vince: Thank you again for your time. Cleveland fans are lucky to have you.

It is comforting to know that the Cleveland sports media has six positive, loyal, hardworking men to steer Cleveland fans in the right direction. It isn't always easy, but these men do it with a grace and showmanship that few can match. The airwaves of Cleveland sports talk will be in good shape for a long time to come.

CHAPTER 10

Bonus: Soccer Returns to Cleveland

Professional soccer made its return to Cleveland in the fall of 2013 when the Cleveland Freeze became a member of the Professional Arena Soccer League. The team was run by a five-man ownership group consisting of Scott Snider, Louis Kastelic, Dave Gaddis, Chris Snider, and Chris Cole. Scott Snider served as president and general manager, while Kastelic was director of team operations. The Freeze played their home games at the North Olmsted Soccer Sportsplex, on Lorain Road at the edge of North Olmsted.

Scott Snider, one of the brightest spots of the team's new ownership, is an entrepreneur with a vast history in ownership—a true leader in the growing brand. He provided a little bit of insight on his background coming into this new and exciting venture:

> *I have always been entrepreneurial. I started my first business when I was 17 years old with my best friend, Mike Gallagher. I was able to grow that business and successfully sold it in 2010 when I was 24 years old. That presented the opportunity to go into business with my father—a lifelong dream of ours—and some other partners. Our goal would be to create a company where we would go out and buy other small businesses where we could invest not only capital but also management and marketing expertise. In 2011, we launched Snider Premier Growth, a family office, where we would do just that. Invest*

in income-producing small businesses and real estate. Today, Snider Premier Growth owns five different companies, one of them being the Cleveland Freeze.

For various reasons, Cleveland fans were excited to have soccer back in town. Scott Snider explained why he decided to join in the fun and the steps he had to take to make the dream a reality:

I have always loved the game of soccer. I've been a manager, a player, and a coach. I grew up watching the Cleveland Crunch and the Cleveland Force and personally, as a player, always had a passion specific to the indoor game. In my more adult playing career, I always was the odd ball out because I would play over the winter and take a break when outdoor season came along, which is quite contrary to the typical soccer season when everyone is playing outside. I played in the Professional Arena Soccer League [PASL], and when the Ohio Vortex closed, it opened an opportunity to launch a Cleveland organization in the PASL. As I think any Cleveland indoor soccer fan would say, since the Force left in 2002, there has been a huge void in our community. A piece of entertainment that presented an affordable price point for families; a fun and electrified atmosphere; and a nonstop, action-packed, on-the-edge-of-your-seat-type game that applied to the soccer fan and non–soccer fan alike: this game called indoor arena–style soccer.

That void created a business opportunity. It coupled with other business opportunities apart from it, such as launching a youth academy, camps and clinics, merchandise, a potential outdoor team, and perhaps even our own indoor soccer training facility. It seemed like a promising business model certainly would fill that 11-year void, and, frankly, it was fun.

I had a choice at age 27 to continue to be a player or become an owner. At the time, our former business partner, Louis Kastelic, and I played together in the PASL. Both sharing the same type of passion and dream, we would talk about owning our own team while in the locker room after a practice or game. When the Vortex closed, it presented the opportunity for our dream to become reality. Louis and I got together postseason with his business partner, Dave Gaddis, and began to combine our business plans for the soon-to-be Cleveland Freeze.

Previously, back in 2011 or so, when Snider Premier Growth was looking for investment opportunities, we actually looked at the I-League, which was a pro indoor league offered by the USL. This league eventually merged with the Major Indoor Soccer League [MISL]. Looking at the platform of the MISL versus the PASL, we thought the PASL presented the better business model and was more workable. It had a larger league and a minor league, the premier league, with some 40 or so teams.

Also, as former players in the PASL, we felt we knew the league. After crafting our business model, we knew we needed more financial support to take this to launch. For me, it started as a personal investment, and then I solicited my business partner—my father, Chris Snider—and this became a Snider Premier Growth investment for our company. In addition, I brought on a friend and notable entrepreneur, someone who was connected to the soccer community, Christian Cole. The five of us invested in and launched the Cleveland Freeze.

Chris Snider, Chris Cole, and Dave Gaddis brought a robust set of skills and wealth of business knowledge as veteran business owners. It complemented the young experience of Louis and me and allowed us to concentrate on operating the business for the group. It took several months to get on board with the new group and get our company and agreements together, but by September 10, 2013, we officially launched the Cleveland Freeze and began a part of the Professional Arena Soccer League just a short two months before the launch of the 2013–14 season.

Louis Kastelic had a storied background and love for indoor soccer from his days of watching the Crunch and Force play. Kastelic explained his history and love for the game:

I have played soccer since I was 5 years old. I started playing in local rec leagues, and from there I advanced on to travel soccer and then premier soccer. My senior year of high school is when I decided that I wanted to focus solely on soccer and pursue a career in college. I earned First Team All-State Honors during my senior season and that helped me get recruited by several colleges. Once I met with Ali Kazemaini, who was the coach at John Carroll University, I decided to attend the university for the next four years between 2005 and 2009.

During my time there, I won one regular season conference championship [2005] and two conference tournament championships [2005 and 2007]. My teams made it to the round of 32 in the NCAA tournament in 2005 and 2007. I set a record for most assists in a game at John Carroll University against Heidelberg with 4 and, until this season, I held the record for most assists in a career at JCU. I honestly did not even know I held the record until one of the guys on JCU, Brian Potocnik, broke the record earlier this season. I could not have been happier that Brian surpassed me, considering I helped him with his college search prior to me even joining the JCU Men's Soccer Coaching Staff in 2011. Brian is a wonderful kid with a fantastic family, and I am so honored that I got to be one of his coaches for the last four years. The hope is that Brian will be an All-American this year.

In 2012, I was signed by the Ohio Vortex midway through the season. This was my first involvement with the PASL and this is when I met Scott Snider, one of the other owners of the Cleveland Freeze who helped form the team.

When I was growing up, my dad was the equipment manager for the Cleveland Crunch and the Cleveland Force during the 1990s and early 2000s. I attended many games and tried to be the ball boy as much as possible while growing up. Without question, Hector [Marinaro] was my idol growing up. I did everything I could to make sure I slapped hands with him from the stands before every game. I always thought growing up that indoor soccer was more entertaining to watch

> *than outdoor soccer, and those Crunch and Force teams were the reasons why I fell in love with the indoor game.*

Kastelic went on to discuss why he chose to join forces with the Snider family and his father-in-law Dave Gaddis to form the Freeze:

> *Ever since the Cleveland Force folded in the 2000s, I always wished and hoped that indoor soccer would come back to Cleveland one day. The games were awesome, and I have always thought that if hockey can be successful in the US, then indoor soccer can succeed as well. It is such a fast-paced game and there is so much excitement and drama. I will never forget those years during the 1990s, and, to this day, the Crunch is still the only professional team from Cleveland to have won a championship since 1964.*
>
> *When I played for the Vortex in 2012, I got to see firsthand how hard it is to run an indoor franchise. Growing up around the Crunch and the Force, I was too young to understand all the hard work that went on behind the scenes, and even though the Vortex did not have a lot of success, I learned a lot about the PASL and the teams within the league throughout the season. At that time, I met Scott Snider and I was intrigued by the idea of forming a team one day, and I learned that he was as well. I learned a little more about Scott's background and discovered that he was a successful, young entrepreneur. After several conversations and meetings with Scott and his business partners, Chris Snider, Chris Cole, and my father-in-law, Dave Gaddis, we thought that we could give it a shot.*

The co-owners hired indoor-soccer legend and Cleveland hero Hector Marinaro to be their head coach. A household name in Cleveland and the perfect man to guide this young bunch, he was beloved locally and is acknowledged as the greatest indoor-soccer player of all time from his days playing for the Cleveland Force and Cleveland Crunch. Marinaro described the differences between the outdoor game, which he coaches currently at John Carroll University,

Vince with Hector Marinaro, the all-time leading scorer in indoor-soccer history

and also what it took for him to come out of retirement in the pro game and coach the expansion Cleveland Freeze: "My biggest challenge is not being able to get on the floor and help my players. As a former player now coaching, you always think, 'What would have I done in that situation?' Then you try to translate that in a way to help today's players. It took some convincing because I wanted it to be very professional and wasn't convinced that this league was that. I also didn't know if I wanted to get back to the grind of road trips and time away from my family."

Marinaro went on to describe some of the changes in the game of indoor soccer from the time he played compared to the way it is now, "Today's game is much faster and more physical than it was back in the day. Today's players are more athletic, but we were much more technical back in the day."

Kastelic explained some of the challenges of finding a roster, a coach, and even a place to play:

> *Finding a roster was not too difficult. I know from experience how much talent there is in the Cleveland area. There are a lot of good players who have played with or against one another for many years. I thought it would be a great story to form a team with mainly Cleveland-based players. Getting experienced guys to join us like John Ball and Allen Eller was also important. I thought their experiences could really help our young team.*
>
> *Finding a location to play was somewhat difficult. Many of the indoor facilities in the Cleveland area have taken down their boards. We were really left with three options: play at the Sportsplex in North*

Olmsted, play at the Multiplex [Word Church] in Warrensville, or get the team into a large arena like Quicken Loans Arena, Wolstein Center, or Public Hall. The last option was the most expensive, and given the fact that we were a newly formed franchise with an extremely small budget, it was impossible for us to afford moving to a larger arena without getting more owners, sponsors, and/or investors. This option was something we talked about looking into in the future.

The Sportsplex and their staff were fantastic. They provided us with so much help, and they understood that we were all trying to work together to put on a show and provide a form of entertainment for everyone to enjoy. Choosing Hector as a head coach was a no-brainer for me. He is an indoor-soccer legend, and he was so important to the success and growth of indoor soccer in Cleveland. The fact that he coached me in college and we work together at JCU helped because I knew what type of person he is and the type of coach he is. He played professionally for over 20 years, and there are not too many guys like him around who have that much experience.

Getting him on board would also help us regain a lot of followers from the days of the Crunch and the Force. When we signed Hector, we were also able to hire his former coach, Bruce Miller, another great mind of the indoor game. I hoped that by hiring Hector and Bruce we could bring instant credibility to our team and organization, and let the fans know that we were serious about our organization and we were here to win!

Scott Snider also gave his feelings as to why it was crucial to bring in a coach with Marinaro's experience:

Hector Marinaro is a legend in the indoor-soccer community nationwide. Locally, he is even more praised. In my opinion, as most I think would share, Hector is the Michael Jordan of indoor soccer. We had several selections for coaches, and when Hector came to the table we knew at very minimum that from a pure creditability standpoint it was gold. To this day I am honored that Hector, as well as Bruce Miller, put their trust and confidence in our group.

Hector came to us through Louis Kastelic, a former partner of ours. He and Hector both coach together at John Carroll University. I think Hector was waiting for the opportunity to get back involved with the professional indoor game and being a part of the Freeze also gave him his first professional coaching opportunity.

Hector was quoted when we announced him as head coach as saying, "I am very impressed with the ownership group that has been put together. I wouldn't get involved unless I felt the ownership group was committed to bringing quality indoor soccer back to this area." That always stuck with us, and we were honored. Beyond Hector's self-made brand, he brought a wealth of knowledge and playing experience of which our players could benefit from. It was a no-brainer when Hector came to the table.

Snider also explained how he handled the challenges of finding a location to play, as well as a little about how the owners went about choosing a name for the team:

We had several names that were in the bucket during our planning stages. What we knew for sure is that we wanted something that pertained to our community, which perhaps described our community in a way or spoke to our history in Northeast Ohio. We obviously also wanted something that was catchy and a name that we could create an atmosphere or culture with for the fans.

It came down to three, and we chose the Freeze because it described our Northeast Ohio snowy and cold winters, our indoor season was played over the winter season, and we could create that atmosphere we liked. We could have a funny mascot, like Mr. Freeze or Lake Effect, we could have someone like a face painter who could paint snowflakes or winter themes, and we could perhaps even have a dance team called the SnowFlakes. We investigated taking on the names of the Crunch or the Force and kind of bringing back the past. However, we chose to create something new that would add to the rich history of indoor soccer that already exists here.

Choosing a location to play was difficult. It came down to three things for us. One, we had a budget to work within. Two, we knew we probably wouldn't get much more than 800 people per game, being a brand-new organization, so we wanted an arena that created a very intimate, close, and exciting feeling that made you feel that you were right there, a part of the game. And three, we wanted a facility that spoke to what we as an organization believed in, which was in part professionalism, cleanliness, and high quality.

The larger facilities like the Wolstein Center were simply out of our budget, as we not only had to pay higher rents but also would have to invest in our own field, turf, and boards. We also felt that they were too big. We didn't want 1,000 people scattered in a giant facility; we'd rather have them packed in and make the experience more intimate and exciting.

The Soccer Sportsplex in North Olmsted really hit all three of our primary objectives. I tip my hat to the owners and staff over there, as I believe it's the cleanest, most professional, and highest quality indoor arena-style facility we have in Northeast Ohio, and I know the staff over there works hard to make it that way.

The Sportsplex also fit some nice bonus objectives. Food and beverage costs were low for our fans, there was free parking, it was right off the highway, our team could practice and play their games on the same field (which was a competitive advantage for us), it provided an opportunity for kids to play on their other fields pre-, during, and post-game, and overall it was in a great community, of which most of them were soccer communities like North Olmsted, North Ridgeville, Olmsted Falls, Westlake, Avon, Avon Lake, Strongsville, Bay Village, and so on. It all just fit well, and it was a great place for us to start our first year.

We packed the place with close to 1,000 people for our home opener and created a fantastic fan experience.

This season would be the sixth in existence for the PASL. It was a 20-team league and the Cleveland Freeze would be part of the Eastern Division, along with the Chicago Mustangs, Detroit Waza, Cincinnati Saints, Harrisburg Heat, and Illinois Piasa. The league consisted of three divisions. One of the two was the Central Division, which played host to the Hidalgo La Fiera, Dallas Sidekicks, Monterrey Flash, Wichita B-52s, Saltillo Rancho Seco, Tulsa Revolution, and Texas Strikers. The third and final division was the Pacific Division, which consisted of the Las Vegas Legends, San Diego Sockers, Toros Mexico, Bay Area Rosal, Turlock Express, Ontario Fury, and Sacramento Surge.

The main goal was to compete for the Ron Newman Cup at the end of the season. The reigning champions, the San Diego Sockers, were not about to relinquish the trophy without one heck of a fight. However, with the league continuing to expand, the challenge would be greater for them to do so.

The Freeze would be coached by a legend in Marinaro, and they put together an impressive roster for their first season in the league. They were led by a dynamic midfielder named Steve Gillespie. Despite standing just 5 feet 9 inches, he had a competitive nature and love of the sport that made him one of the most dangerous players in the game to have to face. Gillespie excelled at soccer while playing at Brecksville-Broadview Heights High School. After an impressive stint there, he chose to attend the University of Mount Union to continue his soccer career.

His time at Mount Union was well spent, as he was voted the 2007 Ohio Athletic Conference Midfielder of the Year. He was also named to All-Great Lakes Region First Team and All-Ohio Athletic Conference First Teams in 2007, as well as the All-Ohio Athletic Conference Second Team in 2006. Perhaps his most important college accomplishment was being voted as a two-time Mount Union soccer

MVP in 2006 and 2007. In college he gained valuable experience, also playing with the Cleveland Internationals of the USL Premier Development League.

Gillespie decided to turn pro and played with the Columbus Crew of the MLS in their 2008–09 season. He also played with the Cleveland City Stars of the USL First Division; was a PASL veteran, with four seasons under his belt; \was captain of the Ohio Vortex for two years. He was developing a strong reputation as someone who could both score and pass. It was the perfect combination for any midfielder.

The other force to be reckoned with on the team was veteran striker Allen Eller. He had attended the University of Akron, where he played on the men's soccer team and from which he graduated in 1998. Eller had experience playing pro soccer in Cleveland as a teammate of Marinaro's in the Cleveland Crunch of the National Professional Soccer League in 2000–01. Eller also possessed championship experience, having been a member of the 2003 and 2004 Baltimore Blast soccer teams that won the MISL championships. On March 29, 2005, the Blast traded Eller and Neil Gilbert to the Cleveland Force for Joel Bailey and Sipho Sibiya. This move allowed Eller to receive even more championship experience—the Force made it to the championship round that season but then lost to the Milwaukee Wave. Eller went on to show his versatility playing with the Croatia Cleveland Soccer Club, from its juniors program to its men's team in the Lake Erie Soccer League, winning several titles throughout the years. Eller brought veteran leadership, sharp skill, and championship experience to the roster.

Eller wasn't the only former Cleveland Force and Crunch soccer player on the roster. The new team also had veteran defenseman John Ball. Ball began his pro career in Cleveland when he was selected by the Cleveland Crunch in the second round of the 1995 National Professional Soccer League Amateur Draft. The team would win the championship that season with Ball as a rookie to learn from the veterans. He remained with the Crunch for the 1996–97 season, during which he was named to the All-Rookie team. He was eligible because he had played only one regular-season game the year before and was still classified as a rookie. Ball played for the Crunch every winter until the team folded in 2005. Along with Eller, he was another veteran leader with valuable championship experience.

The Cleveland Freeze roster was rounded out with defensemen Jared Miller, David Jordan, Mike Green, Josh Grossman, and John Gruden. Other members of the midfield consisted of Louis Kastelic, Stefan Ostergren, Manuel Conde, Cameron Johnson, and Scott Cunningham. Along with Eller, the other forwards were Dean Miller, Chris Green, and Michael Schmid.

The indoor game in general is very different from the outdoor game that many of the Freeze's players were used to. Kastelic talked about the differences, noting, "Indoor is such a fast-paced game compared to outdoor. When you are outdoors, playing for 90 minutes, there are more times for you to relax as a player. In indoor, there is not a whole lot of time to rest, unless you are on the bench. The boards add an entirely new element to the game that you have to prepare for and be aware of, regardless of whether you are on offense or defense. In indoor, players need to have more of an ability to receive the ball in tight spaces and play quickly."

Not only did the soccer team strive for great play on the field, but the ownership team emphasized keeping the fans entertained during the breaks in the action. Scott Snider explained some of their ideas for game-day entertainment:

> *One of the pillars of our company is to provide the community with an affordable and exciting form of entertainment*—entertainment *being the keyword. Whether the team out there is playing baseball, basketball, football, indoor soccer, or having a hot dog–eating contest, they are all forms of entertainment.*
>
> *It's not just about the game that's out there. We hired a part-time game-day operations manager, Ellen Simon, who really I give most of the credit to. For example, on opening day, she was able to organize a*

community partner for the game, the Lake Erie Monsters dance team, fan giveaways and challenging games, a face painter, and a live band. We aimed to have a community partner—a nonprofit organization—each game we could donate to and help promote, and have fan contests or giveaways between each quarter and at halftime as well as some kind of halftime entertainment. All of this combined with our incredible entertainment staff, DJ Six Eight [Nick Day] and announcer Mike in the 216 [Mike Travis], means we put on some great shows.

The Freeze's first game of the season took place on Saturday November 2, 2013, on the road as the team traveled to Detroit to open up the season against the very talented and veteran-loaded Cincinnati Saints. Cleveland held the halftime lead of 4–2, but Cincinnati managed to rally in the second half and win the game 8–7 in a thrilling nail-biter. The starting goalkeeper did his best for the Freeze, allowing only 8 goals on 24 shots. The leading goal-scorer that night for the Freeze was Eller, with two. It was a good effort for their first night as a team, despite the one goal loss.

Their next game was Sunday, November 10, 2013, and it was their home opener in front of a packed house at the North Olmsted Sportsplex. This game provided a matchup with the visiting Harrisburg Heat. Cleveland came out with a strong intensity and controlled the game from the opening minutes. It was a dominating effort by the Freeze as they ran all over the Heat and won the game 11–3. The Freeze were led by Eller as the leading scorer, who put four goals in between the posts and into the net, along with Grossman, who chipped in with three goals and two assists as well. The combination of Grossman and Eller would continue to improve and dominate as the season went on. The defense also looked impressive, only allowing nine shots.

Scott Snider detailed how he will never forget the excitement and emotion of opening day:

It's one of those bittersweet feelings. I was stunned, shocked, and humbled by the incredible support on opening day from the soccer community, family, friends, and colleagues. It was an incredible day that will always rank in some of my top memories of my life. Technically, we actually sold out twice. What I mean by that is, I remember our front desk staff radioing me to come to the front because we technically had ran out of our allotted tickets for the game, but yet there was a line out the door. I rapidly walked up to the front to assess the situation and, just as quick, turned the other way to see where we could potentially fit some more! We found some areas, told people what it was like in there, and sold several more tickets until we literally couldn't fit any more people safely inside. Unfortunately, we had to turn some away, but at the end of the day it was for safety and for fan experience that we couldn't sacrifice either way, and frankly we were already over the limit! I must say we did have a dozen or so people who couldn't see well or felt it was too crowded who we issued refunds to. But overall I think if you were there that day, it was quite a sight to see and an unforgettable experience for most.

Marinaro described the overall emotion of opening night, saying, "It was a great feeling. We really didn't know what to expect, but the turnout was great. Once we took the floor and the players saw the turnout, everybody was pumped up and really excited about that game. For a lot of our players, this was their first-ever professional game, and they all had a lot of family and support in the crowd. Anytime you have a great crowd, you want to make sure you send them home happy so that they come back again. All around, it was a very successful opening night."

Kastelic also shared his memories of the emotional win:

I will never forget that day for the rest of my life. The place was packed, and we actually had to turn people away at the doors because we were full to capacity. As an owner, I was so proud of what our organization had accomplished. To be able to get our team and organization off the ground and running all within a five-month span is truly amazing. As a player, I was so excited to play in front of a huge home crowd, and I was definitely looking for my first win as a pro. When I played for the Vortex, we went winless, so it was great to put a beating on a team that I was used to receiving a beating from. It was also surreal to think that I was playing against a team that Hector and all the former Cleveland Crunch and Force pros I grew up idolizing used to play against in front of large Cleveland crowds. Winning that game was huge, and to do it in the fashion we did helped because I think it showed our fans that this was going to be a fun year.

The Freeze followed up the home opening win with back-to-back wins against Cincinnati at home by a score of 10–9 and then picked up their first road win at Harrisburg 10–7 to improve their record to 3–1. Following their hot three-game winning streak, the Freeze hit their first stumbling block of the season against two of the league's premier teams. The first was a heartbreaking 8–7 loss in Detroit against the Waza. The Freeze was then beaten badly by the best team in the league at home when the Chicago Mustangs showed why they were one of the elite teams with a 13–4 win.

Marinaro described some of the challenges of coaching such a young team against such high-caliber competition as the Waza and Mustangs: "Chicago was by far the best team in the league, which their undefeated record showed. Detroit was the defending champs and a very experienced team. We were very young and still finding what it took to win consistently."

Kastelic also explained why the Freeze had so many issues early on with two of the league's dominant teams: "Detroit and Chicago are two great teams. Chicago was extremely fast, and Detroit was very experienced. Both teams were in the league the year prior, and we still had guys who were only a couple of game into their pro careers."

At 3–3, the season could have gone either way, but the Freeze showed the heart and determination of their head coach and went on a red-hot, six-game winning streak. The tear included road wins against the Cincinnati Saints, Illinois Piasa, and Harrisburg Heat. The other three wins came at home against the Harrisburg Heat, Illinois Piasa again, and Detroit Waza. It was an impressive run that brought their record to 9–3.

Marinaro reflected back on the streak and a decision he made to help get things turned around: "We felt we were getting worn down as games went along, so we decided to go from two lines to three lines and everyone that dressed was playing a regular shift. It helped keep everyone mentally in the games and kept us fresher for the fourth quarter."

Kastelic agreed with the coaches' move to form three lines instead of two: "I think Hector and Bruce made a terrific coaching decision to go to three lines instead of two. This helped guys stay fresh, and at the end of games we were not as tired as we had been in the previous games. We were also playing teams that we should beat during that stretch. We did not have to play Chicago and Detroit during this time, so we felt more confident playing teams we had already proven we could beat."

The biggest win during that stretch came on January 4, 2014, against the Illinois Piasa, the Freeze winning by a score of 27–6. It was an absolute pounding that saw the all-time PASL scoring record set. The Freeze attempted an astounding 47 shots on goal and allowed only 13 to be taken against them. They were also an efficient 2 of 3 converting on power plays. For the Freeze, it was Green, Grossman, and Johnson all securing hat tricks, while Kastelic, Gillespie and Gulden all had 2 goals apiece.

Kastelic also explained what happened on that fateful night, offering, "Illinois's franchise had a lot of problems internally as an organization. They had issues with players on their team not wanting to travel because they wanted to be paid more, and unfortunately, this meant their reserve players had to fill those spots. At that time, our team had hit its stride and we were playing with a ton of confidence."

The Freeze's six-game winning streak came to an end at the hands of the Chicago Mustangs. It was on the road in Chicago, and the Mustangs had what it took once again to cool off the scorching Freeze. The game was never close, and the Mustangs continued to give the Freeze fits with a 20–11 win. The loss dropped the Freeze's record to 9–4, but they remained in the thick of the playoff hunt.

Marinaro voiced his thoughts on the team's struggles against the highly talented bunch from the Windy City, detailing, "As I mentioned earlier, Chicago was the class of the league and they were even tougher at home. We weren't the only team that had matchup problems against them; they were very deep top to bottom." Despite the loss, the Freeze still looked better each time out.

Kastelic shared his thoughts on what made Chicago so good:

> *Our team struggled against them because they were by far the fastest team in the league. Their speed killed us. Guys on our team had run so much by halftime that we had very little left in the tank for the second half. Furthermore, they had the MVP of the league on their team and their players practiced every day. Chicago's franchise owned their practice facility, which meant they could practice any day at any time without costing the team any money. The Freeze practiced twice a week because the fact is, as a first-year team, we could not pay our players enough money to give up their day jobs and put more time into the team. It also would have cost our organization a lot more money to rent out the practice facility since we did not have the luxury of owning our own place. These limitations are things we had to deal with as a first-year team, which makes what we accomplished all that more impressive. The 11 goals that we did score were the most that anyone had scored against Chicago all season long. Unfortunately for us, their offense was too potent.*

It was the longest stretch of the year between games—the Chicago game was played on January 18, 2014, and the Freeze would not take the field again until February 1, 2014. The long layoff between games hurt the Freeze, as they lost in Detroit 13–7. Detroit was another team that the Freeze couldn't seem to get past in the regular season. Marinaro provided his thoughts as to why, saying, "They were a very experienced team that didn't get rattled in games. We were very young, and sometimes it showed, but we gave them a tough game every time we played."

Kastelic shared his thoughts on the Detroit team as well, offering, "Detroit was extremely experienced. Their team knew where to run to and when to run there. Down the stretch, in the fourth quarter, they were able to close the game and we were still trying to figure out how to close games against good teams."

Heading into that Saturday night of February 8, 2014, the Freeze were in a must-win situation. They had a home game against the Cincinnati Saints, and if they won, they would clinch a spot in the PASL playoffs. Considering they were an expansion team, this was a huge accomplishment; several of their players had previously played on the 1–15 Ohio Vortex team the season before.

The Freeze came out that night like a house on fire, ready to destroy everyone in their path and take no prisoners along the way. The Freeze kept the pressure on right from the start and scored at will to take a commanding 8–2 lead by halftime. They didn't let their foot off the gas in the second half either; by the time the game was over, the Freeze walked away with a commanding 17–8 blowout win. It was an amazing night for Grossman, who scored 7 goals, and Eller, who set a PASL record with 8 assists. They truly were the best scoring combo in the PASL.

The Freeze clinched their playoff spot with the win. Marinaro reflected back on the crucial home victory, divulging, "It was pretty simple, we felt we were the better team and we had an opportunity to clinch a playoff spot. That in itself was motivation enough for our guys. You have to remember that some of our guys had played the year before for the Ohio Vortex that went 1–15, so to be looking at a playoff spot was a great achievement and great motivation."

Kastelic was also extremely pleased at how things went that night. He remarked, "We matched up well against Cincinnati. They were another smaller organization, similar to ours, that we were able to have our way with. Ultimately, I think the talent on our team was better than theirs. They had a lot of guys on their team that excelled in outdoor, and the fact is being good at outdoor does not mean you are good at indoor. I do not recall any special adjustments for that game.

I just remember Allen Eller coming up huge for us and then our key guys stepped up big."

The Freeze finished the season with an impressive 10–6 record, a nine-game win turnaround from the previous season that the Ohio Vortex put together with several of the current Freeze players. Eller led the team with 64 points on the strength of a team lead with 34 assists. Marinaro explained the importance of having such a skilled veteran in Eller to lead his team: "I played with Allen way back in the day, and he is a very smart player and nowadays a very experienced player. He was a big-time player for us that came through when needed on most nights. He was a big part of what we were able to accomplish."

The team's leading goal scorer was Stefan Ostergren, with 29 goals. He had a nose for the net and scored in several clutch situations throughout the entire season. Marinaro gives his thoughts on why Ostergren was so effective in finding the net, offering, "He is just a pure finisher. He can hit the ball extremely well with both feet and very accurately. He teamed up really well with Allen on our first line." Grossman was a defenseman, yet was also a prolific scorer, scoring 36 points and an incredible 24 goals. Marinaro gave his thoughts on why a defenseman was able to score so many goals, saying, "Josh has a forward mentality playing defense. He was lethal on fast breaks and has a potent left foot. Had a great year offensively for us coming out of the back."

Gillespie was the team's midfielder and did an incredible job on both sides of the ball, covering a lot of territory. He finished with 12 goals and 15 assists, very impressive numbers for a midfielder to possess. Marinaro gave his reasons as to why Gillespie was able to cover so much territory and be effective doing so: "He is everything you are looking for in a midfielder. He works hard at both ends of the field, very crafty and creative at the offensive end."

The playoffs opened at home on March 1, 2014, on a winning note against the Cincinnati Saints by a score of 11–6. The big win was the first soccer-playoff win in Cleveland in nearly 10 years. Marinaro, who was part of so many big wins in his playing days, including three indoor-soccer league championships, gave his thoughts on how it felt that opening night of the playoffs, saying, "Again, we felt we were the better team and playing at home. The guys were excited and pumped up and really took care of business that night. It was great for the franchise to win a playoff game and send the crowd home happy and wanting more."

Kastelic explained the extra motivation to win that night, disclosing, "The fans were definitely revved up for that night. Our players also knew that if we won, we would have a chance to play Detroit again. This motivated us beyond belief because we had developed a nice hatred for Detroit throughout the season. All of our players played within themselves that night and no one tried to do too much. We knew that if we played our game that we would prevail."

The team then traveled to Detroit and beat them in a nail biter 6–5 to advance to the final rounds. Detroit had been a bit of a thorn in the Freeze's side that season, and Marinaro explained how the team was finally able to overcome them when it counted the most: "Each time we played Detroit, we became more and more confident that we could beat them. It was a great playoff game with a great intensity to it. We were up, but they came back to tie it up late in the game. Then Allen Eller came up big with the game on the line. He was our captain and leading scorer. You look for those kind of players to deliver with the game on the line, and he did big-time."

This was a huge win for the Freeze, and Kastelic couldn't have been more proud of how his team played that night, saying, "This game was the most exciting game of the year. It seems like our team finally learned how to close out a big divisional game. We played great defense this game and got a great effort from our goalie, Mike Mason. Hector and Bruce stayed with the three-line system and then, in the second half, they played the guys who were performing the best."

The team advanced to the championship tournament Final Four, along with Chicago, Hidalgo, and Las Vegas. The Freeze was knocked out of the tournament by the undefeated (and eventual league champions) Chicago Mustangs. Despite not winning the championship, it was still a wonderful season for the Freeze that brought plenty of excitement back to Cleveland. Marinaro did a great job summing up his excitement of the season and what it mean to the future of professional soccer in Cleveland:

> *We beat Detroit in the quarterfinals to reach the Final Four weekend. We were matched up against Chicago in the semifinal and lost to them. They eventually won it all the next day, routing the team from the West. We played Las Vegas in the consolation game and lost in the last seconds of that game. As a franchise, it was a great accomplishment to make it to the Final Four. Our team was made up of all local kids, [most of whom] were getting their first crack at professional soccer. Compared to most every team, our player budget was probably one of the lowest in the league, so I feel we got the absolute most of what we had. It was a tremendous achievement and I am very proud that we made it to the very final weekend of play for an expansion franchise. At the end of the day, we had a very successful season for an expansion team. Considering that the Ohio Vortex the year before was 1–15, we have to be very happy at 10–6. We had a great playoff run, losing to the eventual champion in the league semifinals. We knocked off our Ohio rivals in the first round and then the defending champs on the road in Detroit. The players gave me everything they had, and I was extremely proud of our accomplishments. Professional soccer definitely has the ability to be popular here in Cleveland if the proper product and league is available.*

Scott Snider also reflected back on the excellent first season:

> *I contribute it primarily to players themselves. The talent of the players on the team and the culture they created among themselves as a team and the relentless passion they had to play for and not represent their city but more so their fans. Let's be honest, for the most part, in this current state of professional indoor soccer, you aren't quitting your day job to play professional indoor soccer. It's just not the case for most in this era. Most of our guys had a regular day job, then came to practice in the evenings and played games on weekends. They were dedicated and*

it showed. They were hungry to win. We had a chance to bring a professional championship back to Cleveland, as the Crunch had already brought championships to this city.

I think the guys wanted to be a part of that. The Freeze also had great leadership. Whether it was from our captain and well-respected players like Allen Eller, or the coaching staff of Hector Marinaro and Bruce Miller, or even our ownership group, I think we set the team up for success; they had to perform and get the job done on the field.

As one of the owners, Kastelic took a special pride in the success of the Freeze:

When we beat Detroit, we earned the right to go to the Ron Newman Cup, which was the Final Four. Since Chicago was the host team, they had already earned an automatic bid from our division and, because our team had less wins than the other three teams, we were considered the number four seed. That meant we had to play the number one seed, which was Chicago.

We lost to Chicago in the semifinal game and then we played in a consolation game against Las Vegas. We had the lead for the majority of the game until the fourth quarter when we gave up the game-winning goal in the final seconds. The season and playoff run were amazing. It was our first year of existence, and we were able to make it all the way to the final four.

We accomplished all of this while operating on an extremely small budget and playing in a small venue compared to most of the teams. I do think that soccer can become a popular sport in Cleveland, but only if the league itself is strong and the ownership group is on the same page. The PASL was a young league, so there were learning experiences and curves to overcome, but without question, the league was on the right track.

Playing regional games helps keep costs down, but the fact that the league wanted all teams to be in big arenas within a few years is tough to accomplish, especially if you do not have millionaires running your organization. Cleveland has shown it supports soccer in the past and, with all the recent success of the World Cup and the direction that soccer is headed, I have no doubt it can be successful again.

Kastelic holds a certain sense of pride, as well he should, but never hesitates to give thanks to the fans and hope for the future, saying, "Thank you all so much for supporting us! I am sorry that we could not keep the organization together long enough to see it succeed in the new MASL [Major Arena Soccer League]. Perhaps one day we will see the revival of a new Cleveland team and I definitely hope that I can be part of that journey. Cleveland deserves a team!"

Scott Snider provided an insider look toward the future of the Freeze in Cleveland:

The Cleveland Freeze organization is still open for business, however, after six long and grueling months of review, analysis, debate, and unfortunately some fallout, we decided to put the team on hold for the 2014–15 season for several reasons. At the end of the day, the Cleveland Freeze is a business, and no one that I know is in business to lose money, so we have to be able to feel secure in our investment and show a company that creates value for our investors. This takes diligent planning, and you cannot rush the process. I think our ownership group has shown they have and can create valuable, profitable companies that fill a void in the industry and are committed to the community. I am very confident we have the ability to do the same with an entertainment-based, soccer-oriented company.

The big announcement for the 2014–15 season was the merger of the MISL and the PASL to form a new unified professional indoor league, the Major Arena Soccer League [MASL]. The leagues are very much different from a business standpoint. To the simplest form, the MISL teams have large budgets and the PASL teams have small budgets. They have two different business models in my opinion. Both leagues are great leagues, with fantastic ownership groups and vast amounts of soccer and business knowledge, but nonetheless two different platforms.

I attended the joint annual owners meeting in Baltimore back in May 2014 where they also launched the new MASL. It was a pleasure and a knowledge-gaining experience to be able to meet and talk in-depth with fellow owners and executives of both MISL and PASL organizations over several days. However, at the same time, you could see firsthand some of the difficulties that exist when two businesses merge.

This is close to my heart, as we have experience with this as we buy and integrate companies ourselves through Snider Premier Growth, but even more so we own a national consulting firm that provides exit planning, merger and acquisitions, and value enhancement expertise to clients who are selling or merging their companies. We work with this on, literally, a daily basis, and it's sometimes a struggle.

There were some things the new MASL were doing that we agreed with and others that we did not. A part of us felt that from a pure business standpoint it might be good to hold on to our monetary investment in the new MASL to see how things rolled out and then reanalyze our investment. Our second option was to keep the team active and move them down to the Premier League, which acts as the minor league or development league of the MASL.

The unfortunate part of business in any sense is disagreements among partners. It's just a part of doing business, and I would say it's the part that business owners like the least about owning their own companies. Regardless of which option we wanted to take, our group was confined and limited to what we could do based on our legal agreements among our ownership group. Even more unfortunate, it limited us in communicating effectively with our fans and community of supporters. As our group reanalyzed our situation and worked out some issues, we decided to put the team on hold for the 2014–15 season and focus on building a solid foundation, reorganizing our ownership group, integrating new management, developing young talent for the team, and rolling out new features like a youth academy and a series of camps and clinics.

If we can show the right business model that works, we plan to be active in the 2015–16 season, and we are diligently working on that plan. To do this, we need the continued support of our community, being both the fans and our businesses. We not only need active attendance at our games but also active sponsors and community partners. My call to action to the fans of the Cleveland Freeze would be to spread the word about your experience in the 2014–15 season. We have, without a doubt, demonstrated we can put a winning team on the field and provide a fantastic fan experience. Now we just need the awareness behind all of it to spread across the northeast Ohio soccer and business communities.

Snider went on to say why he thinks that professional soccer can still make it one day in Cleveland:

In my opinion, it's in the eyes of the beholder and what their end goal is. If you are looking at indoor soccer as a business, meaning one, it produces a monetary benefit for its investors, and two, is considered a true professional sports organization where players are paid as professionals, play in professional facilities, and have the large draws for attendance and sponsorships that are consistent with a professional-caliber organization, then indoor soccer cannot succeed on itself alone in Cleveland. The business model calls for a multiple-tiered organization that offers the indoor game, outdoor game, youth academy, camps and clinics, and potentially even a facility. This is what our group seeks to accomplish.

I personally fulfilled a dream when we bought and launched the Cleveland Freeze. Anyone who knows me well knows I am an avid bucket-list keeper for several reasons. Not only was owning a professional team a lifelong dream for me, but a bucket-list item as well. I literally used to tell my dad at Crunch games, "I am going to own and manage one of these teams one day." The essence of being able to own a team is an unforgettable memory. I have three memories, though, that stand out in my mind from our first season.

My first is our home opener at the Soccer Sportsplex. No one really knew what to expect or how the community would take to us. Seeing the Sportsplex, a place where I've played since I was a little kid, packed with Cleveland indoor soccer fans out to support their new team, the Cleveland Freeze, was just a breathtaking moment that I will never forget. I was up in the entertainment deck—the lofted area in the back where our announcer, DJ, stats people, videographer, and online sportscasting team all sat—overlooking the crowd as the music played, the packed house of fans cheered, and the Freeze ended the game with an 11–3 win over the Harrisburg Heat. I remember being teary eyed as I sat there in shock of what we just accomplished that day.

My second is our divisional final win over the Detroit Waza Flo that took us to the PASL Ron Newman Cup Final Four. In our inaugural season, we were able to accomplish what I believed no one thought we could do. In my opinion, we were always shadowed by the experience the soccer community was given with the performance and eventual fallout of the Ohio Vortex. In that moment, I think our shadow went away. Not only did we demonstrate every home game that we could put on a great show, but the collective performance of the Freeze took us to the Final Four.

The game was in Detroit—the Detroit fans are committed and passionate. Their team had won and gone to the Ron Newman Cup consistently since they came into the PASL; Detroit was the favored team. Detroit, without a doubt, collectively had more veteran experience then our younger, newly formed team. It was a battle, soccer fan or not, this was the type of game that had you off your seat, and, if you weren't a soccer fan, you became one that night. We were tied with about a minute or so left to go in the game. I thought for sure we were going into overtime.

With about a minute left, our captain and veteran player Allen Eller gets the ball in the offensive third of the field as we caught Detroit on their substation leaving Eller all alone up top. He received the ball, turned towards goal, drew the goalie out, and put it in the back of the net. The Freeze killed the 60 or so seconds left in the game and won the game 6–5, giving us a Final Four spot in the PASL Ron Newman Cup Championship. I can remember being out on the field with the guys after the game ended, celebrating together. It was another moment that is just burned into my mind, and I won't ever forget it.

My last memory is of the unbelievable outpouring of fan support throughout the season. There are several mini-moments throughout the season that contribute to my overall memory of our fans. Another inspiring and breathtaking moment is just thinking about the fans who came out each weekend night when were played at home. You could sense the rich, committed, passionate indoor soccer history this city has in it. Fans wearing their old Force or Crunch gear from the 1980s and 1990s and even the early 2000s. Seeing some of the old players from the Force and Crunch coming out to support the team was incredible. Having the fans all out on the field to sign autographs, take photos, or simply chat with our players and staff.

Even simple things like following the Facebook feed of what our fans were saying or seeing the pictures or tweets from fans during games. All things that you will never forget and all of this from people who barely knew us—they shook our hands, hugged us, talked to us, and passionately supported us.

The success of the Freeze proved two important things: first, that the fans of Cleveland still remember the glory days of the Crunch and Force and hunger for those winning moments again, and second, that the passionate fans of this town will always support a winner. Marinaro had these final words for the great fans of Cleveland: "It was great to be back in indoor soccer as part of the Freeze, and it was great to see a lot of the fans from the Crunch days. It brought back a lot of memories of the great days of the Crunch. A big thank-you to all that came out and supported the Freeze."

Epilogue

I began working on this book on December 6, 2012. My wife, Emily, had just told me hours earlier that she was pregnant with our first child. It was a roller coaster of emotions that ultimately left me thrilled with the prospect of becoming a father. It also set me to thinking about my 31 years on this earth and the fact that I still had not witnessed a major Cleveland sports championship. I have rooted for Cleveland teams my entire life, often taking me on the same roller-coaster ride of ups and downs. I knew if my loyalty to my unborn child was a strong as my loyalty toward my Cleveland teams, that parenting would be every bit as fun and challenging. It also made me realize that the story of the Cleveland sports fan and the memories we share was one that needed to be told. This is that story.

I started my journey by reaching out to my grandfather Joe DeLuca. He is the oldest and wisest sports fan I know. He went to many Cleveland Barons games and was 15 years old when the Indians won their last World Series. He is a wealth of knowledge that most libraries couldn't match. I spent two nights at his house with my trusty $20 Walmart tape recorder fresh out of the 1980s and picked his brain for several hours about all of his childhood memories. It was evident that his memories were very real and golden.

I was able to track down Hector Marinaro by simply putting his name into a Google search and discovering he was the head soccer coach at John Carroll University in Ohio. I called the school and they put me in touch with him. He agreed to have me out to the campus for an interview that Saturday afternoon. I took my wife and my cousin Frances with me to help ease my nerves. I realized quickly, however, that with Marinaro there would be no need for nerves—he was so friendly I was instantly at ease. It was emotional as he spoke about the relationship he has with his father, listening to him relive the glory days. It was one of the best interviews I have ever done with one of the best human beings I have ever met.

From there I reached out to Joe Charboneau. I had stumbled upon his profile on Facebook and, luckily for me, it was a legit page and he agreed to meet with me at his apartment in Cleveland. I spent a Friday night there and we spoke for hours while sipping on Anchor Steam Beer and playing with his dog, Maverick. Charboneau was honest and humble, and he never took a backseat to any question; he even offered me food out of his own fridge. It was a night that I will never forget.

Charboneau's teammate Len Barker was a bit of a different story. After we agreed to meet in early February, several delays pushed our meeting back. But on May 3, 2013, I finally arrived on the campus of Notre Dame College to meet with the head baseball coach. He was a busy man, but he made enough time for me that day to answer some questions. He has a lot of pride and a vivid memory of a perfect game. The interview was good, but not nearly as good as the classroom of kids I met later that day at North Ridgeville Middle School to promote the message of *Hero*. It's hard to believe anything would trump meeting a perfect-game hurler, but that group of kids did exactly that.

It was an amazing eight months that I will never forget. I learned that you don't need to have the last name of Costas or Gray to be able to ask an important question to an important person in Cleveland sports. You just need to have the heart, the drive, and the willingness to put yourself out there. Sometimes the best moments in life are the ones you create yourself. As novelist and journalist Mark Helprin once said, "The best chance you have if you want to rise to the top is to give yourself up to loneliness, fear nothing, and work hard. One thing you'll discover is that life is based less than you think on what you've learned, and much more than you think on what you have inside you right from the beginning."

Index

B *(continued)*

C

D

E

F

G

M *(continued)*

N

O

S *(continued)*

T

U

V

W

About the Author

VINCE McKEE grew up in northeast Ohio as an avid Cleveland sports fan. His first book, *Hero,* was published in October 2012, forever changing his life and the lives of his family and fans. Vince currently tours as a public speaker to further spread the message of *Hero* whenever he can. He enjoys spending time with his wife, Emily, and daughter, Maggie. Vince is always eager to speak with his fans as well as Cleveland Sports fans and can be contacted by e-mail (**coachvin14@yahoo.com**) or followed on Twitter (**@vincetheauthor**).